TWENTY-FIRST NATIONAL PRINT EXHIBITION

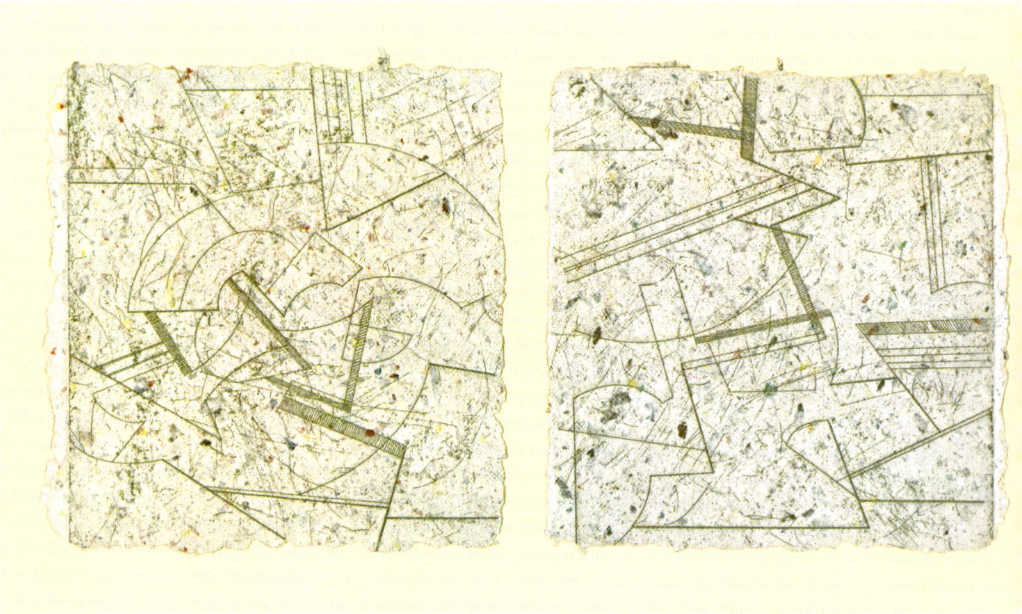

TWENTY-FIRST NATIONAL PRINT EXHIBITION

by Gene Baro

The Brooklyn Museum

Front cover:
RICHARD DAVIS
Bottles [Cat. 27]
1976, serigraph
Image: 56.5 x 73.7 cm.
(22¼ x 29 in.)
The Brooklyn Museum 77.230.2

Back cover:
SHUNJI SAKUYAMA
Prospect Park West [Cat. 114]
1978, lithograph
Image: 66.0 x 50.8 cm.
(26 x 20 in.)
The Brooklyn Museum 78.68.3

Frontispiece:
TAJ WORLEY
Interweave [Cat. 145]
1976, etching and serigraph
Image: 20.3 x 36.7 cm.
(8 x 14½ in.)
Davidson Galleries

Published for the
Twenty-first National Print Exhibition
The Brooklyn Museum
December 9, 1978–February 11, 1979

This exhibition was made possible with the aid of a grant from the National Endowment for the Arts in Washington, D.C., a Federal agency.

Library of Congress Cataloging in Publication Data

Baro, Gene.
Twenty-first National Print Exhibition.
Catalog of the exhibition held Dec. 9, 1978–Feb. 11, 1979 at the Brooklyn Museum, Brooklyn, N.Y.
Includes indexes.
1. Prints, American—Exhibitions. 2. Prints—20th century—United States—Exhibitions. I. Brooklyn Institute of Arts and Sciences. Museum. II. Title.
NE508.B28 769'.973'074014723 78–26421
ISBN 0–87273–072–7

Designed and published by The Brooklyn Museum,
Division of Publications and Marketing Services,
Eastern Parkway, Brooklyn, New York 11238.
Printed in the USA by the Falcon Press, Philadelphia.

24490

Contents

YASUHIRO ESAKI
Fourth Iris [Cat. 35]
1977, etching and aquatint
with hand-coloring
Image: 24.2 x 20.0 cm.
(9½ x 7⅞ in.)
The Brooklyn Museum, Gift of
Mr. David Temple 78.98.1

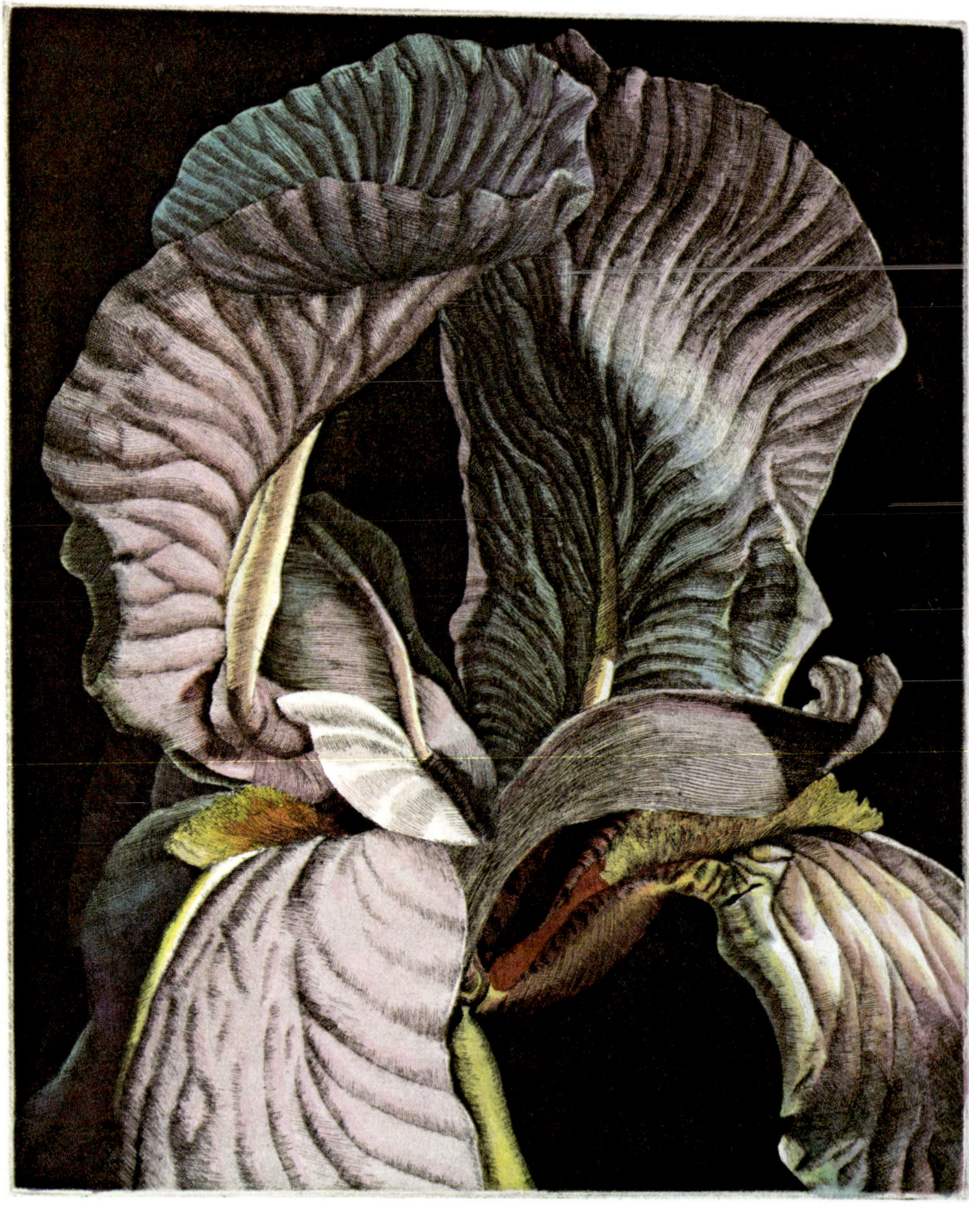

FOREWORD

In 1976, concurrent with the Bicentennial and mindful of the thirty years that the Brooklyn Museum's National Print exhibitions had been showing, with *30 Years of American Printmaking including the 20th National Print Exhibition,* we paused to take a rather expansive look at where we had been and where we were. To be fair, it was necessary for us to take a broader view of the enormous print production of those years. Also, it was necessary to review the American print scene of the past two years or so; that is, the currents in place or developing since the Museum's *Nineteenth National Print Exhibition.* The result was an exhibition more than twice the size of the usual Brooklyn Museum Print National. We combined a review of the past with an assessment of the present. But this was, in effect, a one-shot affair.

The *Twenty-first National Print Exhibition* returns us to an older concept of this series, where, typically, concern focuses upon preoccupations and practices in the printmaking art of a few years. There is a real

Michael Botwinick
Director
The Brooklyn Museum

luxury derived from this approach. If it seems impossible, empirically, to deduce, present, and explain the complexities of current print production in any single exhibition project, the National releases one from the necessity of doing so. The Museum's commitment is to an extended presentation of important developments and issues in American printmaking. We remain acutely aware of the fact that we can never encompass the whole of the field in a given National, but, while we do not aim at comprehensiveness, we do intend to reach out to vital printmaking wherever it appears in America. The exhibition organizer works toward the presentation of what seems valuable in the many-faceted national print scene and not merely toward the presentation of what is already accepted and established. With our exhibition series itself, we feel that we have created a tradition. Each year the focus shifts—sometimes imperceptibly. Some years a strong undercurrent runs through the production of prints, and the concerns of the artists give a direction to the exhibition. In other years, conscious decisions or circumstances may lead the curator in other directions. We believe that an ongoing look at prints, never codified into a single point of view from year to year, contributes importantly to our understanding, awareness and appreciation of the medium.

As we have this year, we will always try to be straightforward about what conclusions we have made and what preconceptions governed our activity.

Gene Baro is the individual whose vision has shaped the past two National Print Exhibitions. Their diversity reflects his breadth of vision. Mr. Baro's present endeavor was aided by the generosity and willingness of people and institutions throughout the United States. A project of this scope requires the help of many and special mention should be made of Joann Moser, Curator of Collections at the University of Iowa Museum of Art, and

Richard Claude Ziemann, artist. A substantial proportion of the works in the *Twenty-first National* were lent by the artists. To them and to the other lenders we give our thanks. This exhibition was made possible through a grant from the National Endowment for the Arts in Washington, D.C., a Federal agency.

We hope that the *Twenty-first National Print Exhibition* will be stimulating and informative. As sure as there was a *Twentieth National Print Exhibition,* so there will be a twenty-second.

STEPHANIE WEBER
Reliquary IX [Cat. 140]
1978, etching and embossing
with collaged Xerox and
hand-coloring
Image: 15.9 x 19.1 cm.
(6¼ x 7½ in.)
The Artist

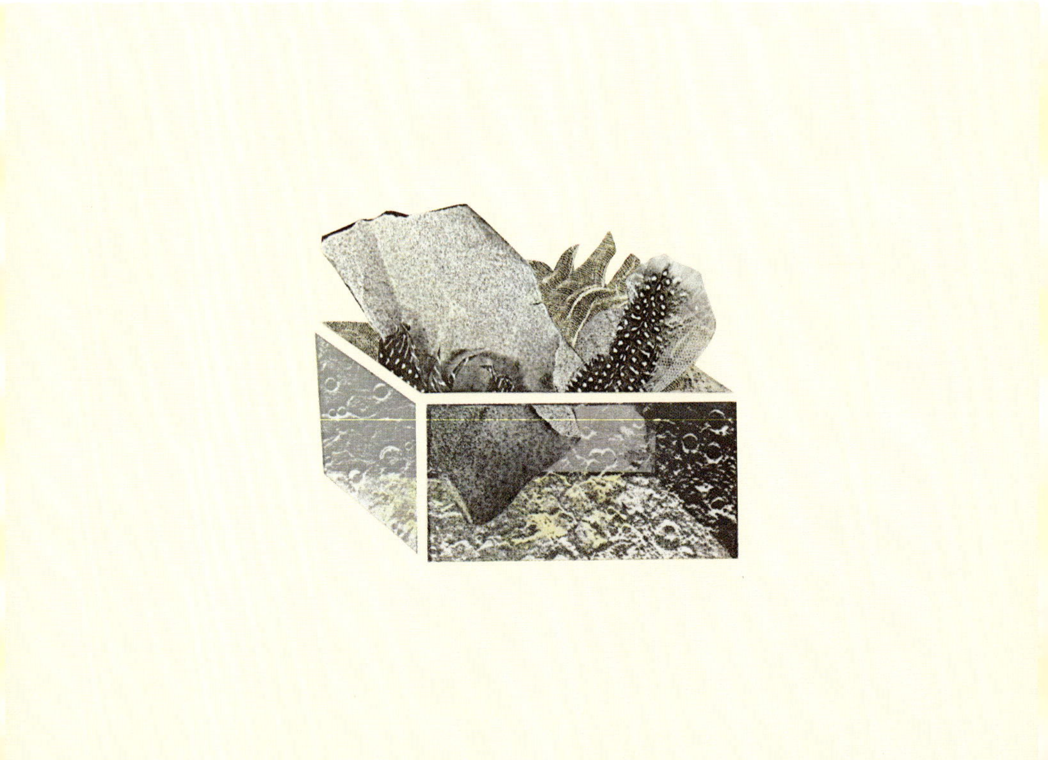

INTRODUCTION

Gene Baro

The Brooklyn Museum's *Twenty-first National Print Exhibition* presents two works each of seventy-five artists previously unrepresented in this series. The decision to reach out to new artists, or at least to artists unknown to the series, developed from my perception of the abundant, high-quality printmaking available in the United States, printmaking not necessarily confined to the so-called centers of art or to the well-publicized print workshops.

The interesting artists who work in the print mediums are not inevitably the ones we've heard most about. Many new artists of worth are out there, as well as many artists of solid achievement who have worked long with perhaps only local recognition. The print field is many fields, with many factors of production, communication, and marketing affecting what becomes known to a broad public. We are accustomed to learning of merit in printmaking through the many national, regional, and local printmaking competitions and invitational exhibitions; and sometimes we learn of the same artists and even of the same prints over and again. We are accustomed to accord importance to what is advertised and disseminated. We don't trouble to find the artist who prints small editions in a home studio and addresses a small circle. We don't look for the adventuresome press or listen when financial stringencies are about to close its doors.

Of course, even among artists who live in great cities or who are or were attached to university art departments, art schools, or print workshops, there are many who labor at their art in isolation. City life can separate artists intent upon personal vision and deflect others into counter-productive competitiveness. The pressures and busyness of academic institutions often frustrate a meaningful exchange of artistic ideas and a useful critical dialogue among colleagues. And the pressures of the workshop, where commercial success is the issue, can inhibit aesthetic judgment and point to slick solutions.

Some artists cannot depend upon their established reputations as painters or sculptors to excite public interest in their prints. If they make prints only, they are unlikely to gain attention from major art magazines, weeklies, or newspapers. The artist who settles for the designation of printmaker seems to many worthies of the art world to occupy a no-man's-land between craft and art.

Formalist critics tend to regard printmaking as secondary artistic activity, too concentrated upon craftsmanship and technique to engage the concerns of high art. But not long ago all the arts were similarly grounded in firm craftsmanship and technical expertise. It's only recently that the public has accepted critically and with ready money ill-made paintings and sculptures, works whose deficiencies of facture are thought to be validated by, or at least compensated by, moral and aesthetic superiority.

The fact is, printmaking has no limitation that cannot be transformed or transcended by the right artist. The mediums themselves, singly and in combination, form a palette sufficient to the most sophisticated visual ideas and the most profound feelings. Of course, some printmakers are not artists in the large sense but are precisely as alleged—purveyors of craft, repetitious demonstrators of their own technical abilities. But banal practitioners exist in every discipline. Technique is the proper beginning of art and not its rationale; necessarily, the best printmakers are among the best artists.

For the museum professional concerned with prints, there can be little comfort in the vastness of the contemporary American art scene. My own practice is never to refuse to look at work, whether I am organizing an appropriate exhibition or not, and I actively seek out unfamiliar work on the same basis. But also I am always conscious of opportunities missed. What is possible with the best intentions and commitment of one's energies at most times seems inadequate.

In preparing The Brooklyn Museum's *Twenty-first National Print Exhibition,* I traveled extensively, visiting studios, workshops, print publishers, art schools, university art museums and art departments, independent printmaking facilities, and commercial galleries in many states. In addition, open viewings were arranged for me at the Museum's Department of Prints and Drawings. No limitation was placed upon the number of prints an artist might submit, so long as these were produced no earlier than 1975. No limitation was made as to size or medium.

In all, I examined roughly fifty prints for every one selected, for a total of around seven thousand. The project went on for the better part of a year, with some months devoted substantially to travel and print reviewing. There were obvious limitations of time and budget and other obligations to the department that I had to meet. In the field, I

EVA POKORNY
My Life [Cat. 103]
1978, monotype
Image: 18.1 x 12.7 cm.
(7⅛ x 5 in.)
The Artist

EVA POKORNY
In the Ravine [Cat. 104]
1978, monotype
Image: 17.8 x 12.7 cm.
(10⅛ x 8 in.)
The Artist

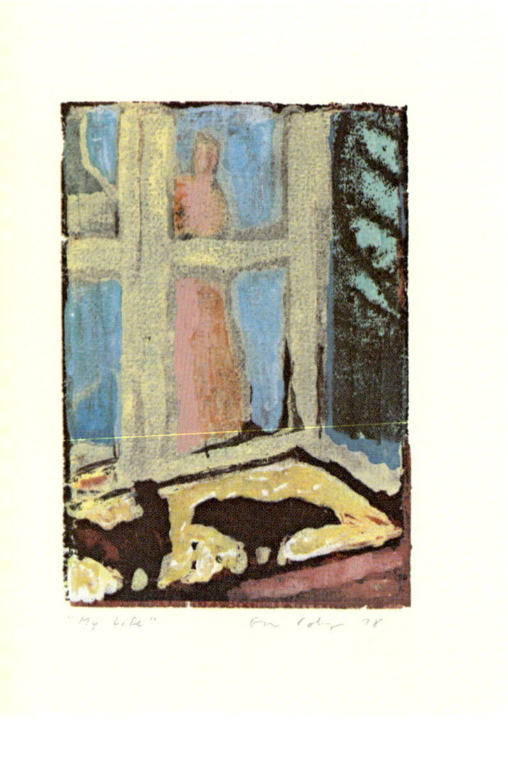

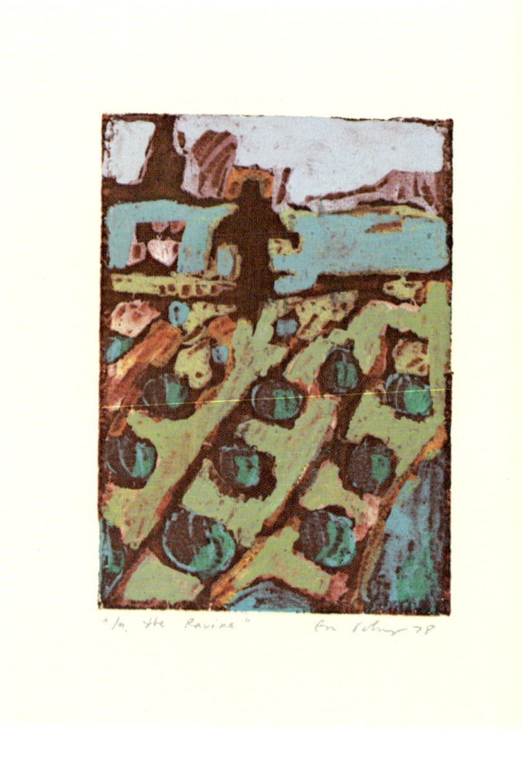

encountered the usual hazards: artists gone away, workshops closed, late planes, missed appointments, too hospitable hosts. At last there were catalogue deadlines to consider and the need to finish.

I had determined to choose work that dealt seriously with printmaking processes. The subject need not be serious so long as the artistic approach to it was. I was not after aridly perfect prints but after interesting artists. I wanted to see something in the work that established accomplishment but that also suggested further possibilities for individual development. I looked for artistic intention sensitive to medium, consistent with it, fulfilled by it. Choosing two prints from each artist, I tried to balance my selections to show a spectrum or range of concerns or, failing that, a concentration of them. With two prints from each contributor, one can hope to make a statement in an exhibition.

Although I organize many exhibitions and jury others, I tried to keep the task of the *Twenty-first National Print Exhibition* a separate issue, without preconceptions. I wished the exhibition to shape itself by association, its themes, if there were to be any, emerging as I chose print after print. I wanted to see what was visually of importance to printmaking artists, to see what pattern might manifest itself, conscious all the while that pattern is more often imposed than self-generated.

But apart from what this particular exhibition might reveal, I faced a situation uncomfortably clear. The number of American artists with professional aspirations increases year by year, and in no discipline is this more apparent than in printmaking. The audience for art is very large in the United States, but still not large enough to absorb aesthetically, let alone financially, the volume of professional-quality work being produced. Much of value remains unknown and even more remains too little known to bring the artist sustaining recognition or financial independence.

As to changes of emphasis in the printmaking art, some things came clear readily and comfortably. The work I reviewed contained a far smaller proportion of outsized prints than would have been typical a few seasons ago. Really big prints seem, with very few exceptions, to be the present prerogative of the workshops and commercial establishments. Some repudiation of size itself was evident through the large numbers of artists who are now working small, within a foot. The scale may be generous, but the size is intimate.

The quality of the small work was also remarkable for concentration, intensity, and directness of effect, as if a determinedly more personal approach were again being attempted in spite of the available dazzling technologies of the workshops. The impression of a return to the personal was reinforced by the prevalence of small editions, sometimes only of five or ten prints, in the growth of interest in monotype, which yields a unique image, and in the work of mixed mediums in sequences that produce editions variées, with each print having a different aspect within a controlling imagery.

On the whole, serigraphy seems to have suffered some decline in popularity (but not in quality) to the benefit of intaglio processes. Photography is less directly evident in printmaking than it was a few years ago, though there is now some interesting experimentation with photo-etching and photo-lithography as a stage of print production or for special fineness of registration. Photographic process is no longer used as often for its own sake but seems to be in the service of more inclusive concepts.

During the 1960s a number of well-known painters and sculptors discovered or rediscovered printmaking, under the pressure of a market demand for their work or out of an interest generated by the commitment of their colleagues. They were generally better funded than the artist with a small press in the basement, and they were more ambitious. A complex printing technology was available to them for hire, along with master printers and other support technicians out of commercial shops and manufacturing establishments. And their projects were regarded by entrepreneurs as solid investments with the added attraction of a speculative potential. The results were usually either deplorable, replications of images for people who couldn't afford the original whatever-it-might-be, or the prints were startling and innovative, the reaction of talent to a fresh medium within an essentially collaborative context.

Traditional printmakers, fine artists though they might be, were suddenly confronted with the competition of printmaking-as-big-business, not only with ingenious works but with hard-sell marketing. Most of them simply went on as before, hoping for the best; but young artists, in school or newly out of it, went off in pursuit of the technologies and the blockbuster image.

The Brooklyn Museum's *Twenty-first National Print Exhibition* suggests a retreat from advanced processing and aggressive showmanship (still coming at you from the big print workshops and superb at its best) to more traditional methods and images and to a more personal way of working. To some extent, this is a matter of economics. Many didn't make it to the high-priced market, which, if it didn't contract, didn't expand enough to accommodate the aspirations of a new generation. Then, too, many talents may not have been served well in the rush to succeed.

Be that as it may, the present exhibition attests, with some exceptions, to the resurgence of a more intimate art, lyrical and fanciful, gentle and witty, technically adept but understated, serious but not self-important.

PHILIP E. MULLEN
ADI Blue [Cat. 96]
1977, serigraph
Image: 60.4 x 41.6 cm.
(23¾ x 16⅜ in.)
The Artist

CATALOGUE

NOTE In the catalogue entries, dimensions are in centimeters (inches are in parentheses); height precedes width. The collection is given in italics.

Andell's imagery can be delightfully amusing or more soberingly affecting. She works gracefully in etching and monotype, varying her attack between the linear and the painterly. *Picnic at Crane's Beach* suggests appetite taking over in the form of a number of autonomous teeth. The artist used drypoint, etching, and spit-bite, a process where diluted nitric acid is brushed directly on the plate in order to achieve a watery effect. She printed on Rives BFK paper.

1
Nancy Andell
(b. Boston, Massachusetts, 1953)
Picnic at Crane's Beach
1976, etching with drypoint
and spit-bite, edition: 5
Image: 11.1 x 13.4 (4⅜ x 5¼)
Sheet: 23.2 x 26.7 (9⅛ x 10½)
Impressions Workshop, Inc.

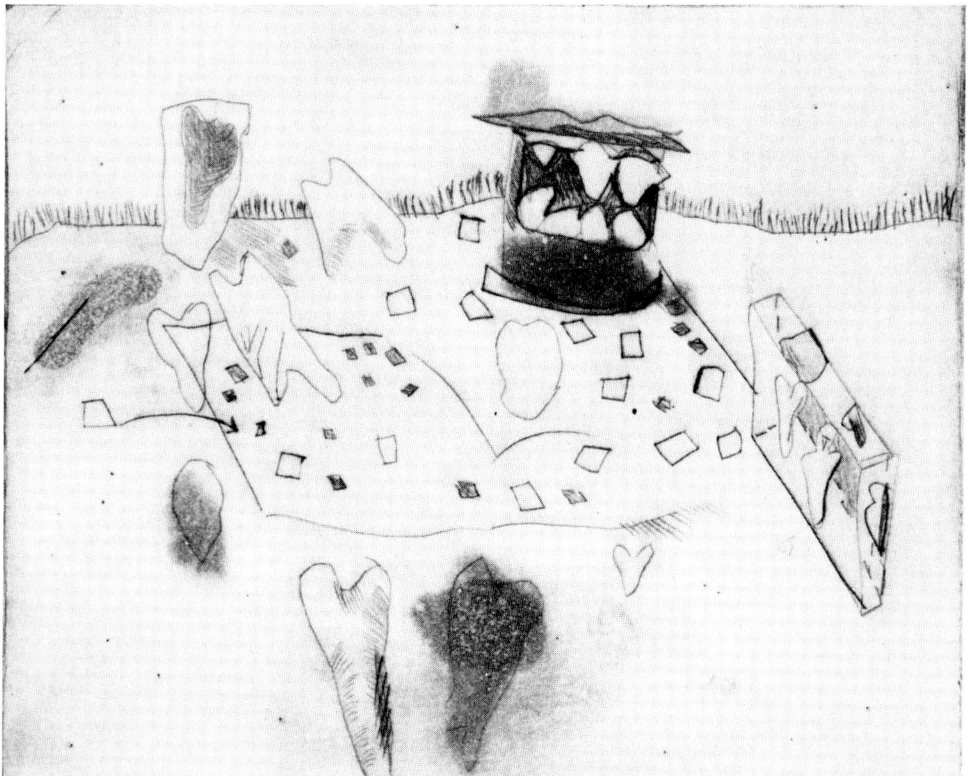

2

Nancy Andell

(b. Boston, Massachusetts, 1953)

Around 4:00 P.M. in November 1977

1977, monotype, edition: unique

Image: 62.5 x 29.8 (24⅝ x 11¾)

Sheet: 74.9 x 52.1 (29½ x 20½)

Impressions Workshop, Inc.

Andell is attracted to monoprint for its spontaneity and for the painterly effects possible in the medium. Here she has worked from two zinc plates. She printed in one press run on Rives BFK paper.

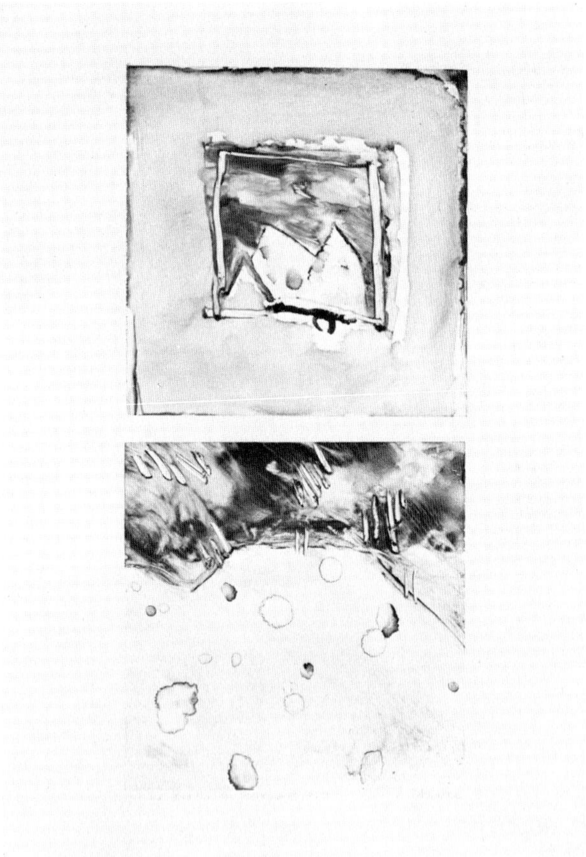

Baczek has brilliantly combined embossing and aquatint to render an urban landscape as seen through a bank of windows, perhaps, but not inevitably, the windows of the studio. The apparently realistic cityscape is played against the formal framing device, with its strong suggestion of abstraction. The cityscape is seen arrested, enhancing the sense of stopped time, the mood of reverie. Aquatint is managed with great subtlety and skill to enhance the feeling of space proposed by the drawing and to create atmosphere both literal and imaginative. Printing was by the artist on Rives BFK paper.

3
Peter Baczek
(b. Webster, Massachusetts, 1945)
Lombard Street Triptych
1977, aquatint and embossing, edition: 20
Image: 29.9 x 66.6 (11¾ x 26¼)
Sheet: 43.0 x 74.9 (17 x 29½)
ADI Gallery

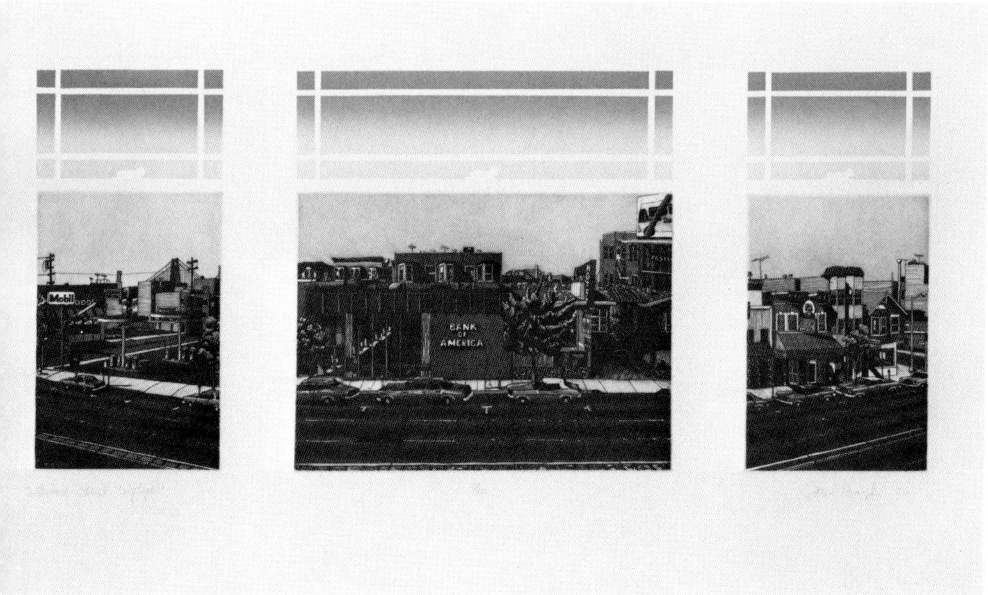

4

Peter Baczek

(b. Webster, Massachusetts, 1945)

Duboce Street

1978, aquatint, edition: 50

Image: 38.2 x 28.3 (15 x 11⅛)

Sheet: 38.2 x 28.3 (15 x 11⅛)

ADI Gallery

Baczek sometimes works from photographs in developing detailed drawings for his plate, but he avoids photomechanical processes in the production of his prints, preferring, as he puts it, "to retain a human quality." Preliminary sketches taken directly from the subject are another source of his images. When the detailed drawing is achieved, it is transferred to zinc plates. Aquatint is then applied by hand or by box, and the plate is etched in a twenty to one solution of nitric acid. Printing was by the artist on Arches Cover buff.

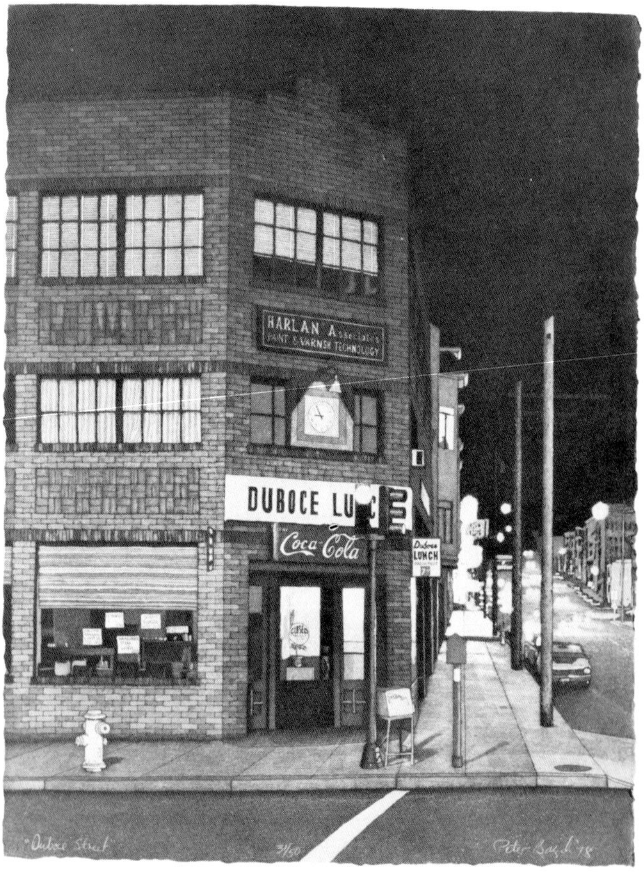

5
Andrew G. Balkin
(b. Niagara Falls, New York, 1947)
Life's Flight into Water: Harmony
1976, aquatint, engraving, mezzotint, soft-ground, and drypoint, edition: 35
Image: 44.8 x 60.4 (17⅝ x 23¾)
Sheet: 56.6 x 70.8 (22¼ x 27⅞)
The Artist

Balkin's imagery often depends upon the close interaction of abstract elements and forms that depict or allude to real objects. The tensions created can seem physical, the image aggressive and dynamic despite a harmonious disposition of apparently neutral forms. This print, the third image in a suite of five titled *Life's Flight into Water,* is a case in point. The print, which incorporates three plates, each carrying part of the image, involves drypoint, soft-ground, mezzotint, aquatint, and engraving. The plates were inked to separate colors and run through the press wet on wet with nice attention paid to registration. Charbonnel inks were used, and the artist printed on Arches cover white.

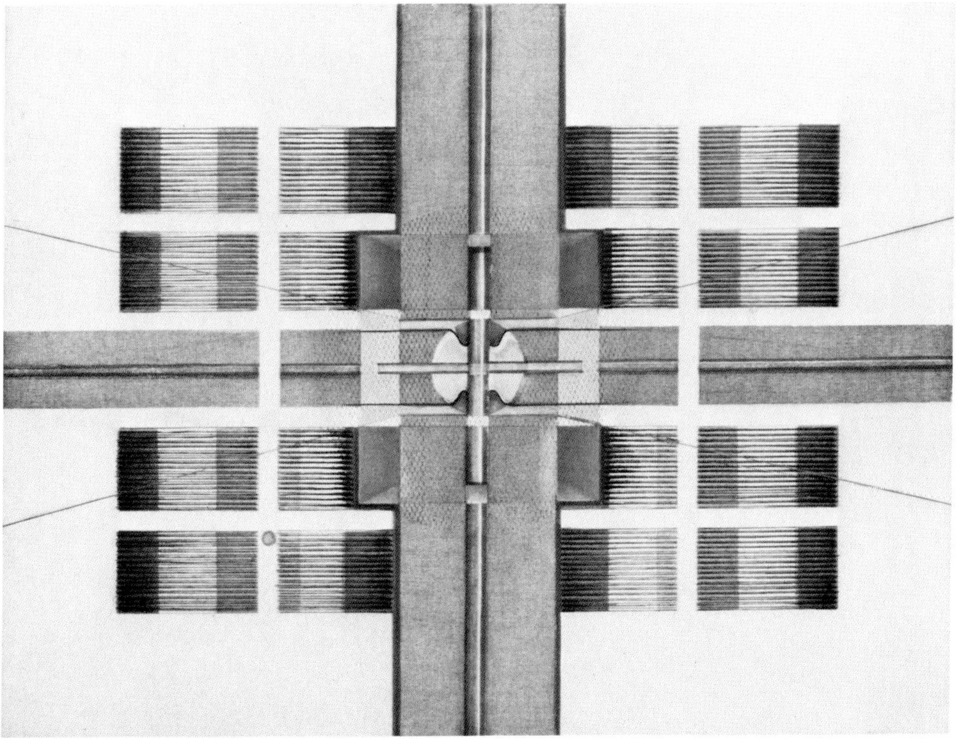

6

Andrew G. Balkin

(b. Niagara Falls, New York, 1947)

Future Memories I

1977, aquatint, engraving, mezzotint, soft-ground, and drypoint, edition: 35

Image: 60. 1 x 44.8 (23⅝ x 17⅝)

Sheet: 74.3 x 56.5 (29¼ x 22¼)

The Artist

Balkin is seen in this print as capable of lyrical and meditative imagery. Here again there is a tension implicit in the centered forms that project an energy at variance with that of forms that seem to float and hover in an ambiguous space. The plate was developed with aquatint, engraving, mezzotint, soft-ground, and drypoint, and the colors (Charbonnel intaglio inks) were dropped onto the plate à la poupée. The plate was then hand-wiped. The artist printed on Arches Cover buff in a single press run.

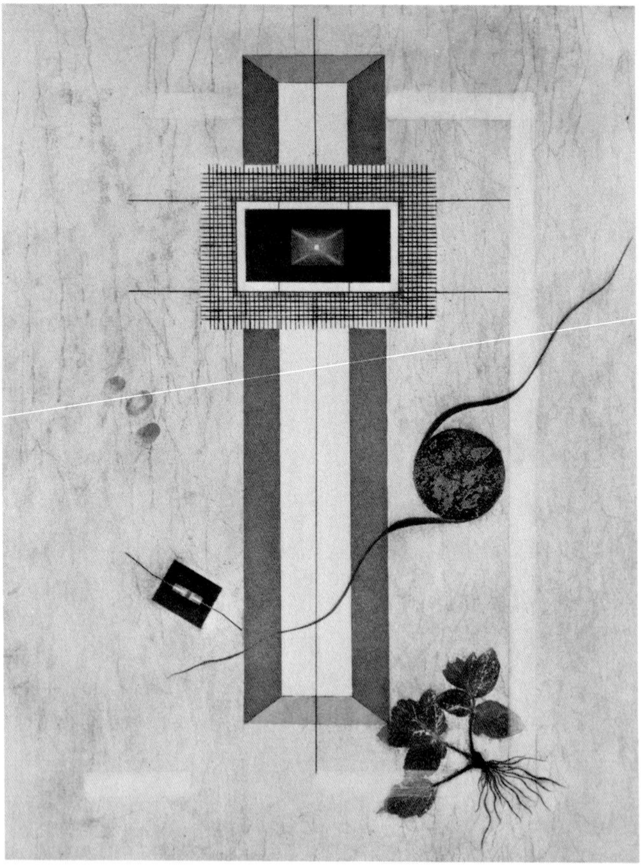

7
Susan Hamilton Bolt
(b. Edinburg, Texas, 1949)
Declination Reparation
1977, serigraph, edition: 18
Image: 35.6 x 43.0 (14 x 17)
Sheet: 48.3 x 55.9 (19 x 22)
Associated American Artists, Philadelphia

Bolt has a distinctly personal feeling for serigraphy. Although the linear elements in her prints—the drawing, as we might think—seem to dominate, the visual dynamic is shared absolutely with color. The disposition of the inks, the many inflections between transparency and opacity, between mutedness and intensity, articulates and animates the space described by the drawing. This serigraph results from thirty-eight printings. The base colors were laid down in three printings as follows: pale gray-pink; pale green; pale brown. Additions of pigment reinforced and intensified the color. More opaque ink was used for complements which were printed as small plates overriding transparent areas. Then still more opaque lines were added. The printing moves from transparency to opacity, from matteness to intensity. Bolt printed on Rives Heavyweight white.

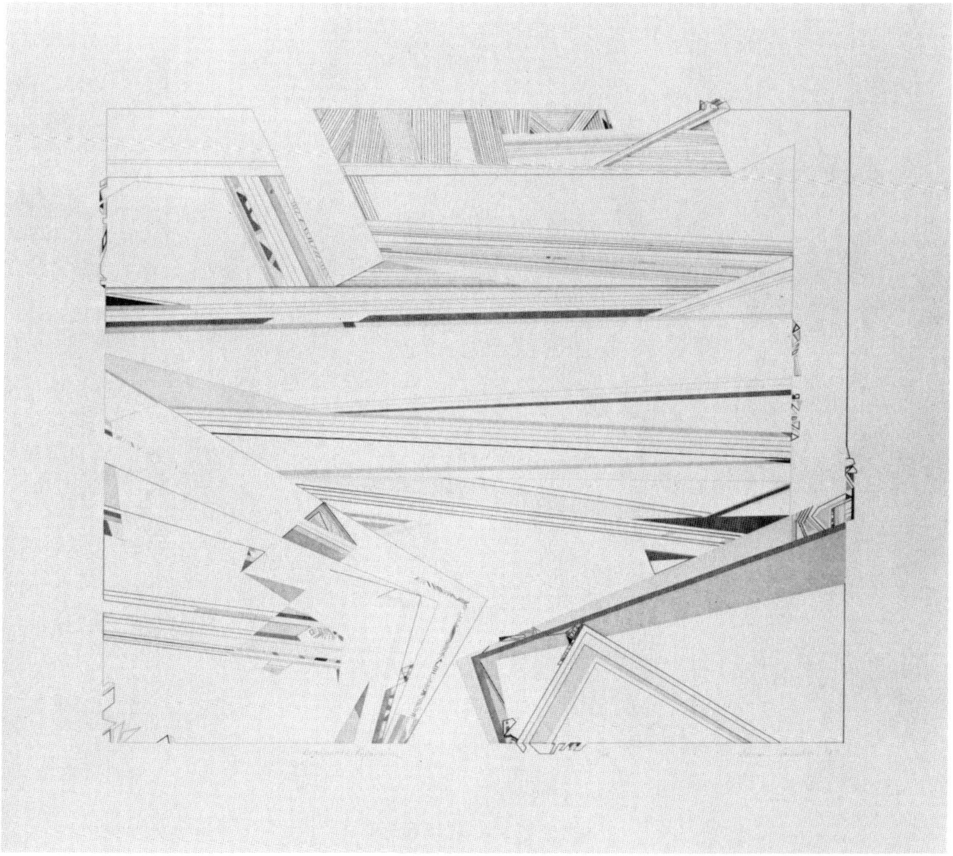

8
Susan Hamilton Bolt
(b. Edinburg, Texas, 1949)
Box Making
1978, serigraph, edition: 15
Image: 46.7 x 38.4 (18⅜ x 15⅛)
Sheet: 46.7 x 38.4 (18⅜ x 15⅛)
Associated American Artists, Philadelphia

Bolt is conscious of her paper as area and as a field for spatial exploration. She can discover the space of the sheet, or she can take that space as a given and fill it. In *Box Making*, imagery invades and occupies a territory; the pressure is upon the paper both as area and spatial field. The spirit of the piece is impending; the concern is with being and becoming. This serigraph is the result of forty printings, the first a split-fountain on the border area, ranging from yellow-orange to orange and followed by red and green. Transparencies were printed, gradually increasing the density of pigments in relation to transparent base and binder. Line work was done last with light values printed first, the artist working to darker, more intense colors. She printed on Arches Cover white.

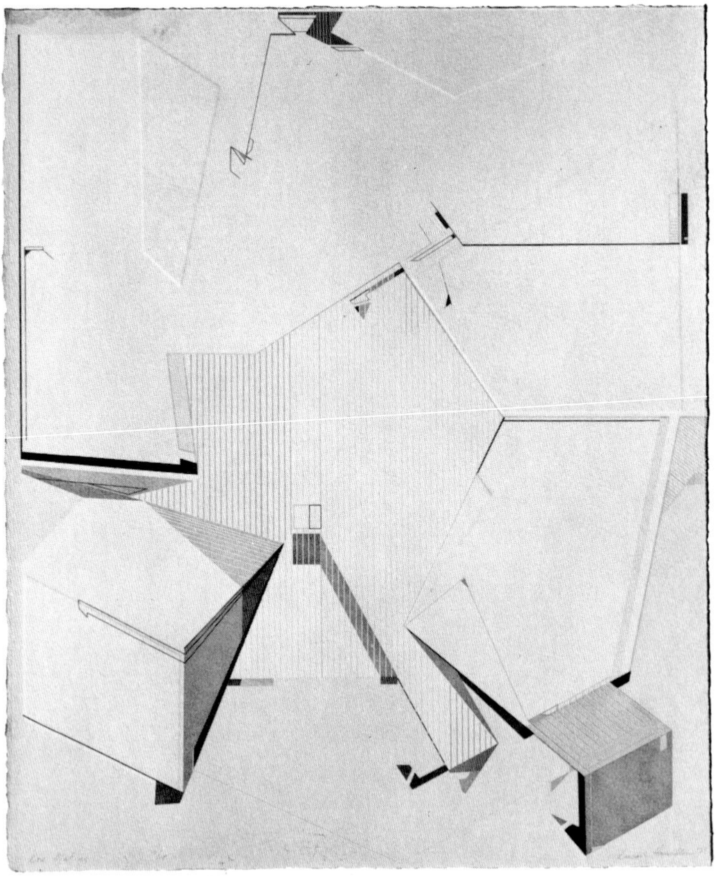

Boyle's imagery often exploits ingredients intrinsic to printmaking processes: repetition, reversal, mirroring. Added to this are ambiguities of scale and of form that render complex the interrelationships of a few elements. In *Wan Was Wax,* the image of the reversed page with its casually drawn moons and explicit language evokes turning and changing as repeated and consistent episodes within a continuum. Image stands for process. The artist used open-bite with line etching on a zinc plate. Color printing ink was applied by brush in the mode of monotype, and the words "Wax" and "Wan" were drawn on the print using a transfer technique. The artist printed on Lana, a French paper.

9

Martin Boyle

(b. Columbus, Ohio, 1952)

Wan Was Wax

1977, open-bite with etching, edition: unique

Image: 30.2 x 45.1 (11⅞ x 17¾)

Sheet: 52.3 x 70.8 (20⅝ x 27⅞)

The Artist

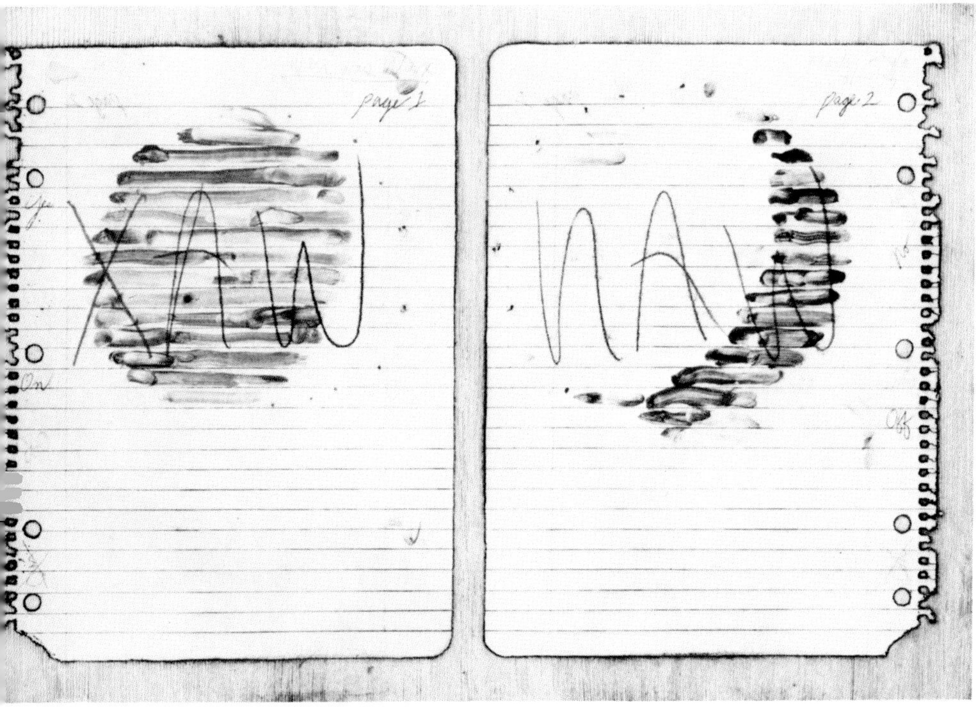

10
Martin Boyle
(b. Columbus, Ohio, 1952)
Triptych: Conundrum I, Omnidirectional Translator, Conundrum II
1977, etching, edition: 10
Each sheet:
Image: 127.0 x 90.3 (50 x 35 $^{9}/_{16}$)
Sheet: 127.0 x 90.3 (50 x 35 $^{9}/_{16}$)
The Artist

Boyle's *Triptych* creates a sense of the celestial, not only through its drawn shapes calling to one another over the distances of paper but by the printed language proposed both as literal meaning and as visual metaphor. The sense of floating is very strong, enhanced by the linear treatment within hemispheres, which have their own internal space to play against the spaces that seem to contain them. But which is greater? Two infinities seem proposed. The plates were inked intaglio and the color rolled on. Smaller images were then screenprinted on the finished etchings, and words were hand-printed with metal type. The artist printed on American Etching paper.

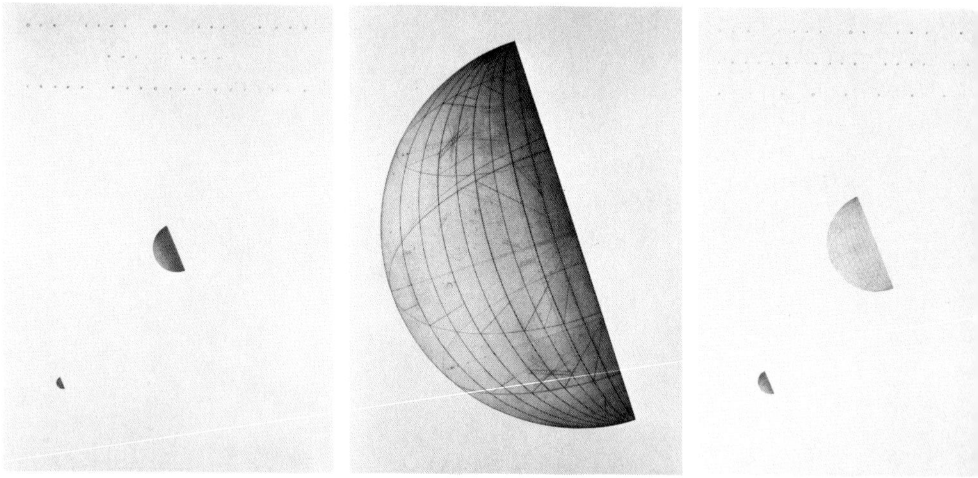

Brill's prints address some fundamental visual issues. How do we perceive surface activity independent of form? How does form relate to what we yet perceive as an invariable surface, a thing that is essentially the same in all its parts as, for instance, water is the same through its infinite configurations and activities, the same tissue of surface whether mobile or still? In *Cranbrook Series, Black Hanging #1,* Brill has proposed a surface doubly flowing, flowing in its overallness and flowing simultaneously in the discreet lift and thrust of its collage strips with their toothed edges. This lithograph was printed from stone. The artist created texture by using gum arabic stop-out. He then rolled-up the image in black (the marks made by the gum arabic remained white). The background textures were printed on a 22 by 30 inch sheet of Rives newsprint gray. The hanging forms were printed on an identical sheet of Arches Cover white, which was then cut into strips with pinking shears and fixed to the background sheet. Printing and assembling were by the artist.

11
Glenn F. Brill
(b. New York, New York, 1949)
Cranbrook Series,
Black Hanging #1
1978, lithograph and collage,
edition: unique
Image: 79.3 x 55.5 (31¼ x 21⅞)
Sheet: 79.3 x 55.5 (31¼ x 21⅞)
The Artist

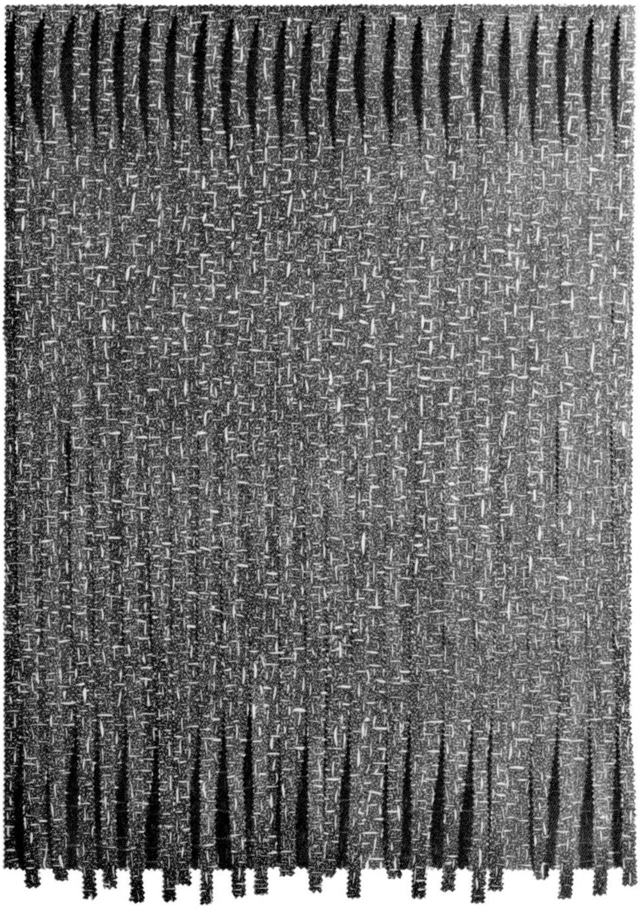

12
Glenn F. Brill
(b. New York, New York, 1949)
Cranbrook Series, Collage #5
1978, lithograph and collage,
edition: unique
Image: 25.4 x 32.7 (10 x 12⅞)
Sheet: 25.4 x 32.7 (10 x 12⅞)
The Artist

Brill imparts a persuasive painterliness to this lithograph-collage. The collaged elements declare themselves explicitly, the long strips overhanging the rectilinear form. But they are wedded to the surface by the artist's controlled, shallow space and by his mediating color. This lithograph was printed from two aluminum plates and three stones as follows: aluminum (orange-brown), aluminum (pink), stone (blue), stone (purple), then stone (blue). Gum stop-out was used on the aluminum plates and the last stone; crayon was used with the two remaining stones. Printed collaged strips were treated with hand-coloring in pencil. The artist printed on Arches Cover white.

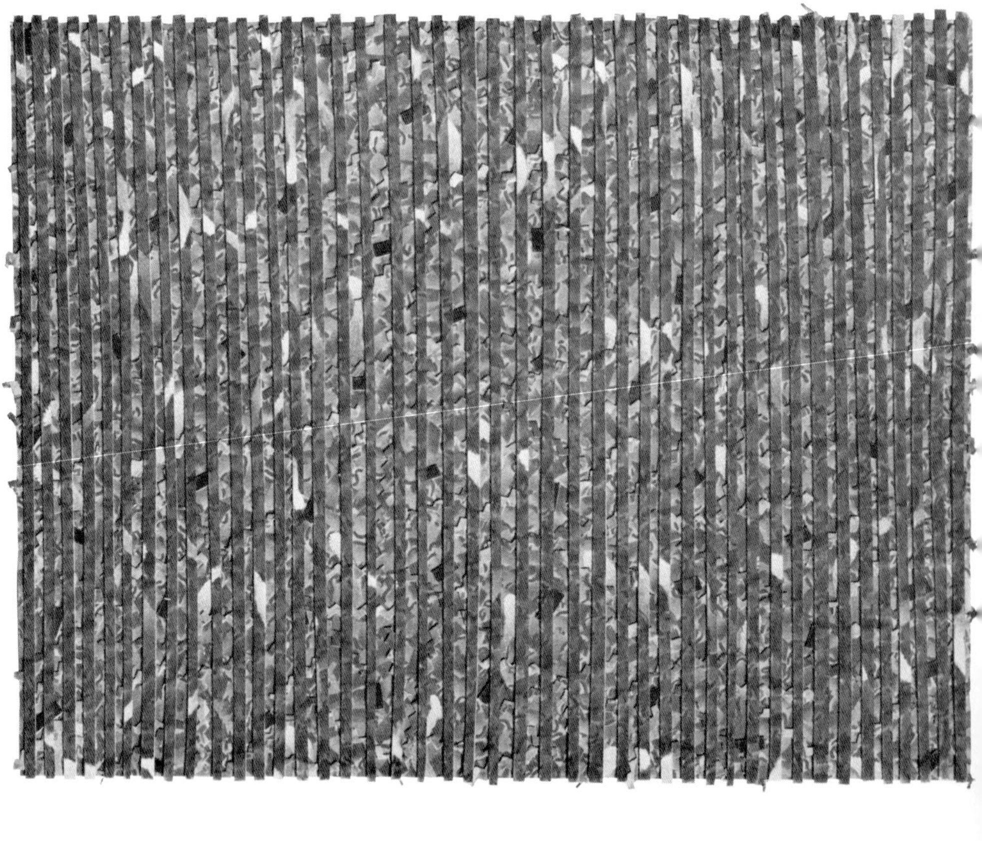

13
David Bumbeck
(b. Framingham, Massachusetts, 1940)
An Actress
1977, photo-etching, aquatint, engraving, etching, scraping, and burnishing, edition: 100
Image: 36.2 x 42.5 (14¼ x 16¾)
Sheet: 48.2 x 54.6 (19 x 21½)
The Artist

Bumbeck uses photo-etching in a peculiarly sensitive way, as a point of departure for draughtsmanship or as a constituent in his richly worked and differentiated surfaces. The signature of this artist is the skill with which he harmonizes the individual stylistic distinctions and technical means that enrich particular areas of his plate. At his best, he achieves a visual unity that conveys an immediacy of feeling, a unity of effect, at the same time as he suggests underlying tensions, as if the elements brought together successfully existed only through pressure. The artist describes the figure in *An Actress* as "an invention dealing with structural rhythms." The not quite comfortable pose of the voluptuous body, the spiky shrubbery, and enigmatic image of the resting cat convey a disquiet whose meaning lies inward. The artist has used aquatint, line etching, and engraving. As is usual with his plates, there is extensive scraping and burnishing. Printing by the artist was on Arches Cover white.

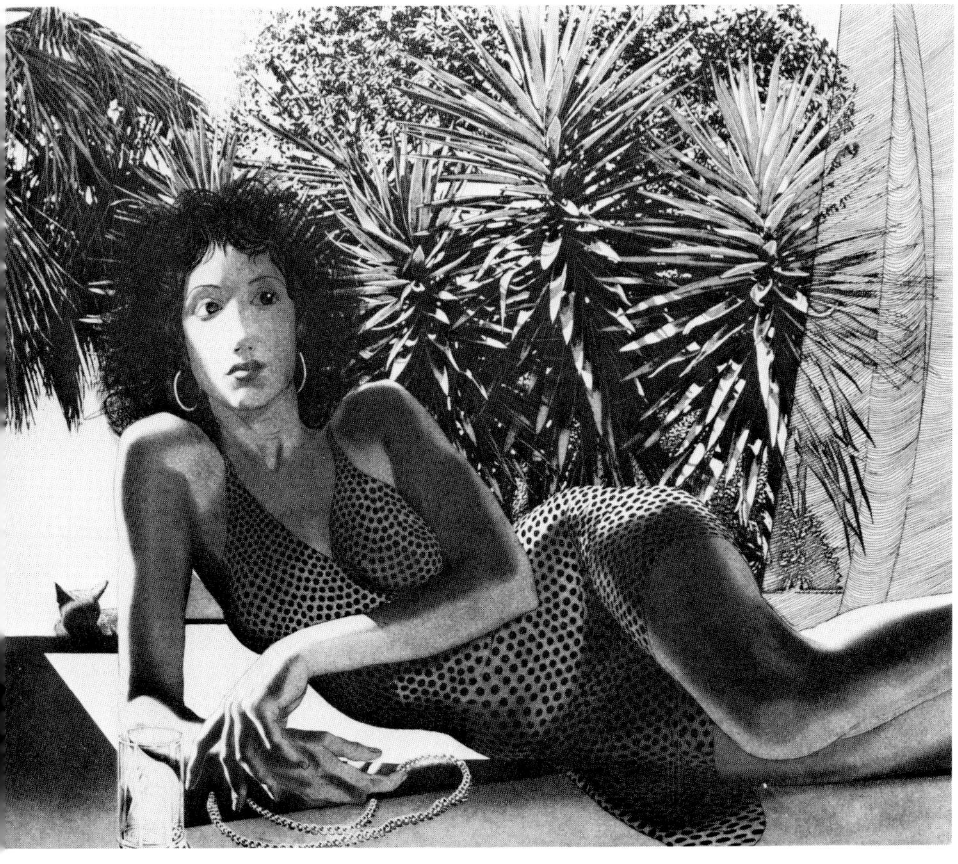

14
David Bumbeck
(b. Framingham, Massachusetts, 1940)
Moods of Miss J
1978, photo-etching, aquatint, engraving, etching, open-bite, scraping, and burnishing, edition: 80
Image: 36.5 x 42.5 (14⅜ x 16¾)
Sheet: 48.2 x 52.4 (19 x 20⅝)
The Artist

Bumbeck excels in projecting the enigmas of human per- sonality. Whether he is dealing with stylized figures tha exist in a dreamlike landscape or with a series of relate images, as in *Moods of Miss J,* he manages to compel in- volvement. Here there is an appealing vulnerability that i as unsentimental as it is captivating. This is perhaps becaus the artist has extrapolated the evolving image from photograph, getting deeper into his own feelings as h describes and invents. In addition to photo-etching, th plate is worked with aquatint, engraving, and open-bit etching. There is much scraping and burnishing. The tw color elements are inserts rolled in relief. The artist printe on Arches Cover white.

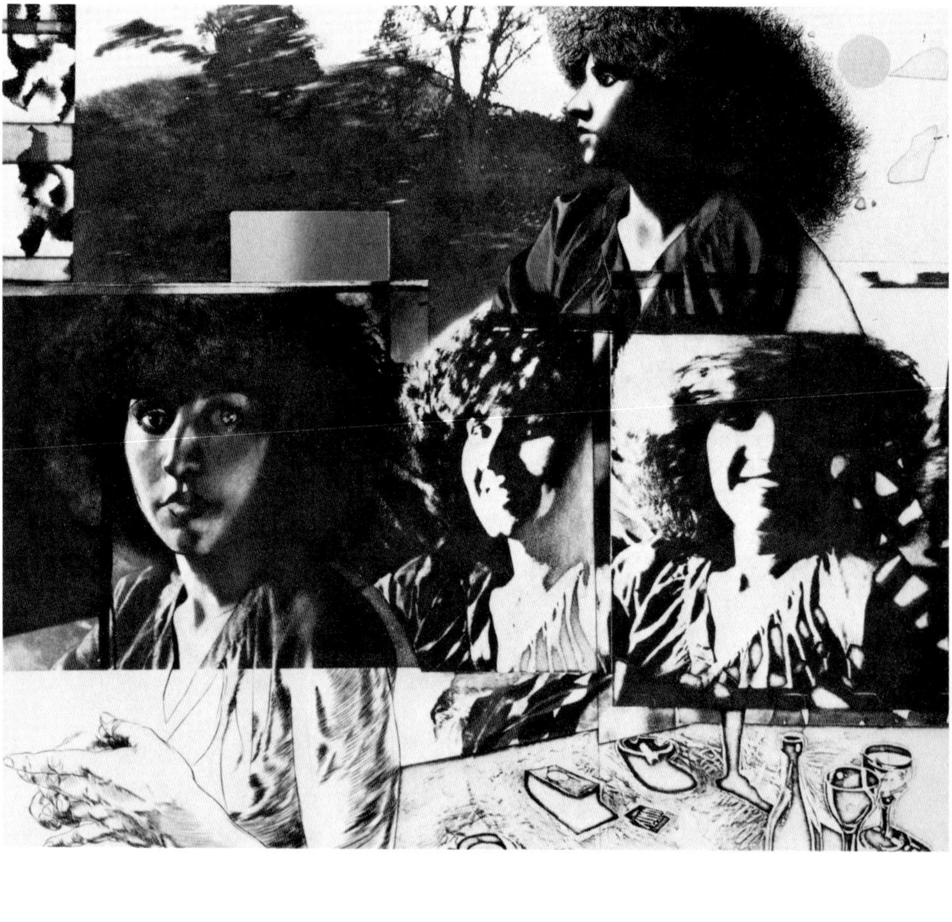

Chrzanowski, a former student of Vincent Longo, reflects some of her teacher's preoccupations in intaglio but of course has her own sensibilities and commitment to color. The result is a painterly use of the etching medium with grid-related structures and other linear episodes denied, absorbed, or modified by depth of etch as expressed in varying ink transparencies, in aquatinting, and in over-printing. Three zinc plates involving etching, aquatint, and soft-ground were used in the production of this plate. The artist printed on Arches Cover white. Ink was hand-made.

15
Romola Chrzanowski
(b. Huntington, New York, 1946)
Untitled
1977, etching, aquatint, and soft-ground, edition: none
Image: 39.8 x 29.5 (15⅝ x 11⅝)
Sheet: 75.5 x 56.1 (29⅝ x 22⅛)
The Artist

16
Romola Chrzanowski
(b. Huntington, New York, 1946)
Untitled
1977, etching, aquatint, and soft-ground, edition: none
Image: 39.8 x 29.5 (15⅝ x 11⅝)
Sheet: 75.5 x 56.1 (29⅝ x 22⅛)
The Artist

Chrzanowski has developed a number of proofs from a group of four plates printed in successive states in combinations of two or more plates. She has varied plate combinations and colors and the order of printing both of plates and colors. Both prints here result from this experiment. This image was developed from two zinc plates that involved etching, aquatint, and soft-ground. Again, the artist printed on Arches Cover white with hand-made ink.

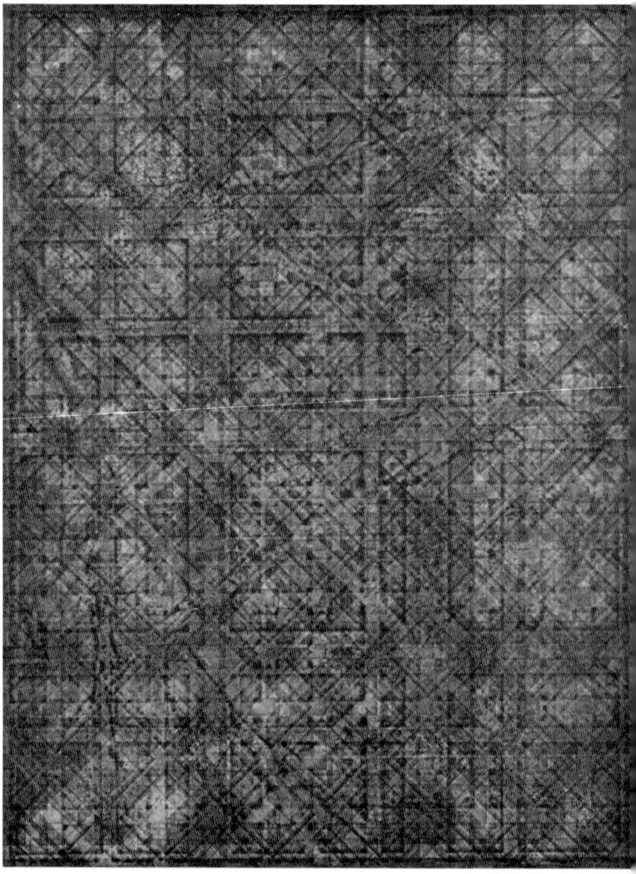

Clinton's *Cave Painting* was produced at Graphicstudio at the University of South Florida in Tampa, where he worked as a master printer. The print takes a lithographic stone as its central image and plays color against the stone's surface, its grain and fractures, to create an illusion of space, a kind of film of light that both denies and probes the stone's materiality. There were seven press runs. The first three runs involved colors airbrushed on aluminum plates, the last four involved photo-images of the litho stone. The printing order was yellow, red, black, green and blue, orange and red, and violet. The artist printed on Arches Cover white.

17
Paul A. Clinton
(b. Salem, Oregon, 1942)
Cave Painting
1976, lithograph, edition: 8
Image: 52.7 x 73.6 (20¾ x 29)
Sheet: 57.0 x 76.4 (22½ x 30 1/16)
The Artist

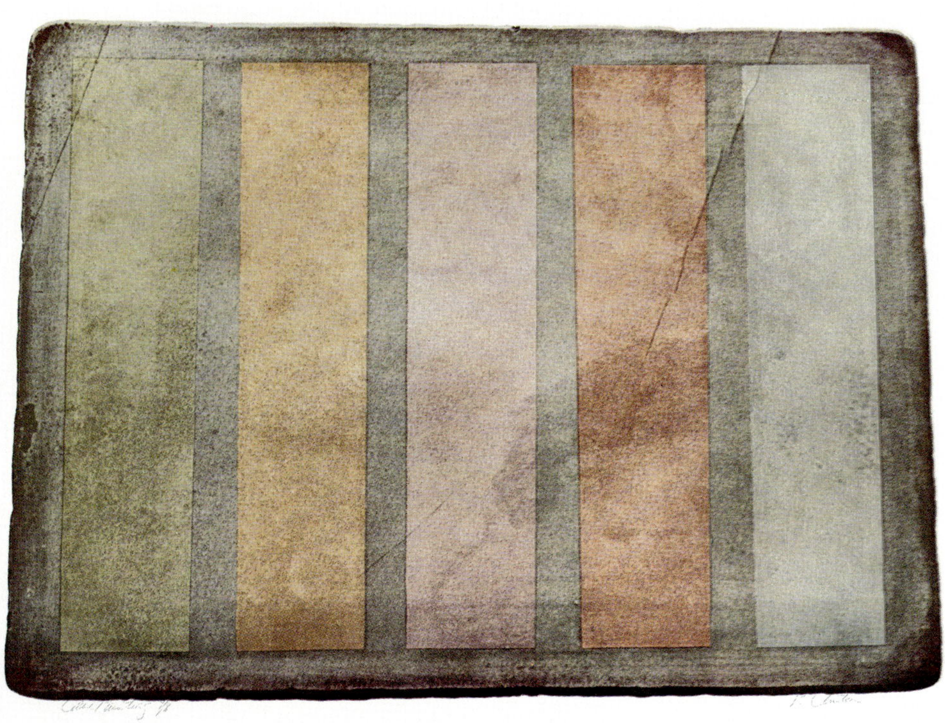

18
Paul A. Clinton
(b. Salem, Oregon, 1942)
Lithophyte (Blue II)
1977, lithograph, blue-print, and hand-coloring with color pencil, edition: unique
Image: 26.7 x 64.7 (10½ x 25½)
Sheet: 30.3 x 68.0 (12 x 26¾)
The Artist

Clinton is a master printer who has collaborated with such artists as Robert Rauschenberg, Frank Stella, James Rosenquist, and Ellsworth Kelly. As an artist in his own right, he has taken printmaking techniques and characteristics as his subject matter, developing aesthetic attitudes out of his raw engagement with the process. In this sense, he is like the painters who see their engagement with paint as the rationale for their art or the sculptors who proclaim the truth of materials. Clinton's prints have a quietude and refinement that masks their complexity and thoughtfulness. *Lithophyte (Blue II)* involves five press runs and the combination of lithography and blue-print with hand-coloring (color pencils). Colors printed are in order: blue, airbrushed yellow, airbrushed orange, airbrushed blue, brown. Printing was by the artist on Rives BFK paper.

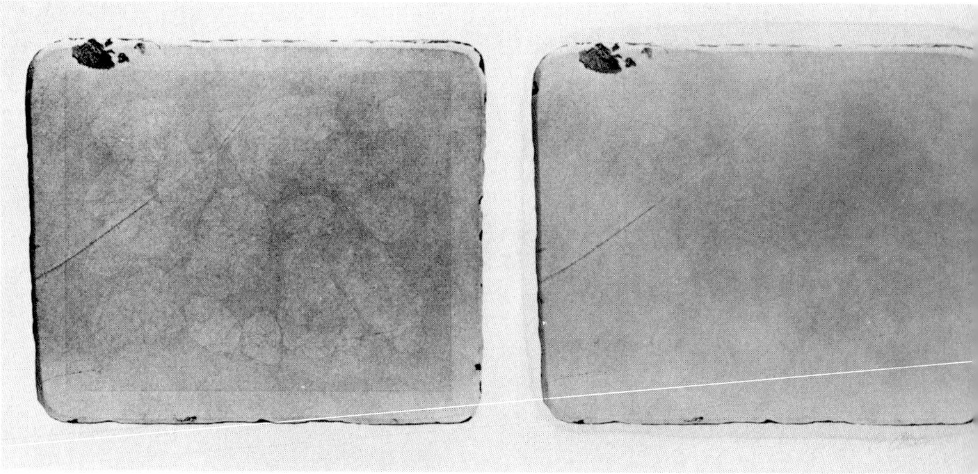

Crabb's obsessive draughtsmanship, a kind of meticulous doodling, projects a fantastic world enlivened and enriched by fine intaglio technique. In *No Deposit, No Return,* tonal richness enhances the ambiguity of scale. Aquatint, engraving, dry-point, and etching lend power and variety to the drawing. The image suggests physical manipulation, as perhaps a straight drawing of the subject would not. The artist has worked on a magnesium plate and has printed with Graphic Chemical Dark Brown no. 545 on Arches Cover white.

19
James Crabb
(b. Merced, California, 1947)
No Deposit, No Return
1976, aquatint and etching with drypoint and engraving,
edition: 25
Image: 21.9 x 14.6 (8⅝ x 5¾)
Sheet: 56.5 x 37.7 (22¼ x 14⅞)
Davidson Galleries

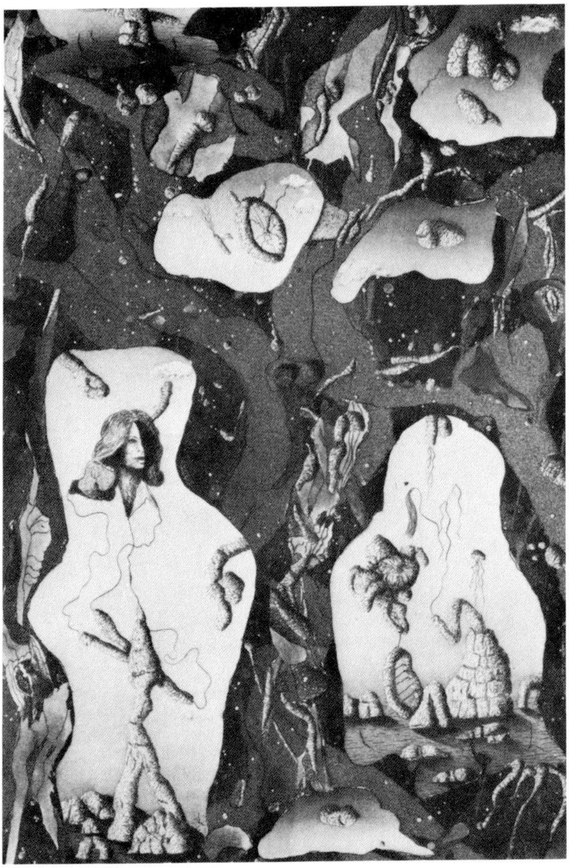

20

James Crabb

(b. Merced, California, 1947)

Departure #8

1977, aquatint and etching with drypoint and engraving, edition: 22

Image: 39.8 x 34.5 (15⅝ x 13⅝)

Sheet: 76.2 x 56.4 (30 x 22¼)

Davidson Galleries

Crabb's forms are biomorphic, a populous growth over the surface of the plate that itself seems to show erosion, wear and tear, marks of passage. These threadlike and convoluted forms seem to be going nowhere and everywhere and, on close inspection, organize into reminiscent anatomies as if we dealt with shorthand creatures. The print was developed from two zinc plates with aquatint and etching and with some drypoint and engraving. The first plate, wholly of aquatint, was printed by the artist in hand-ground yellow-ochre. The second plate, both etching and aquatint, was overprinted in Graphic Chemical Black no. 514 on Arches Cover white.

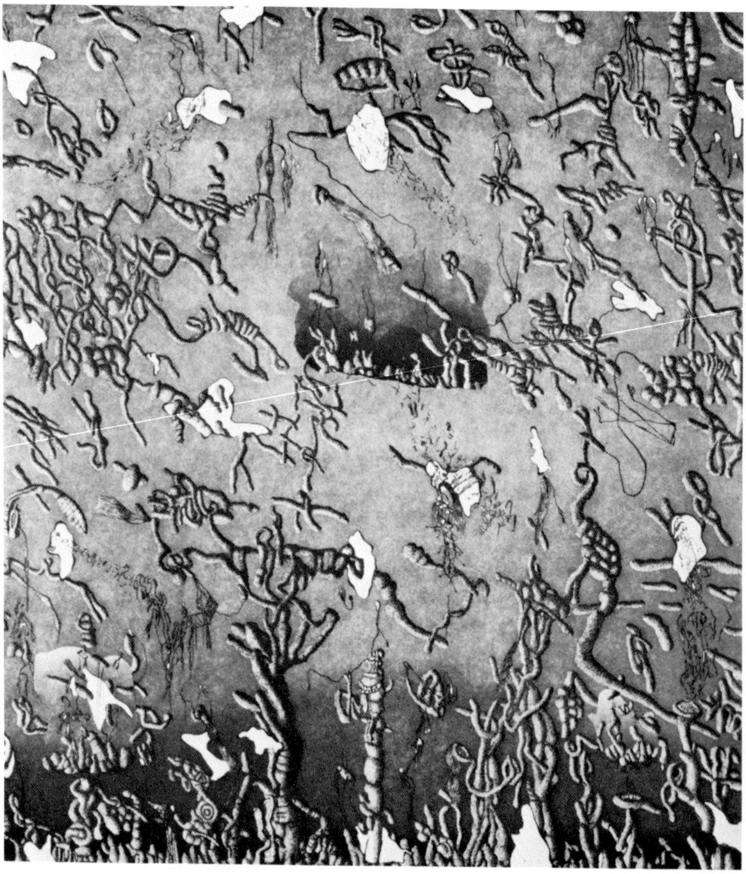

21
Jack Damer
(b. Pittsburgh, Pennsylvania, 1938)
Main Line
1977, lithograph, edition: 10
Image: 63.5 x 86.6 (25 x 34⅛)
Sheet: 63.5 x 86.6 (25 x 34⅛)
The Artist

Damer is fluent in the lithographic medium, but a continuing preoccupation in a variety of his images is the flow of energy across the paper sheet, the energy of line, of color incident, and of black and white drawing. The energy activates the field or becomes the field itself, getting beyond the perception of area to space as force or pure extension. *Main Line* consists of five printings from a single stone. Lines were printed first in stone black followed by yellow, red, blue, and black. After printing the format of transparent black lines, the artist removed the grease from the stone with carbolic acid and gasoline. Grease receptivity was destroyed but the optical image remained. The stone was counter-etched to reestablish its grease sensitivity, and the artist drew the next color (yellow) with autographic ink in pen using the lines from the first printing as a guide. After the yellow was processed and printed, the procedure was repeated for successive colors. Registration was managed by commercial registration buttons cemented to the stone. The paper was hole-punched to accommodate these pins. The artist printed on Arches Cover white.

22
Jack Damer
(b. Pittsburgh, Pennsylvania, 1938)
Xacto Facto
1977, lithograph, edition: 3
Image: 62.2 x 75.4 (24½ x 29¾)
Sheet: 62.2 x 75.4 (24½ x 29¾)
The Artist

Damer's commitment to richly activated surface is demonstrated in *Xacto Facto*. The image, a color plate that was used in another print, here appears alone printed in black. In this form, the print is the first of three states executed by reduction. The artist printed on Arches Cover white.

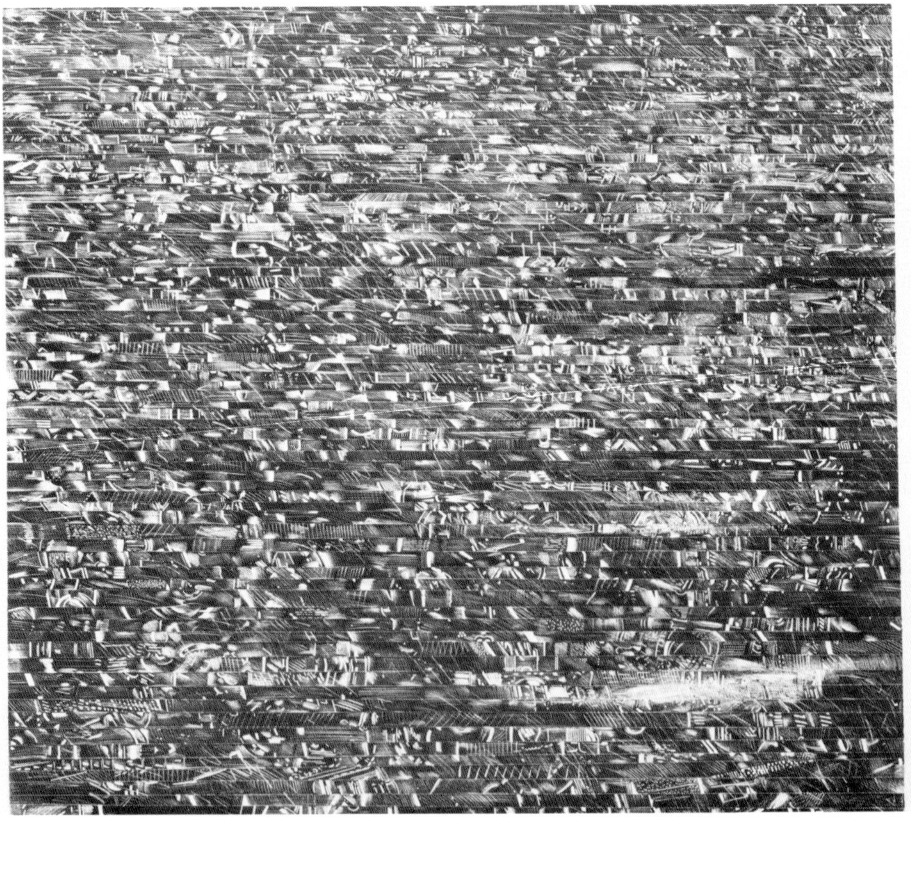

Danner's serigraphs seem to reconcile impulses out of the traditions of collage with formal devices that suggest iconographic art. In *I Bombed the Taj Mahal with Art (What's Steven Got in His Hand),* random elements are peppered over a formalized landscape, while below, a gesture unfolds as if in the frames of a film or in the narrative panels of a religious triptych. The artist has written: "This print pays homage to separate yet related fantasies. One fantasy improvises off of an architectural landmark, the Taj Mahal, and the other presents the interpretation by a friend of a Groucho Marx gesture. In the combination of these two directions, the activity of expression, not the form, takes precedence." But the formality of presentation seems also a potent part of the expression, balancing as it does the smaller and larger gestures and rationalizing a variety of spaces and scales. The serigraph was printed from nineteen paper stencils on index paper.

23
Robert William Danner
(b. Milwaukee, Wisconsin, 1948)
I Bombed the Taj Mahal with Art (What's Steven Got in His Hand)
1976, serigraph, edition: 45
Image: 55.9 x 81.0 (22 x 31⅞)
Sheet: 55.9 x 81.0 (22 x 31⅞)
The Artist

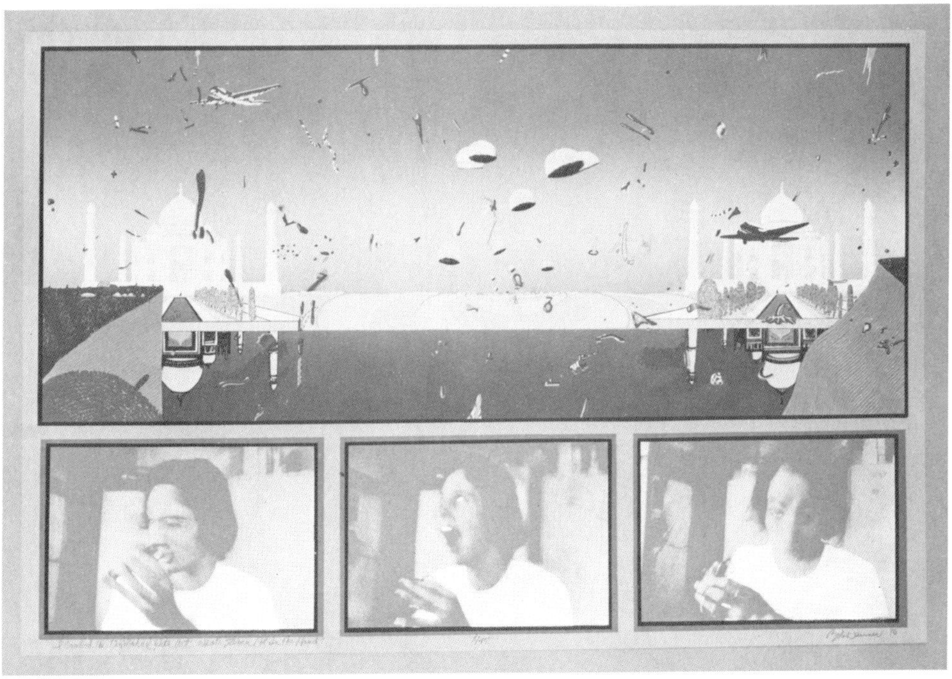

24

Robert William Danner

(b. Milwaukee, Wisconsin, 1948)

1973 Birdnest, Rose, and Capital

1977, serigraph, edition: 35

Image: 58.5 x 43.3 (23 x 17 1/16)

Sheet: 58.5 x 43.3 (23 x 17 1/16)

The Artist

Danner has written about *1973 Birdnest, Rose, and Capital:* "This print documents the hair style 'Birdnest.' It was one of the total of thirty different styles I used to celebrate the cutting of my hair in 1973. From 1970–1975, I structured a number of interactions using my hair as a focal point. Since hair is used as a means of defining identity, the rituals opened me to introspection." Again, the image balances formal and informal elements in a manner that seems to present the subject. Using paper stencils, the artist printed nineteen screens on index paper.

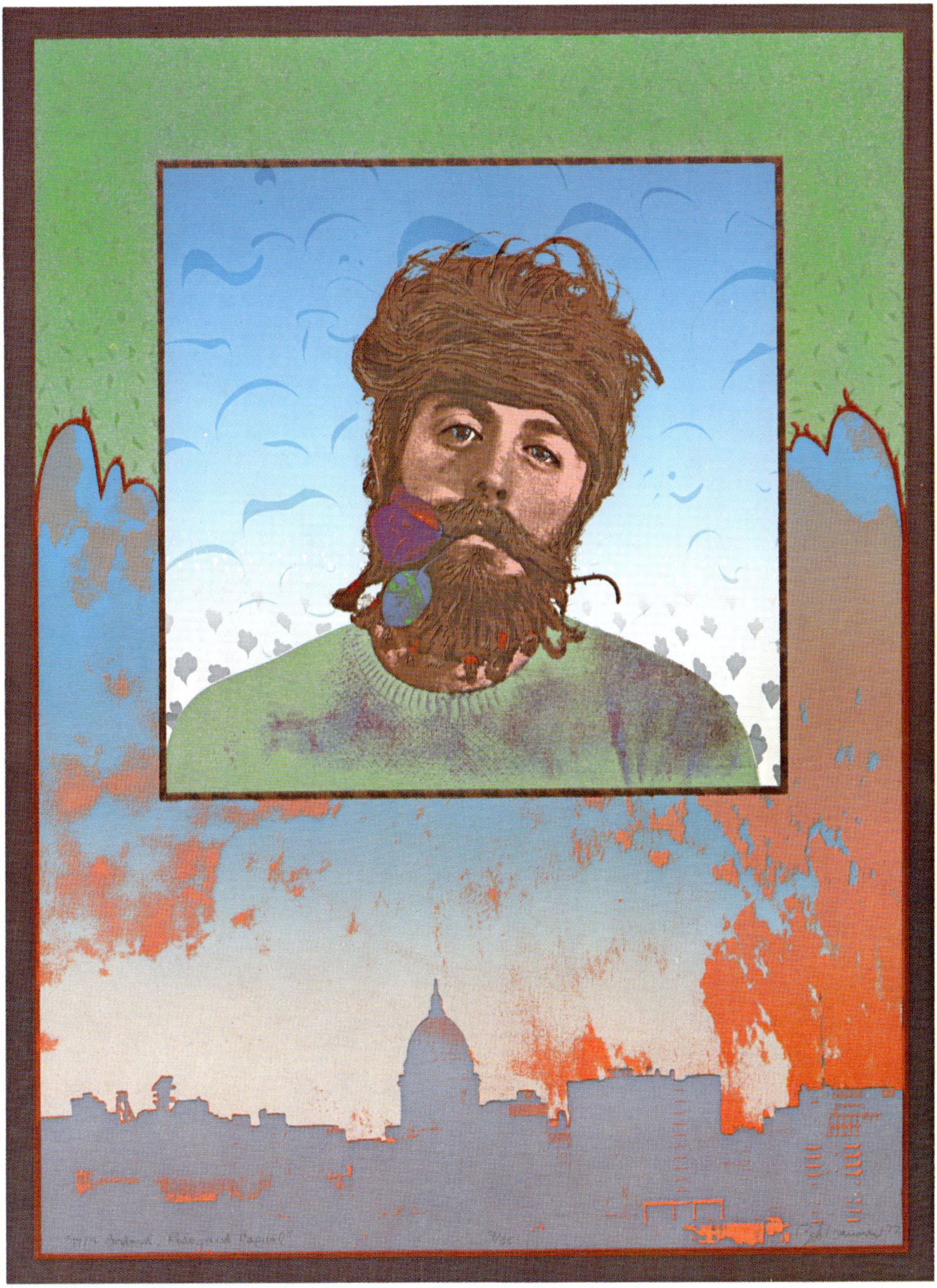

25
Paul S. Davidson
(b. Ticonderoga, New York, 1951)
Untitled
1977, lithograph, edition: 10
Image: 38.1 x 26.7 (15 x 10½)
Sheet: 38.1 x 26.7 (15 x 10½)
The Artist

Davidson's lithographs provide dark glowing surfaces whose muted radiance suggests ambiguous space and indeterminate scale. Like diffused light come upon unexpectedly at night at a distance, they locate themselves as sensation. Their energy derives from the tension of transparent borders and matte areas inflected only enough to activate the central field. In the present print, the image is bled. There were four press runs from ball-grained, deep-etched aluminum plates. First, the full sheet was printed in a solid brown-black; next, the border was printed in a transparent blue-green. The central rectangle was printed first with a dark gray crayon drawing, then with a pale purple tone gray crayon drawing. Printing was by the artist on Copperplate Deluxe.

Davidson uses essentially simple procedures to achieve lithographs that are visually subtle. This print was achieved in three press runs from ball-grained, deep-etched aluminum plates. The image area was printed first as a solid dark brown, then a transparent blue border was printed, and finally a semi-transparent red crayon drawing was overprinted on the central field. Press work was by the artist. The paper is Arches Cover white.

26
Paul S. Davidson
(b. Ticonderoga, New York, 1951)
Untitled
1977, lithograph, edition: 10
Image: 48.2 x 30.4 (19 x 12)
Sheet: 56.7 x 38.2 (22⅜ x 15)
The Artist

27

Richard Davis

(b. Middletown, New York, 1947)

Bottles

1976, serigraph, edition: 210

Image: 56.5 x 73.7 (22¼ x 29)

Sheet: 63.5 x 97.2 (25 x 38¼)

Reproduced in color on the front cover

The Brooklyn Museum 77.230.2

Davis's serigraphs are of the highest technical order and are also works of art of lucid strength and elegance. *Bottles* seems absolutely wedded to the paper, declaring its own space and atmosphere in a way that serigraphs rarely do. The image was printed from twenty screens. The artist made all photo-stencils by painting opaquing ink on Mylar, using small, very fine brushes. He printed with silkscreen inks thinned with transparent base and binder varnish on Lenox paper, then overprinted with clear silkscreen varnish. Hand printing of the edition, a five-month undertaking, was entirely by the artist.

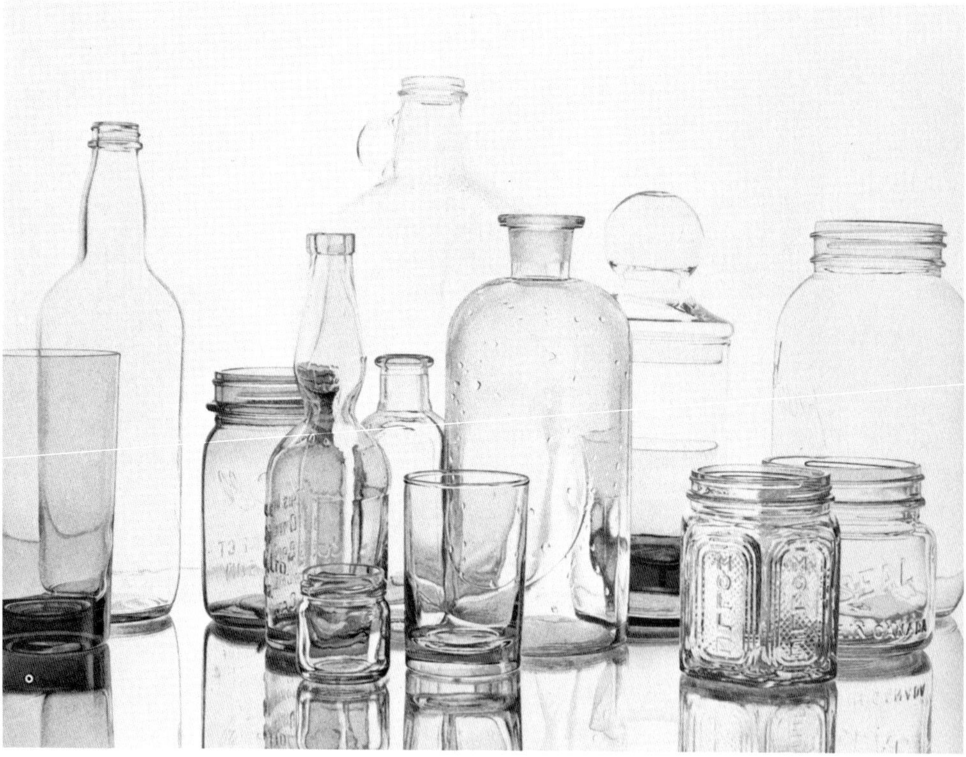

Davis's *Outcrop* was a year in the making. The complex image required thirty-one screens, all by photo-stencil. The artist, a perfectionist, hand-printed the entire edition on Strathmore white wove paper.

28
Richard Davis
(b. Middletown, New York, 1947)
Outcrop
1978, serigraph, edition: 290
Image: 58.4 x 78.4 (23 x 30⅞)
Sheet: 71.0 x 91.4 (28 x 36)
ADI Gallery

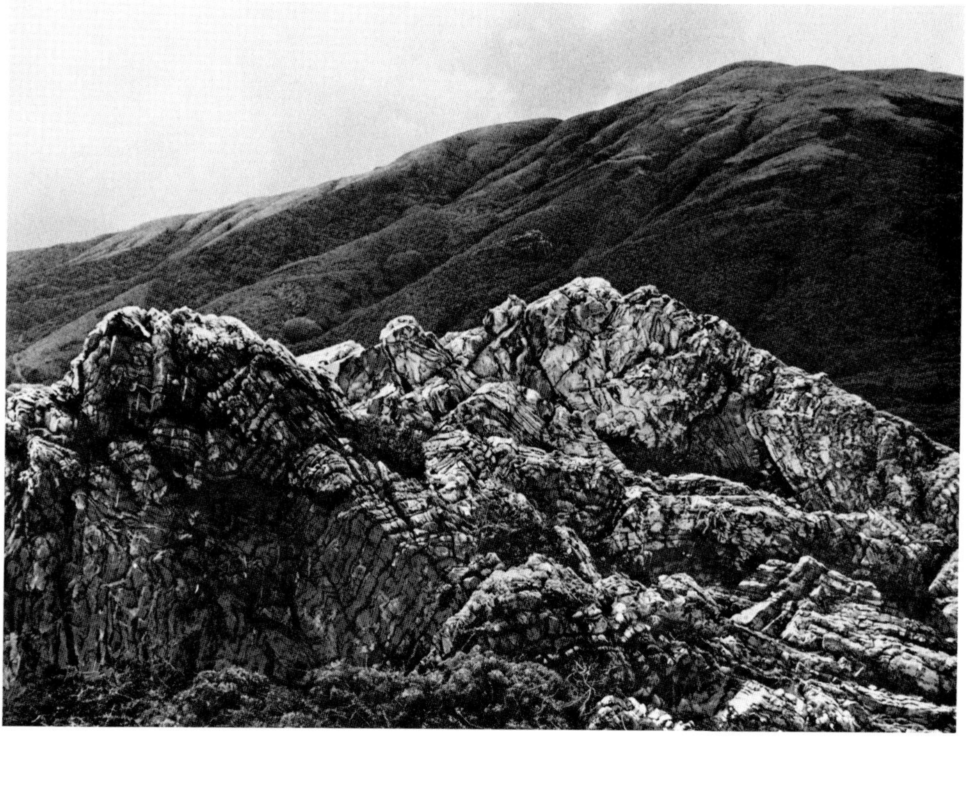

29

Craig Dennis

(b. Lansing, Michigan, 1950)

Cross-Reference

1977, photo-etching, edition: 14

Image: 34.5 x 54.3 (13⅝ x 21⅜)

Sheet: 52.4 x 70.5 (20⅝ x 27¾)

The Artist

Dennis's prints often involve an image of the physical self both as knowledge and as mystery. In *Cross-Reference,* the image of a hand appears as an analogue of a map of Michigan. The artist has written elsewhere in these pages: "I want to see a map of my hand, because it knows things that I don't." The compelling thing in this art of ideas and intuitions is that it operates visually, on a level of unified impact. There is a story, of course, and explanation, but image dominates. *Cross-Reference* was produced from a photo-etched plate with hand alterations to the photo-transparency and to the plate itself. The artist printed the edition on Rives BFK using 75% Graphic Chemical Etching Black no. 514 and 25% Graphic Chemical Intense Black no. 1117.

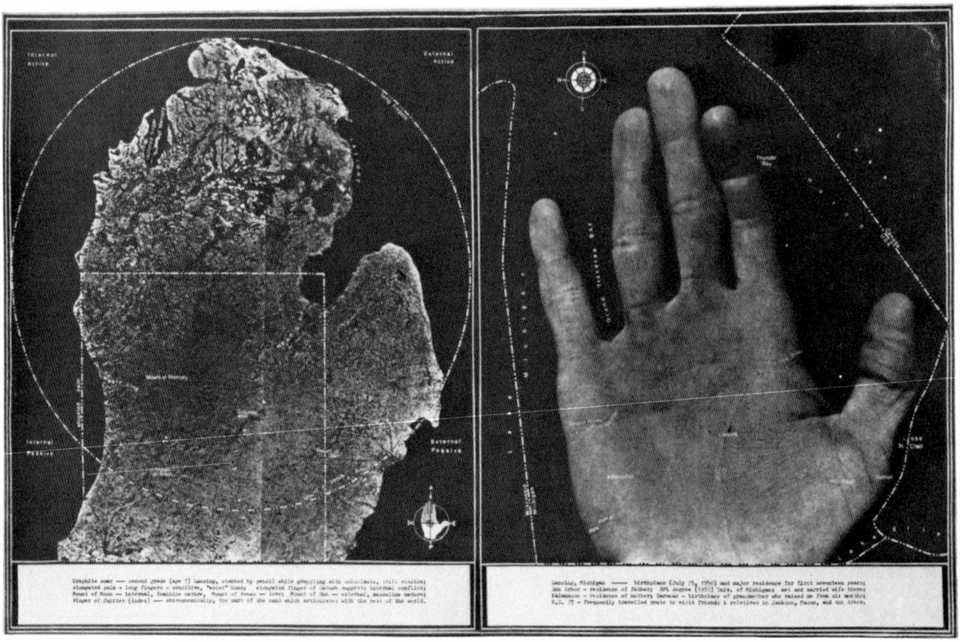

Dennis's *Stones/Bones* redistributes parts of the body in a grid pattern. It is as if these sub-images were tiles of a wall wearing down into a kind of indeterminacy. The surface seems scarred and eroded, the separate panels sometimes seeming to push out, scored away by graffiti, marked by wear and tear. Images of structure and of loss are projected simultaneously—one image after all. This lithograph was printed from five aluminum plates, the first three drawn in no. 2 crayon, the fourth painted with lithotine tusche, and the fifth a photographic plate (133-line half-tone) with hand manipulations and additions to the negative. Colored inks were by Hanco. The artist printed on Arches Cover white.

30
Craig Dennis
(b. Lansing, Michigan, 1950)
Stones/Bones
1978, lithograph, edition: 14
Image: 57.8 x 40.7 (22¾ x 16)
Sheet: 76.2 x 56.5 (30 x 22¼)
The Artist

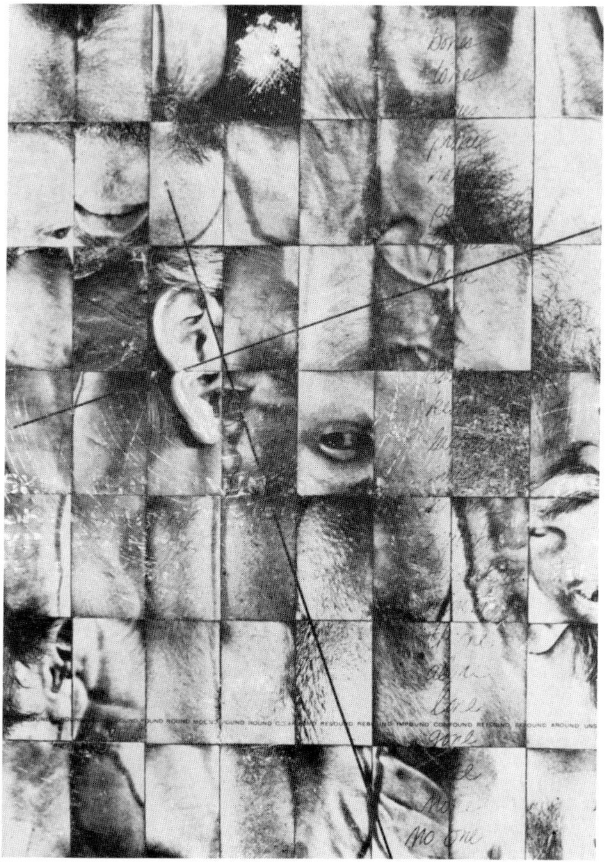

31
Michael Di Cerbo
(b. Paterson, New Jersey, 1947)
Untitled (77A)
1977, aquatint and etching,
edition: 10
Image: 49.2 x 39.7 (19⅜ x 15⅝)
Sheet: 59.8 x 48.0 (23½ x 18⅞)
The Artist

Di Cerbo has turned his sense of urban grandeur and power into a loose geometry of forms, patterns of intense light and velvety darks that allude to the soaring architecture of skyscrapers or to the huddle and mass of office blocks seen from a high window. New York, particularly, is a source of inspiration, but the images are of energies and of forces and not of identifiable locations. This print was developed on a zinc plate with line etching and aquatint. The artist printed with Weber's Intense Black ink on Arches Cover white.

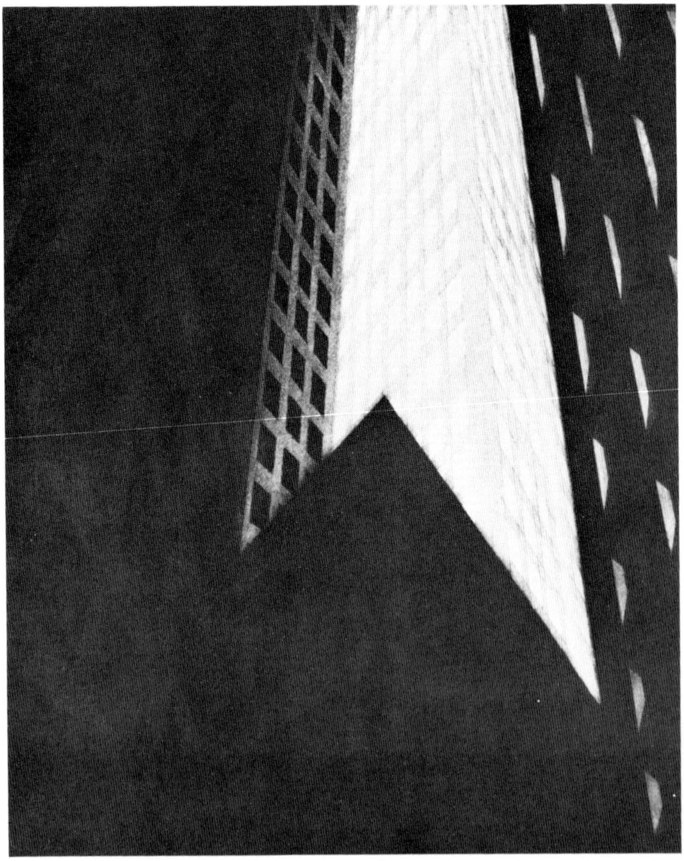

Di Cerbo's imagery varies, but his technique remains fundamental. The artist develops his zinc plate with etching and aquatint. He prints with Weber's Intense Black ink, in this instance on Stonehenge white.

32
Michael Di Cerbo
(b. Paterson, New Jersey, 1947)
Untitled (78C)
1978, aquatint and etching, edition: 10
Image: 37.8 x 49.6 (14⅞ x 19½)
Sheet: 50.2 x 59.8 (19¾ x 23½)
The Artist

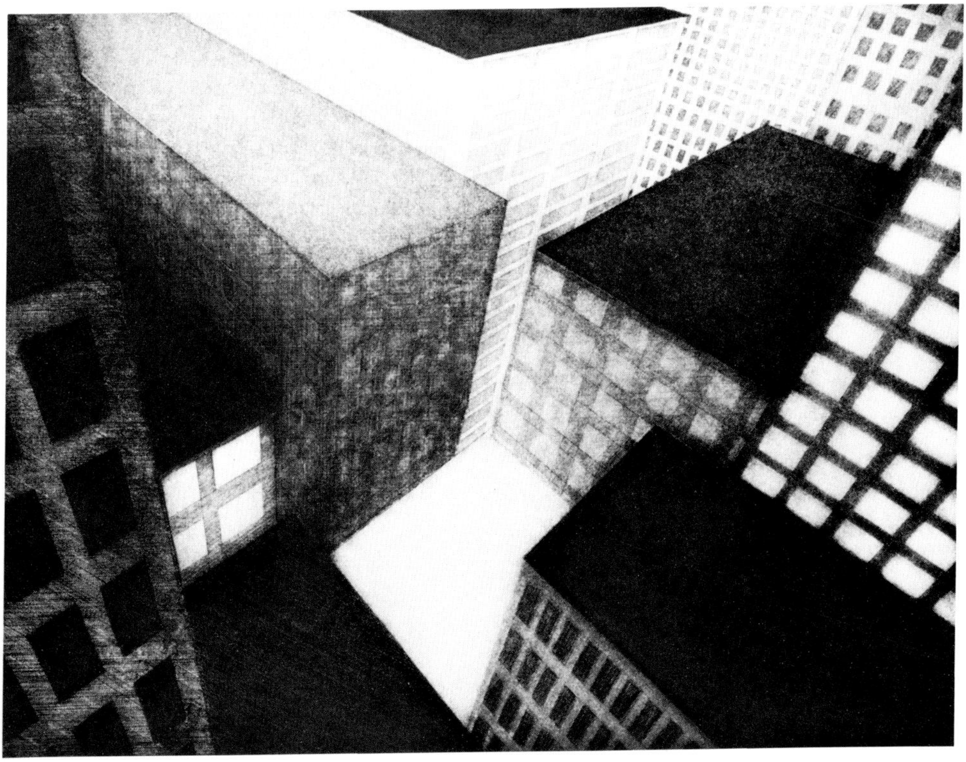

33
Martha Erlebacher
(b. Jersey City, New Jersey, 1937)
New Potatoes
1978, lithograph, edition: 60
Image: 55.6 x 76.1 (21⅞ x 30)
Sheet: 66.2 x 84.2 (26⅛ x 33⅛)
Associated American Artists, New York

Erlebacher's lithographs spiritualize the delights of the table. There is none of the gross indigestibility of cornucopia art, but cool arrangements suavely realized in the meticulous idiom of realistic illustration. The artist claims a symbolic content, and there is no doubt that some epiphany is reached through contemplation of her sensuously realized forms and flowing colors. For *New Potatoes,* the artist drew on a stone and on four aluminum plates. The printing sequence was as follows: black (stone), yellow, and red with the same blue printed on the third and fourth aluminum plates. Printing was by Landfall Press Master Printer Jack Lemmon on Arches Cover white. The edition was co-published by Landfall Press, Chicago, and G.W. Einstein Co., Inc., New York.

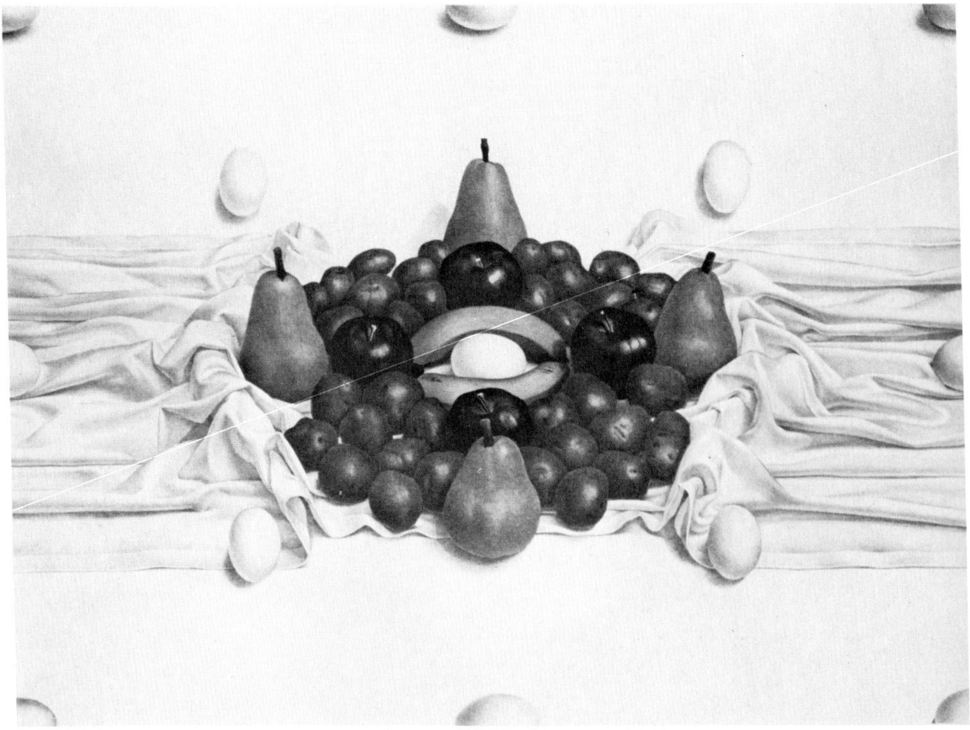

Erlebacher's lithograph *Homage to Bacchus* suggests a kind of chaste voluptuousness. Fruit, plates, napery, glasses, and bottles have a svelte roundness; the air seems to hug these shapes, the light to polish them. Yet what seems so near and available comes across finally as remote, immaculate, even dust-free. The tempting untouchableness of it all is punctuated by ranks of floating cherries and other fruits—all with a panache of Renaissance carvings. The symmetry gives an altar-like consistency to the whole. The artist drew on one stone and four aluminum plates, which were printed black (stone), yellow, blue, light red, and dark red. Printing was by Landfall Press Master Printer Jack Lemmon on Arches Cover white. The edition was co-published by Landfall Press, Chicago, and G.W. Einstein Co., Inc., New York.

34
Martha Erlebacher
(b. Jersey City, New Jersey, 1937)
Homage to Bacchus
1978, lithograph, edition: 60
Image: 55.6 x 76.1 (21⅞ x 30)
Sheet: 66.0 x 85.7 (26 x 33¾)
Associated American Artists, New York

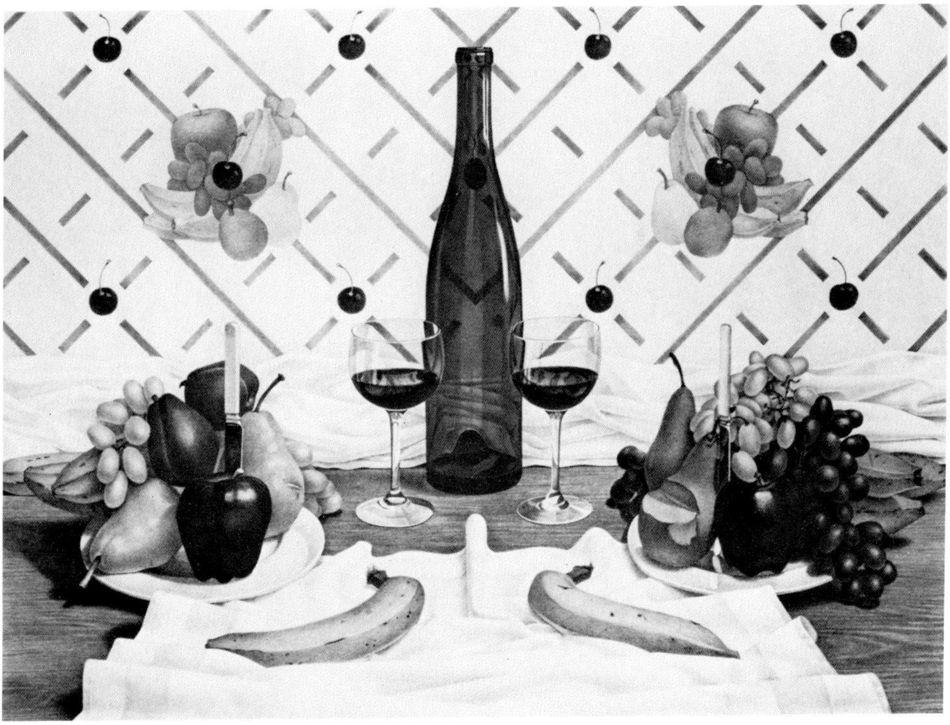

35
Yasuhiro Esaki
(b. Kyushu, Japan, 1941)
Fourth Iris
1977, etching and aquatint
with hand-coloring, edition: 25
Image: 24.2 x 20.0 (9½ x 7⅞)
Sheet: 56.5 x 37.8 (22¼ x 14⅞)
Reproduced in color on page 6
The Brooklyn Museum, Gift of Mr. David Temple 78.98.1

Esaki has a fine sensitivity to the intaglio technique and a sure sense of scale in the presentation of his images. Inevitably, it seems, he presses the boundary of the paper sheet, giving a sense of fullness and abundance. His effective detail is wholly subordinate to the central image. In *Fourth Iris* the artist worked on a copper plate with line etching and aquatint. The edition was printed by Kay Bradner on Lana and hand-colored with watercolor by the artist.

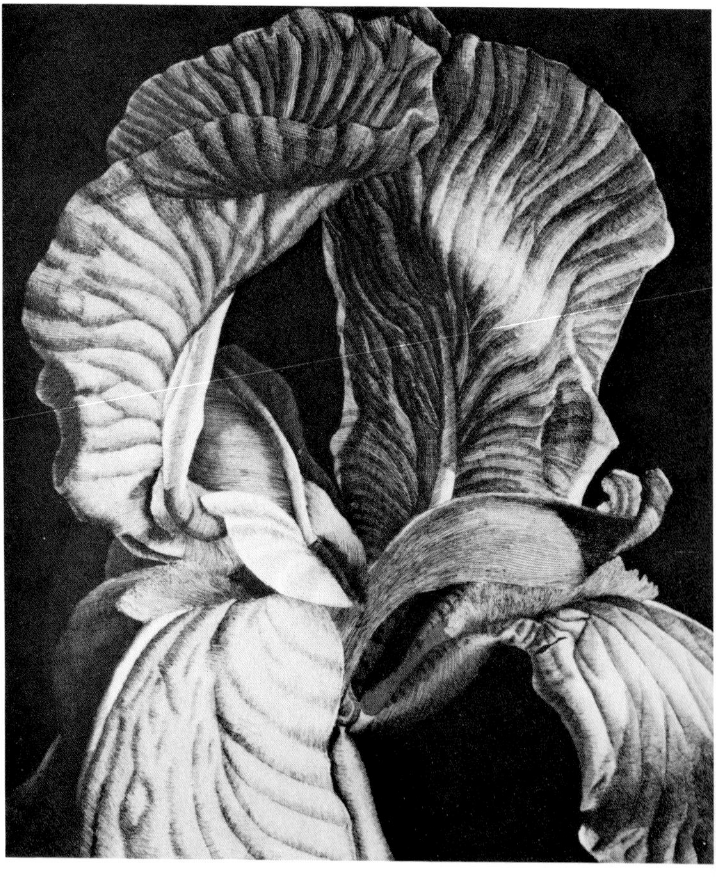

Esaki's *Jacket* is the latest of several of his prints dealing with this article of clothing. Again, the image exerts an outward pressure. The rhythm of the lines heightens our sense of the object itself, which balances abstract and realistic tendencies. The artist worked with line etching on a copper plate. He printed the edition on Arches Cover white.

36
Yasuhiro Esaki
(b. Kyushu, Japan, 1941)
Jacket
1978, etching, edition: 25
Image: 32.1 x 29.9 (12⅝ x 11¾)
Sheet: 61.9 x 47.0 (24⅜ x 18½)
The Artist

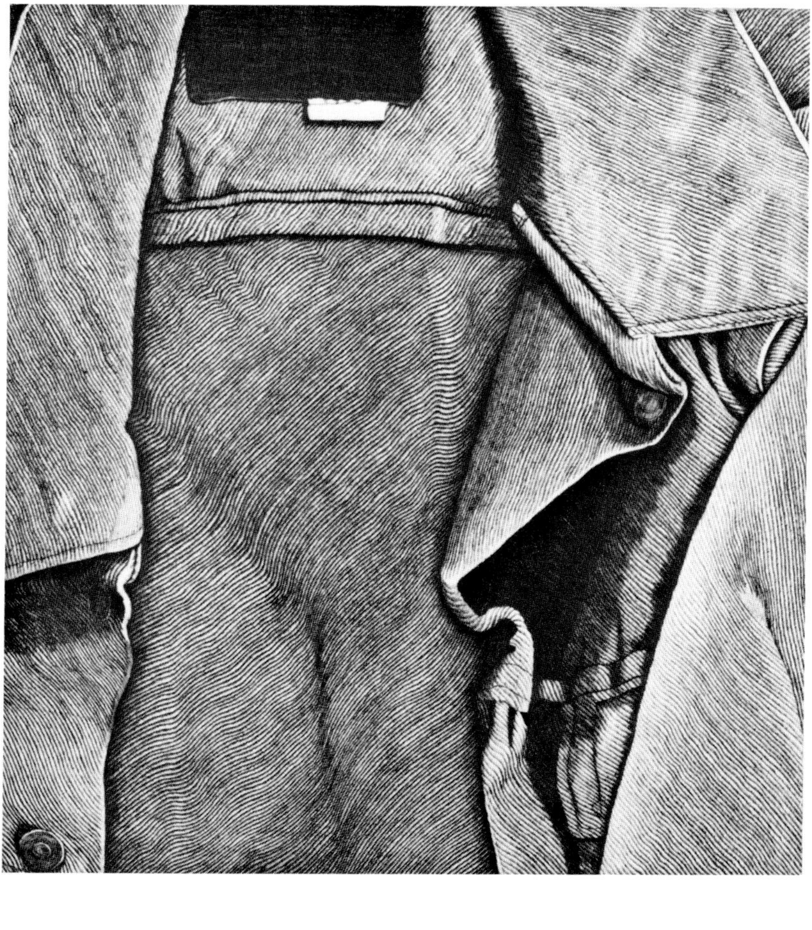

37
Maurine Farmer
(b. Sharon, Pennsylvania, 1952)
Summer Salads
1978, photo-transfer on serigraph ground, edition: unique
Image: 45.7 x 60.3 (18 x 23¾)
Sheet: 56.5 x 76.2 (22½ x 30)
Van Straaten Gallery

Farmer's images vary but not her photo-transfer technique. In fact, this technique is available to everyone and is a standard form of self-discovery on the part of art students. The pleasure here is in the artist's touch, her choices, her deployments. Through the banal technique of photo-transfer, she has succeeded in making personal statements of aesthetic appeal. *Summer Salads* was produced by the artist using the same technique as that for *Little Floaters*. The print is on Arches Cover buff.

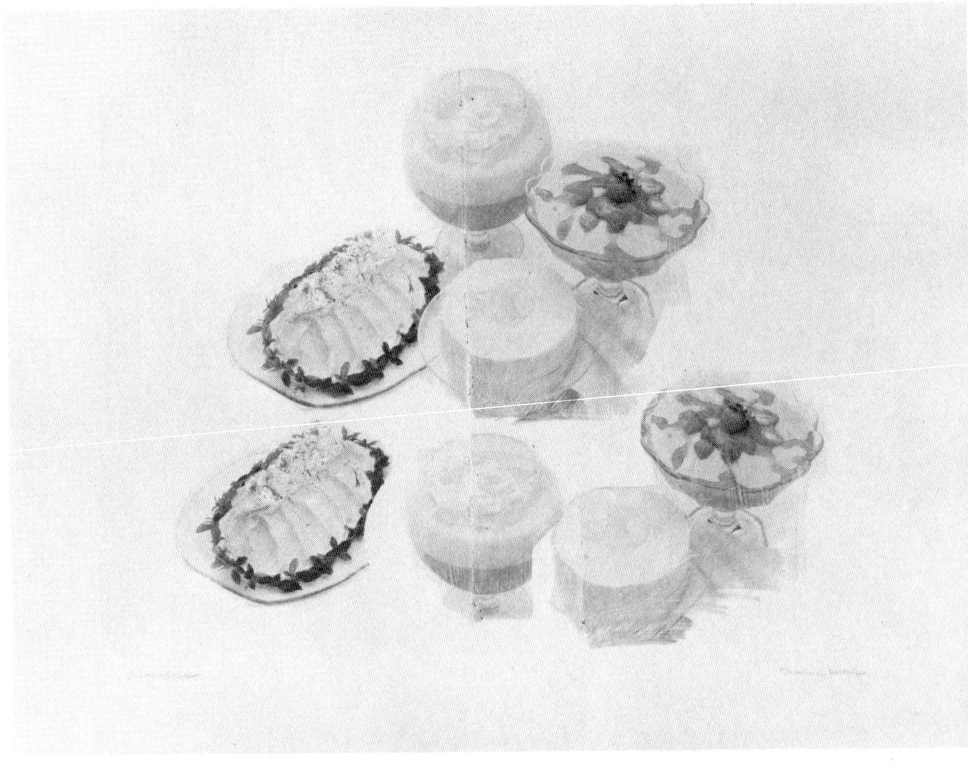

Farmer finds her imagery directly in advertising art, more particularly in magazine illustration. A preferred subject is food. She rearranges her found images to give a variety of patterns or episodes that animate the page. Her prints are produced upon a flat serigraph background. The artist dampens the freshly selected magazine page in oil and then rubs the back of the desired photograph with a pencil until the colors and the image are transferred. Occasionally, she will draw back into the rubbing with a pencil to darken an area, but she usually prefers to leave the transfer undisturbed. *Little Floaters* was produced by the artist on Arches Cover white.

38
Maurine Farmer
(b. Sharon, Pennsylvania, 1952)
Little Floaters
1978, photo - transfer on serigraph ground, edition: unique
Image: 60.3 x 45.1 (23¾ x 17¾)
Sheet: 76.2 x 56.8 (30 x 22⅜)
Van Straaten Gallery

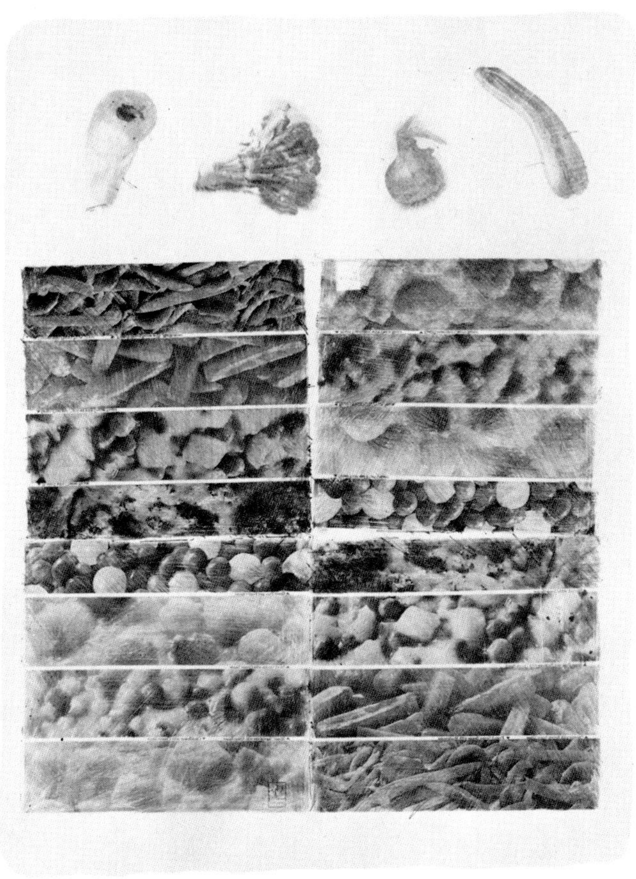

39
Freddie Fong
(b. Canton, China, 1952)
Black and Newsprint Grey
1977, lithograph and collage,
edition: 50
Each image:
35.6 x 28.3 (14 x 11 1/8)
Sheet: 56.8 x 76.2 (22 3/8 x 30)
ADI Gallery

Fong's lithograph-collage *Black and Newsprint Grey* plays an image against itself. It is printed with different colors on different papers; both are fixed to a support sheet so that the top of the one is the bottom of the other. One version of the image was printed on Arches Cover black, with peach as the key color. Another printing of the image was on Rives BFK newsprint gray in dark brown, with pink for the highlights. The images were collaged on Arches Cover white.

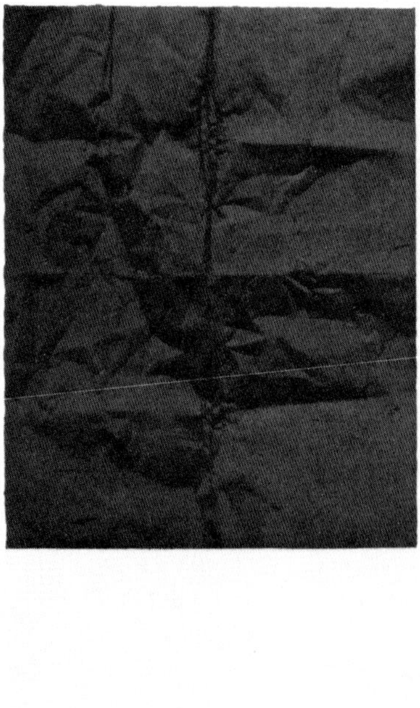

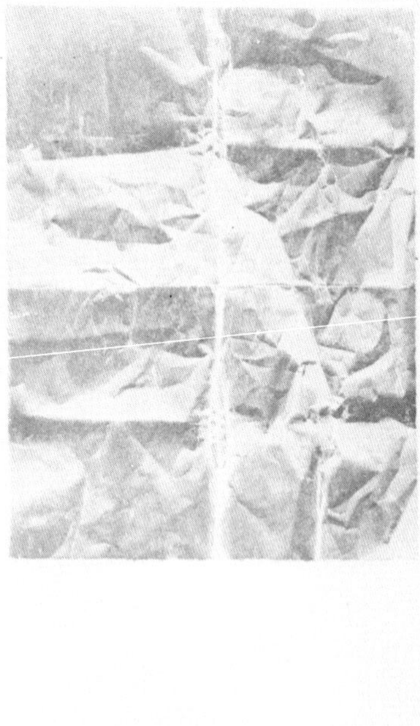

Fong's prints involve a dialogue between the physicality of paper and the illusion of his image, which is of a paper sheet or sheets. In *Candy Wrappers IV* the image of overlaying tissues seems breathed upon the black Arches. At the same time, there is no separation in our perception between the illusionary and the real sheets. The artist printed transparent inks off-register to enhance the tissue-like reference. The printing sequence was red, orange, and blue.

40
Freddie Fong
(b. Canton, China, 1952)
Candy Wrappers IV
1977, lithograph, edition: 30
Image: 40.6 x 48.5 (16 x 19⅛)
Sheet: 51.1 x 68.5 (20⅛ x 27)
ADI Gallery

41
Sondra Freckelton
(b. Dearborn, Michigan, 1936)
Tulips
1977, lithograph, edition: 75
Image: 66.0 x 50.8 (26 x 20)
Sheet: 71.1 x 55.0 (28 x 21⅝)
Brooke Alexander, Inc.

Freckelton is one of a number of artists who have turned to offset lithography for the subtleties of registration and clarity of tint that the process allows. The artist's imagery—flowers, plants, and domestic settings—has the luminocity of watercolor, and in fact washes and overlays of color are what concern Freckelton in her lithographs. *Tulips* was hand-drawn by the artist on seven aluminum plates. The edition was printed on Rives BFK by Joseph Petruzzelli, Siena Studios, New York. The publisher is Brooke Alexander, Inc., New York.

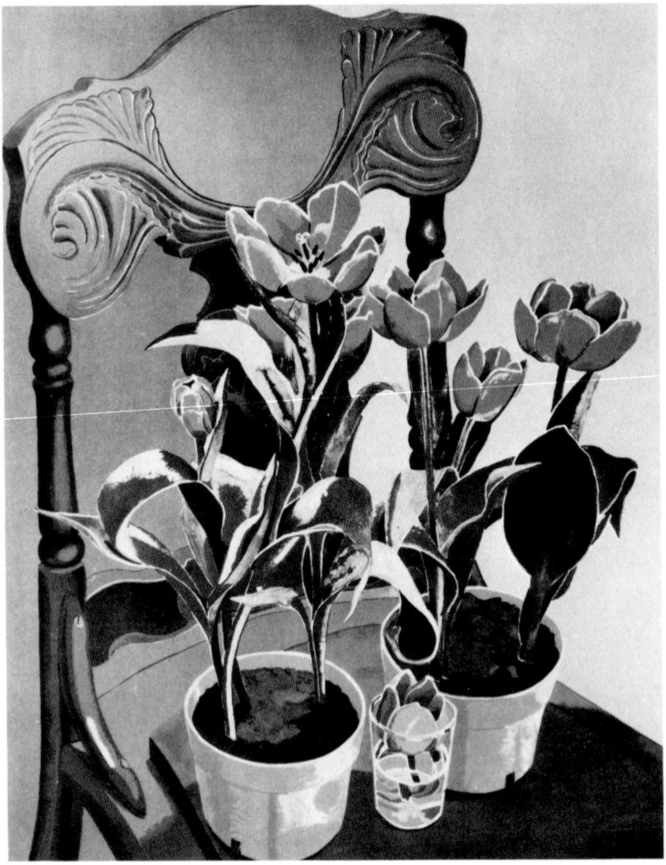

Freckelton's *Begonia with Quilt* has the luminocity and verve of watercolor, partly the result of the thin inking. The print was produced from eight aluminum plates drawn by the artist and was printed by offset press on Johannot paper at Siena Studios in New York. The publisher is Brooke Alexander, Inc., New York.

42
Sondra Freckelton
(b. Dearborn, Michigan, 1936)
Begonia with Quilt
1978, lithograph, edition: 97
Image: 66.0 x 52.4 (26 x 20¾)
Sheet: 69.3 x 54.7 (27¼ x 21½)
Brooke Alexander, Inc.

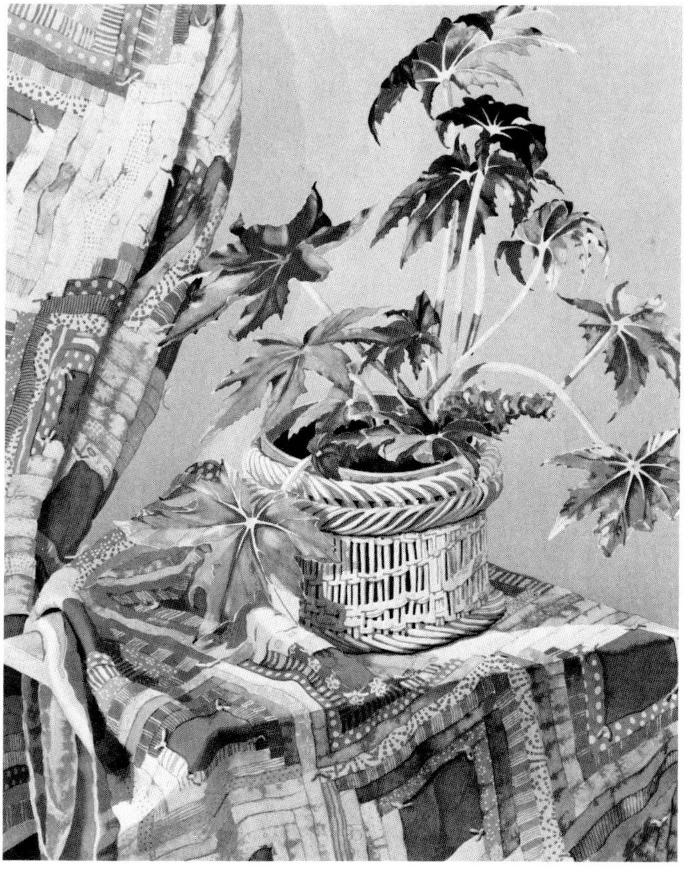

43
Deborah Grobman Furnback
(b. Philadelphia, Pennsylvania, 1944)
Straight Strokes V
1976, lithograph,
edition (varied): 15
Image: 31.2 x 38.2 (12¼ x 15 1/16)
Sheet: 31.2 x 38.2 (12¼ x 15 1/16)
Straight Strokes VI
1978, lithograph, edition: 17
Image: 33.0 x 45.8 (13 x 18 1/16)
Sheet: 33.0 x 45.8 (13 x 18 1/16)
The Artist

Furnback has declared herself concerned with image-making. However, the standardization of the image has no overriding appeal for her. The subject matter of brushstrokes in isolation and relationship, as real things in themselves or as constituents of illusion, makes an edition variée pertinent to this artist's aims. *Straight Strokes V* is part of an edition variée with the image developed up to the total of six press runs, but with each print resulting from at least four runs. There were two background color runs and two runs for shadow shapes. Each print was produced with different combinations of these runs. However, some of the prints in the edition have areas that are cut and removed. Some of the prints have been cut so as to be dimensional. The present print was left uncut. There were four runs in *Straight Strokes V,* a blend of three colors (pale pink to pale cream) for the base color of the strokes, a lavender-gray background, a medium gray shadow—all done from aluminum plates. The key image of tusche brushstrokes was printed in black ink from a stone. *Straight Strokes VI* was printed in four identical runs but standardly editioned. The artist printed both images on Arches Cover white.

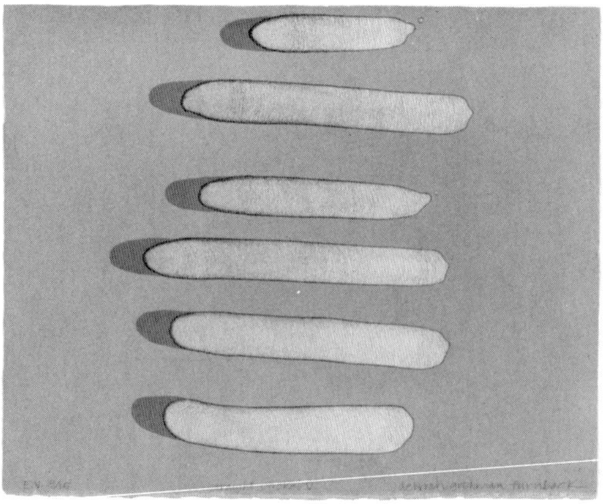

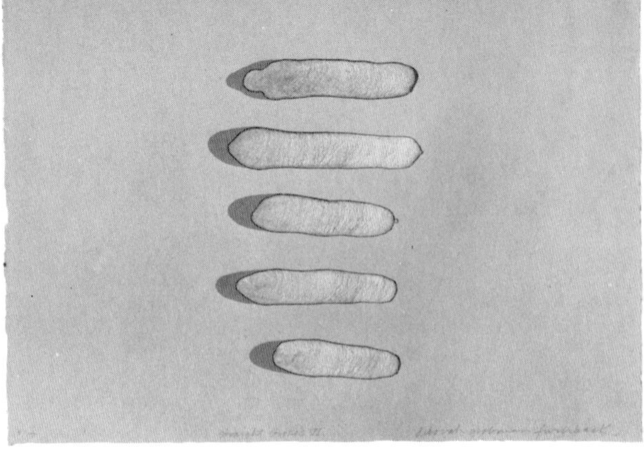

urnback's *Strokes Given Linear Momentum by Hand* is part f the *Hayward Portfolio,* a collection of prints by faculty and tudents at California State University at Hayward. The mage derives from a rubber stamp that the artist ordered to e made photographically from a lithograph of one of her usche brushstrokes. For each print in the edition, she rinted the rubber stamp through a paper stencil, insuring orrect registration. The rubber stamp strokes were then and-colored by the artist in pencil. Paper is Arches Cover vhite.

44
Deborah Grobman Furnback
(b. Philadelphia, Pennsylvania, 1944)
Strokes Given Linear Momentum by Hand
1977, rubber stamp print with hand-coloring,
edition (varied): 50
Image: 27.9 x 35.4 (11 x 14)
Sheet: 27.9 x 35.4 (11 x 14)
The Brooklyn Museum, Gift of California State University at Hayward *78.103.7*

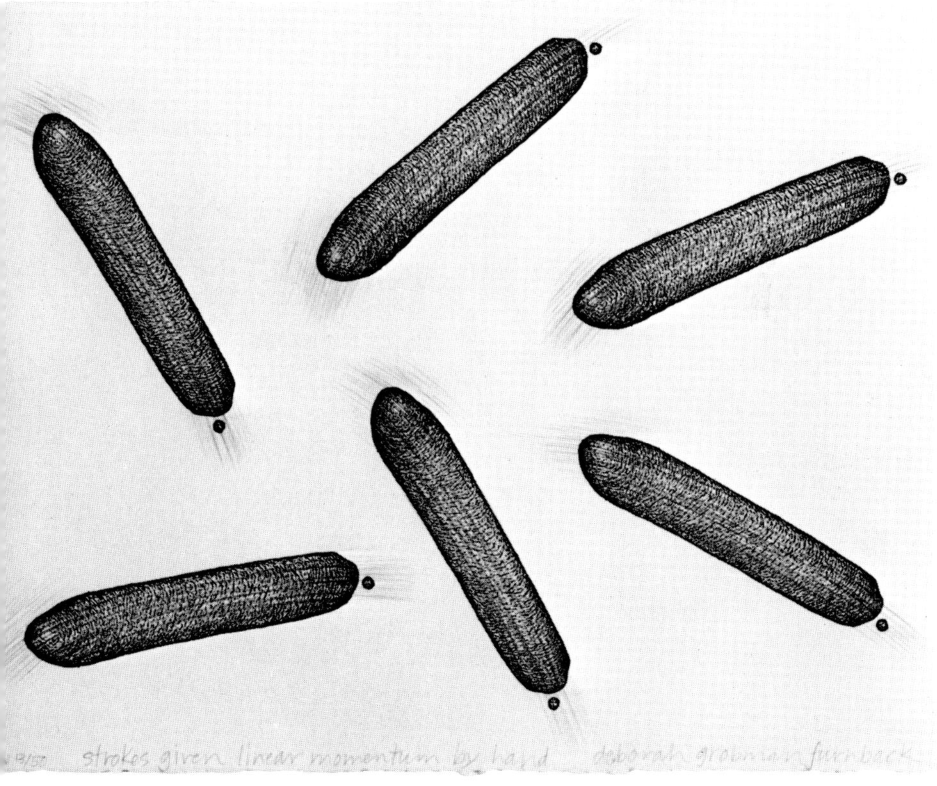

45
Anita Gelman
(b. Detroit, Michigan, 1952)
The Serpents
1976, photo-etching with aquatint and etching, edition: 15
Image: 27.4 x 22.2 (10¾ x 8¾)
Sheet: 45.5 x 35.2 (17⅞ x 13⅞)
The Artist

Gelman is not your buttoned-down printmaker. The inta glio medium is wrestled with to provide potent expression The medium is bent to service, and the sense of engagemen contributes to the atmosphere of the prints. *The Serpents* i witty and abrasive. The artist produced her effects with combination of photo-etching, etching, and aquatint. Sh printed a single copper plate in two colors, black and tur quoise, applied à la poupée in one press run on J. Barchan Green paper.

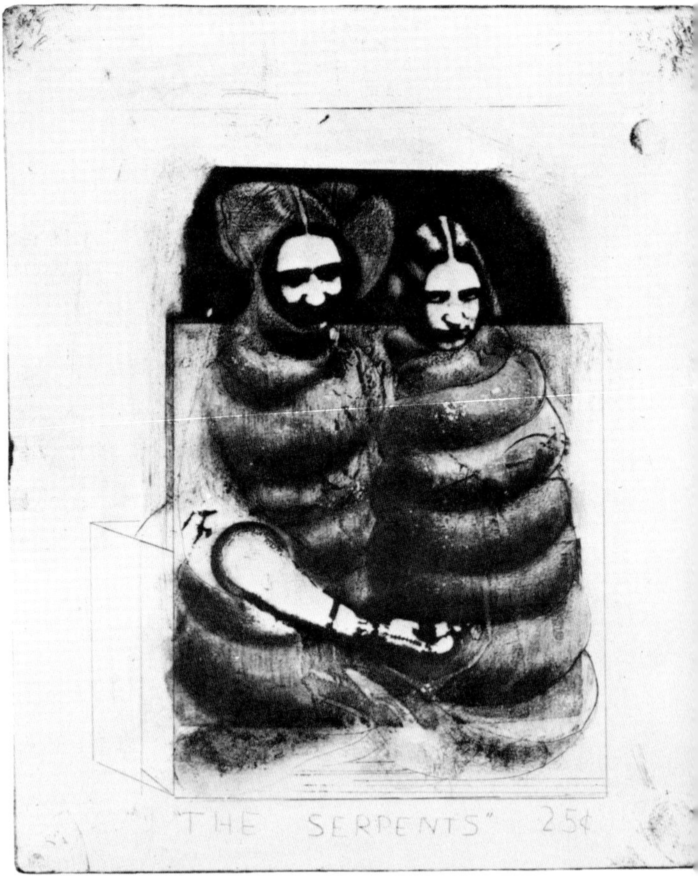

46

Anita Gelman

(b. Detroit, Michigan, 1952)

Self Portrait II

1977, photo-etching with soft-ground, edition: 10

Image: 35.2 x 29.6 (13⅞ x 11⅝)

Sheet: 53.9 x 39.2 (21¼ x 15⅜)

The Artist

Gelman's *Self Portrait II* reflects an obsession with the medium. The image is all but obliterated in the making of it and a new image emerges—a new self, perhaps, or a self rediscovered when others are etched away. The compelling result is induced by the artist from three zinc plates printed by her in ochre, cool brown, and black on German Etching paper.

Illustrated in color on the next page

Cat. 46

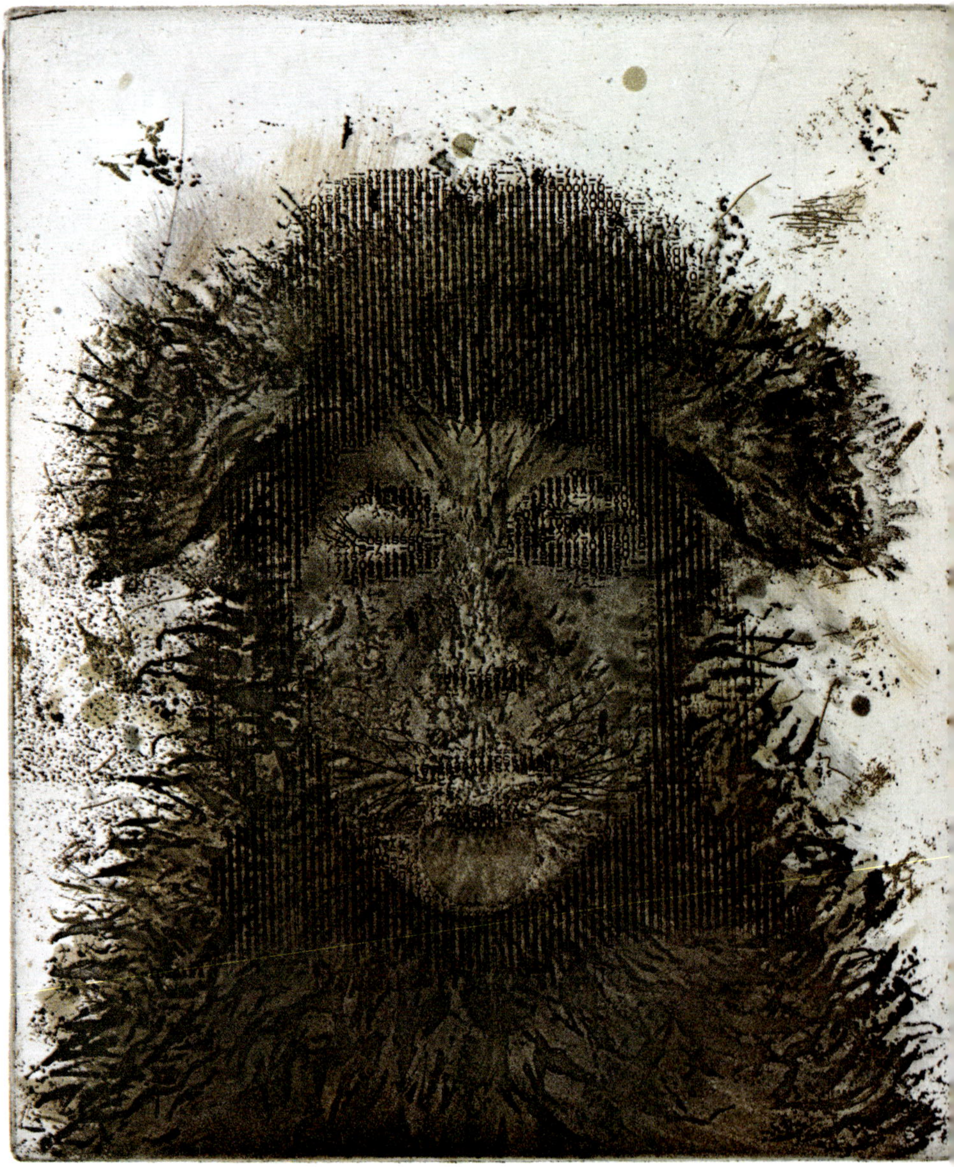

Goldman's images have the dreamlike fixity of things looked at intensely or for a long time. In fact, they are autobiographical subjects rediscovered in the printmaking process, which is a kind of meditated reaction to them. It is as if the artist were tugging these images out of her own feelings, simply by having to deal with them in a concrete way. *Norris Court #4* is houses across the street from where the artist lived in Madison, Wisconsin, but you might recognize them as many places in America, so deeply are they seen. The print is a four-color etching from a single zinc plate. The image was photo-etched from a pencil drawing by the artist and reworked by her through aquatints. The plate was painted on the surface with Graphic Chemical Inks and oil and run through the press. This removed most of the ink. The plate was then run through the press with a fresh piece of paper, and the ghost image was set aside. The plate was cleaned and inked intaglio and printed over the ghost image. Paper was Rives BFK.

47
Jane E. Goldman
(b. Dallas, Texas, 1951)
Norris Court #4
1977, photo-etching with aquatint, edition: 50
Image: 27.3 x 47.9 (10¾ x 18⅞)
Sheet: 39.0 x 56.7 (15⅜ x 22¼)
The Artist

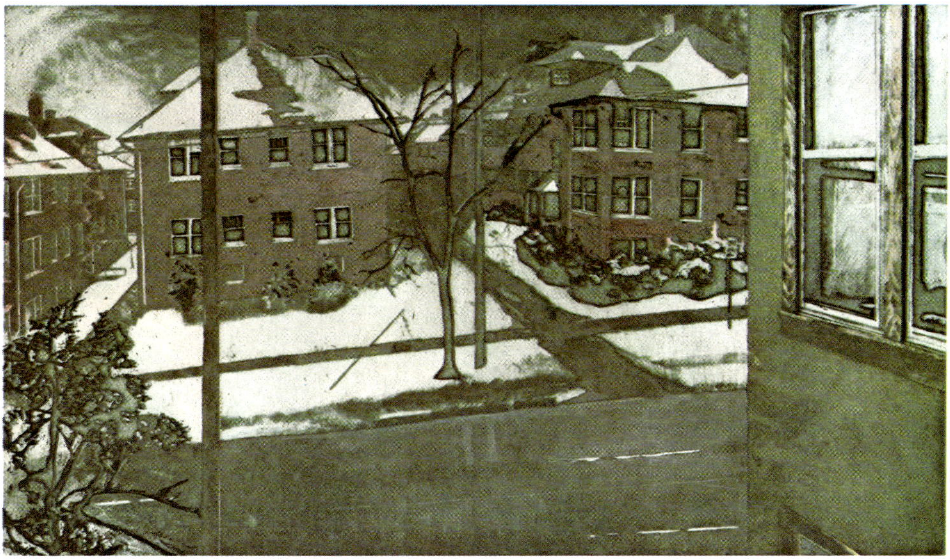

48
Jane E. Goldman
(b. Dallas, Texas, 1951)
Castle Place Reflections #1
1978, etching and aquatint with some roulette, edition: 50
Image: 60.0 x 60.0 (23⅝ x 23⅝)
Sheet: 75.9 x 75.0 (29⅞ x 29½)
The Artist

Goldman's *Castle Place Reflections #1* is perhaps the most delicately lyrical of her prints. The simple patterns seem to hesitate on the page. There is a sensation of watery light, a medium in which the shadows of the leaves seem to float or swing. All is delicately managed to suggest that a common corner of her house and its pot and foliage may have a life of their own, a separate involvement with time. This image, with etching, aquatint, and some roulette work, was printed intaglio on Rives BFK from three zinc plates inked à la poupée and printed by the artist.

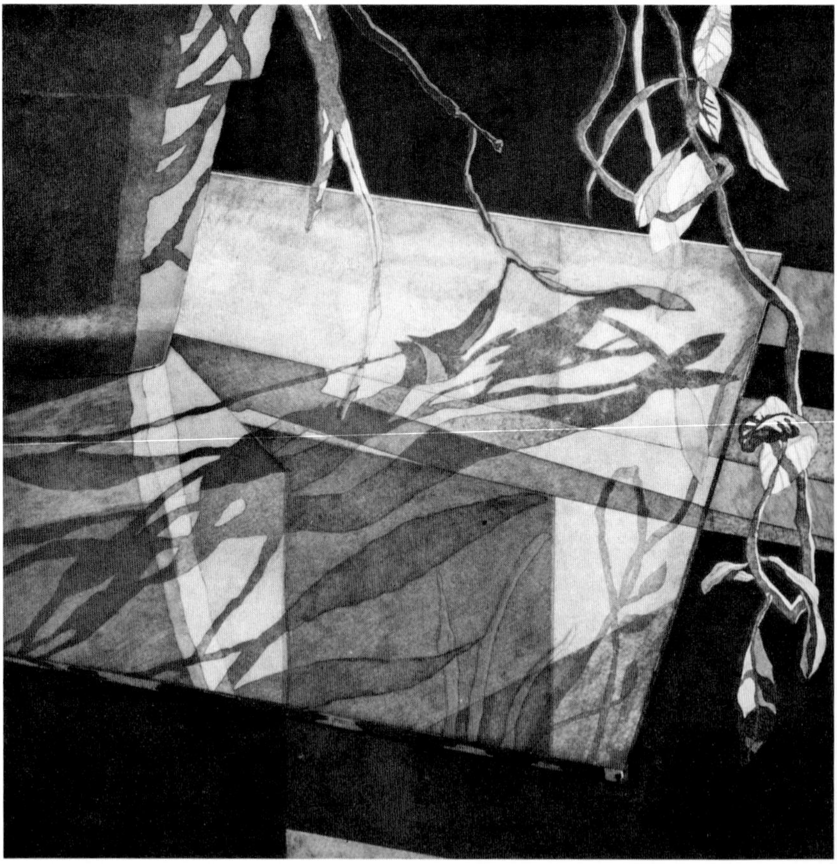

Gordy is a painter whose ideas are strikingly graphic. In screenprinting he has found a vehicle that perfectly translates his painting style without simply imitating it. The bold pattern, the flat color immaculately managed in a single key, and a feeling of surface integrity are characteristic of Gordy's idiom and are integral also to screenprinting capability. *Dog* is a screenprint in four colors, two blends in five runs. All screens were hand-cut and hand-printed on Arches Cover white at Weldon Workshop, New Orleans, Louisiana.

49
Robert Gordy
(b. Jefferson Island, Louisiana, 1933)
Dog
1976, screenprint, edition: 75
Image: 48.0 x 76.2 (18⅞ x 30)
Sheet: 57.8 x 86.0 (22¾ x 33⅞)
The Artist

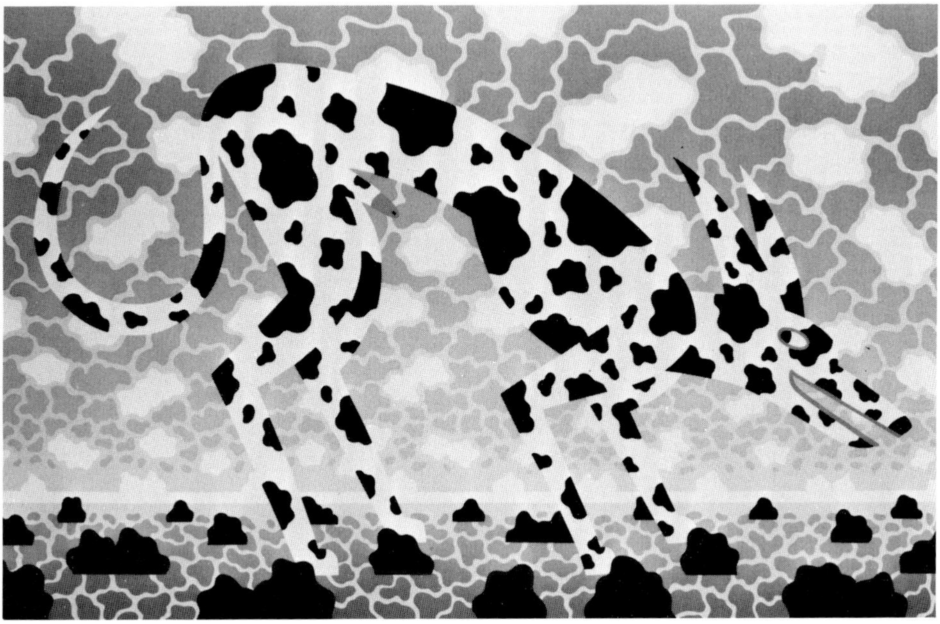

50
Robert Gordy
(b. Jefferson Island, Louisiana, 1933)
Sister Act
1977, screenprint, edition: 65
Image: 81.2 x 90.1 (32 x 35½)
Sheet: 81.2 x 90.1 (32 x 35½)
The Artist

Gordy's *Sister Act* shows him to be a master of the black-white continuum. The force and energy of the image has as much to do with tonal virtuosity as with explicit subject matter. The wit of the piece gives another dimension of pleasure. The screenprint was done in four colors. All screens were hand-cut and hand-printed by Weldon Workshop, New Orleans, Louisiana, on Arches Cover white.

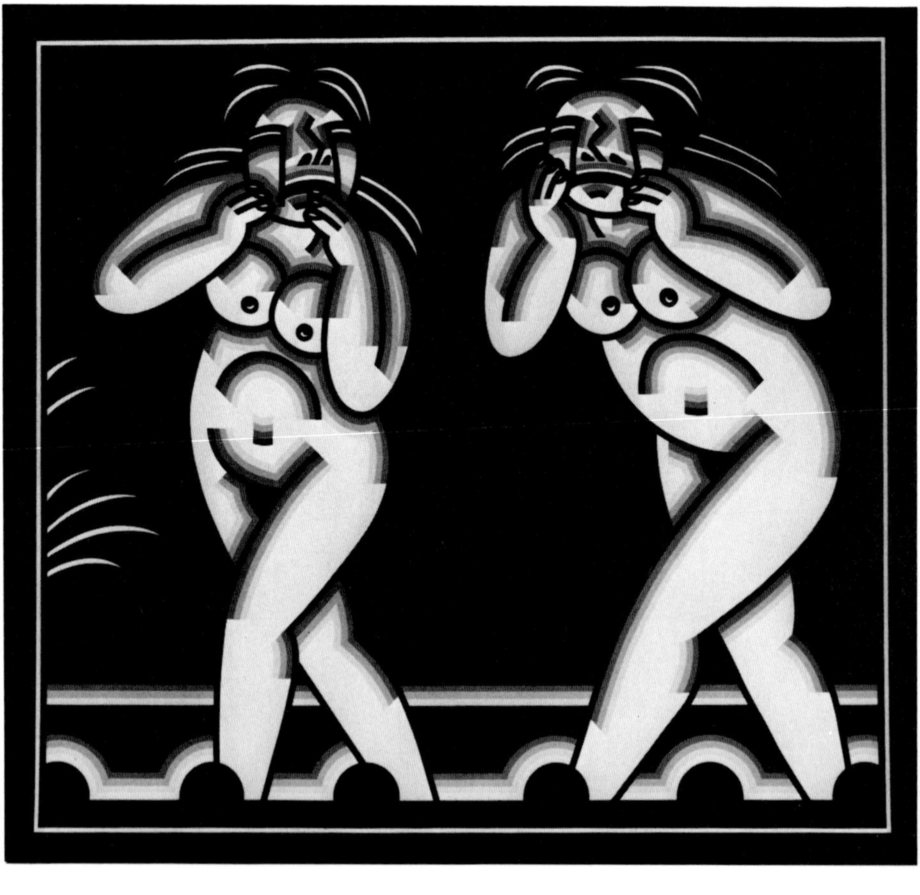

51
John Greene
(b. Paterson, New Jersey, 1955)
Untitled
1978, etching, edition: none
Image: 20.3 x 15.6 (8 x 6⅛)
Sheet: 59.0 x 46.4 (23¼ x 18¼)
The Artist

Greene is preoccupied with marking systems, or pattern equivalents, as these appear in nature and art. He understands that the particular surface is made up of abstract marks and that visual quality carries tactile suggestion. The same line or mark may move in upon itself to the non-representational (representing only itself) or it may move toward description (beyond itself to an external reality). The artist drew with a steel etching needle on a zinc plate covered with hard-ground. The plate was etched for eight minutes in a bath of ten to one diluted nitric acid and was constantly brushed while etching. The artist used black ink (Graphic Chemical no. 514) and printed on special handmade paper using an American-French Tool Etching Press.

52
John Greene
(b. Paterson, New Jersey, 1955)
Untitled
1978, woodcut, edition: none
Image: 20.0 x 16.0 (7⅞ x 6 5/16)
Sheet: 62.2 x 49.8 (24½ x 19⅝)
The Artist

Greene cut a soft pinewood block for this print. He applied etching ink (Graphic Chemical no. 514) with a gelatin brayer. The image was hand-printed on Mulberry Paper using a spoon. For the red-brown coloring, the artist mixed his black ink with Windsor and Newton Burnt Sienna oil paint. The mixture was then thinned with turpentine to a watery consistency. A paper template was used to cover the entire sheet of rice paper except where the inner rectangle carried the image. The artist applied the colored solution by running his thumb over a tooth brush wet with it; the color was thus flung over the whole surface in tiny specks. These eventually bled together and covered the area with color.

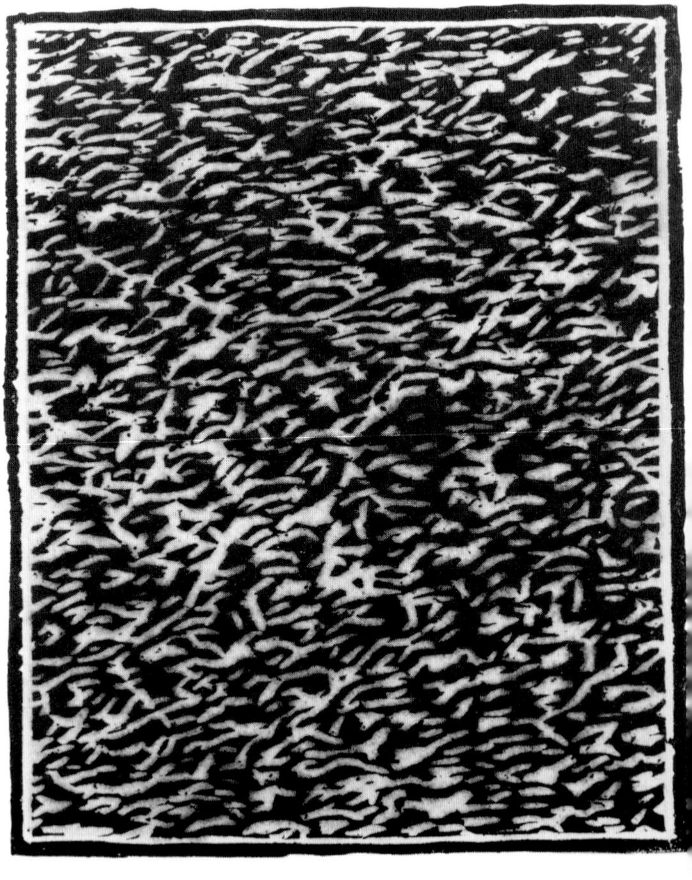

Gura's prints express a variety of illusions. In *Box Series II* her image is self-sustaining, a readable box, at the same time that it is questioned by color and by the disposition of shapes within the dominating form. The interaction of color with embossing is sensitively managed so as to keep the question of illusion completely to the fore. The artist escapes didacticism in the grace of the work. For this print, Gura embossed Arches Cover white to which she collaged lithograph rice paper in various colors. The print is a part of an edition variée in which colors differ from print to print.

53
Kathy Gura
(b. Streator, Illinois, 1951)
Box Series II
1977, lithograph with chine collé and embossing, edition (varied): 10
Image: 50.9 x 76.1 (20 x 30)
Sheet: 50.9 x 76.1 (20 x 30)
ADI Gallery

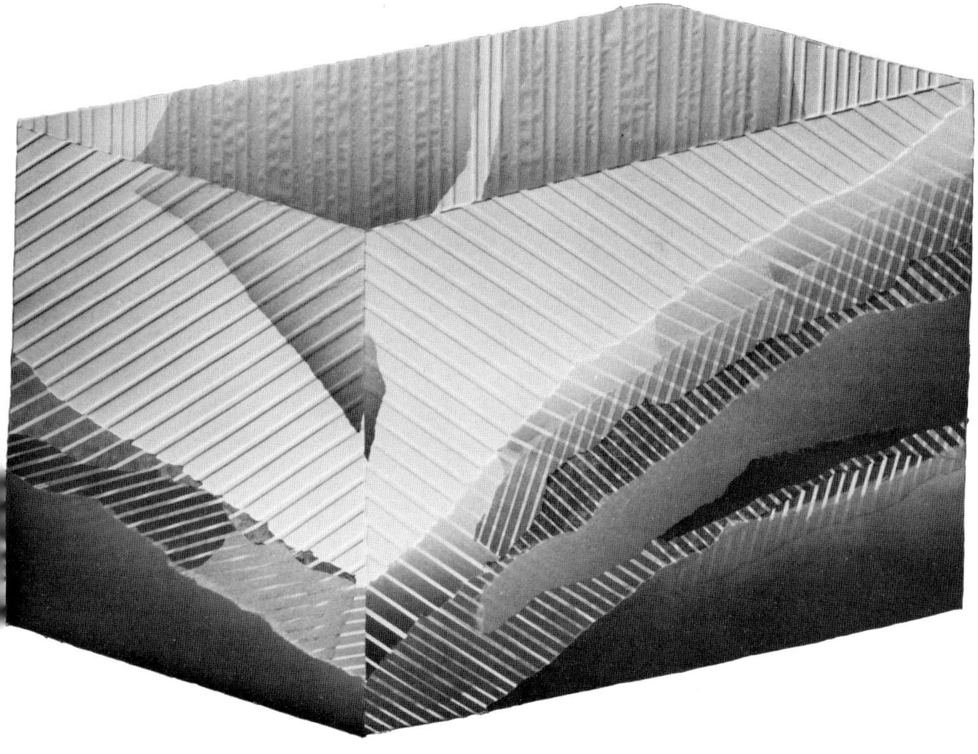

54
Kathy Gura
(b. Streator, Illinois, 1951)
Square Site I
1978, lithograph with
chine collé, edition: unique
Image: 25.4 x 25.4 (10 x 10)
Sheet: 56.5 x 40.3 (22¼ x 15⅞)
ADI Gallery

Gura's *Square Site I* is the first piece in an ongoing series of unique prints that was begun by the artist in April 1978. Production of the image involved embossing and lithographed elements applied chine collé from Japanese rice papers. The basic paper was Arches Cover white.

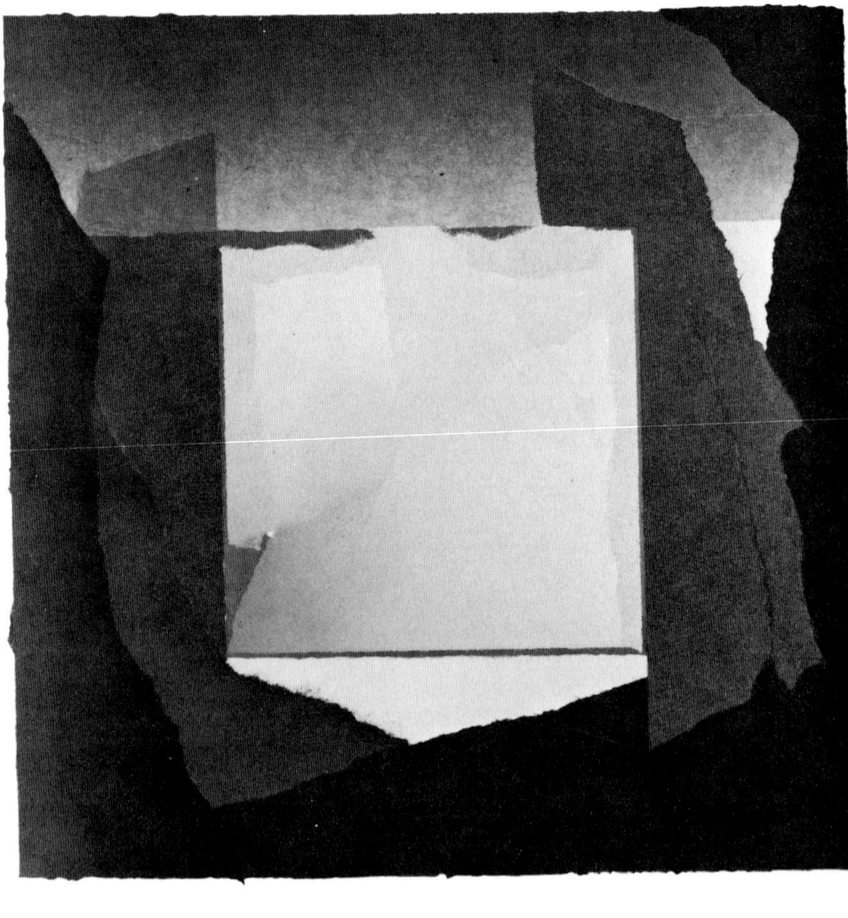

Hansmann's prints have great freedom and fluency based on his gift for, and understanding of, draughtsmanship. He is capable of working with large scale and feeling in small formats. For the present print, the artist modeled acrylic paste and rice paper with pencil and palette knife on a chipboard base. He printed intaglio with Charbonnel ink on Copperplate Deluxe paper.

55
Gary Hansmann
(b. San Diego, California, 1940)
Ghost Dancer
1975, collagraph, edition: 5
Image: 8.2 x 17.4 (3¼ x 6⅞)
Sheet: 21.0 x 32.6 (8¼ x 12 9/16)
The Artist

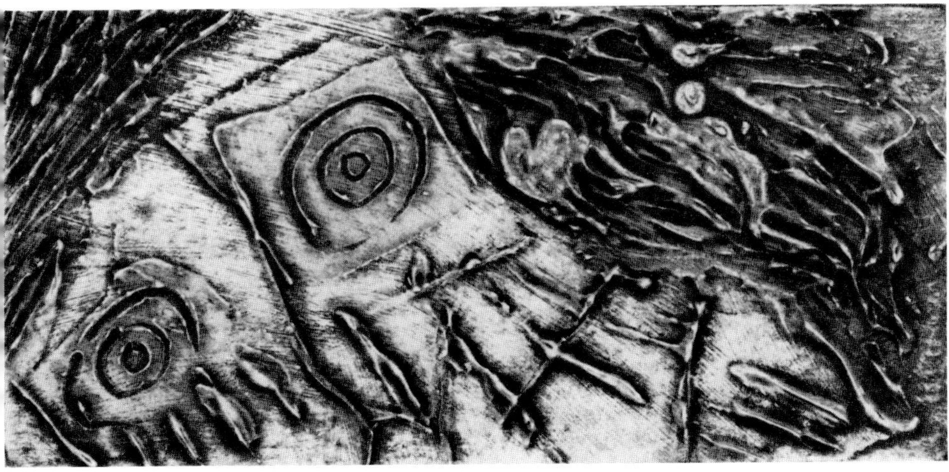

56
Gary Hansmann
(b. San Diego, California, 1940)
The Ancestor
1977, monotype, edition: unique
Image: 30.5 x 23.5 (12 x 9¼)
Sheet: 60.0 x 44.7 (23⅝ x 17⅝)
The Artist

Hansmann is preoccupied with monotype, where the spontaneity and energy of his draughtsmanship show well and where he can pursue painterliness without losing print quality. *The Ancestor* was produced with oil-based intaglio inks and printed on Rives BFK heavyweight. The artist used an intaglio press.

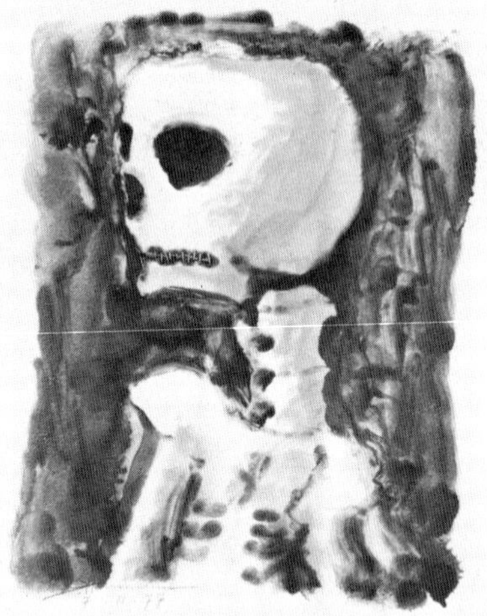

Harelson has a personal touch with serigraphy, both in concept and in finish. In his prints we do not find the flat color and the powdery varnished surfaces that are current clichés of the medium. In *Locking Horns* all is dust and tackiness, an extraordinary exploration of gray and black. In this print, pattern is space and energy; inks are wedded absolutely to that image; wit and style are one. The artist printed in two colors on Strathmore Aquarius watercolor paper.

57
Clint Harelson
(b. Baton Rouge, Louisiana, 1947)
Locking Horns
1977, serigraph, edition: 13
Image: 51.5 x 66.7 (20¼ x 26¼)
Sheet: 55.9 x 76.1 (22 x 30)
The Brooklyn Museum 78.64

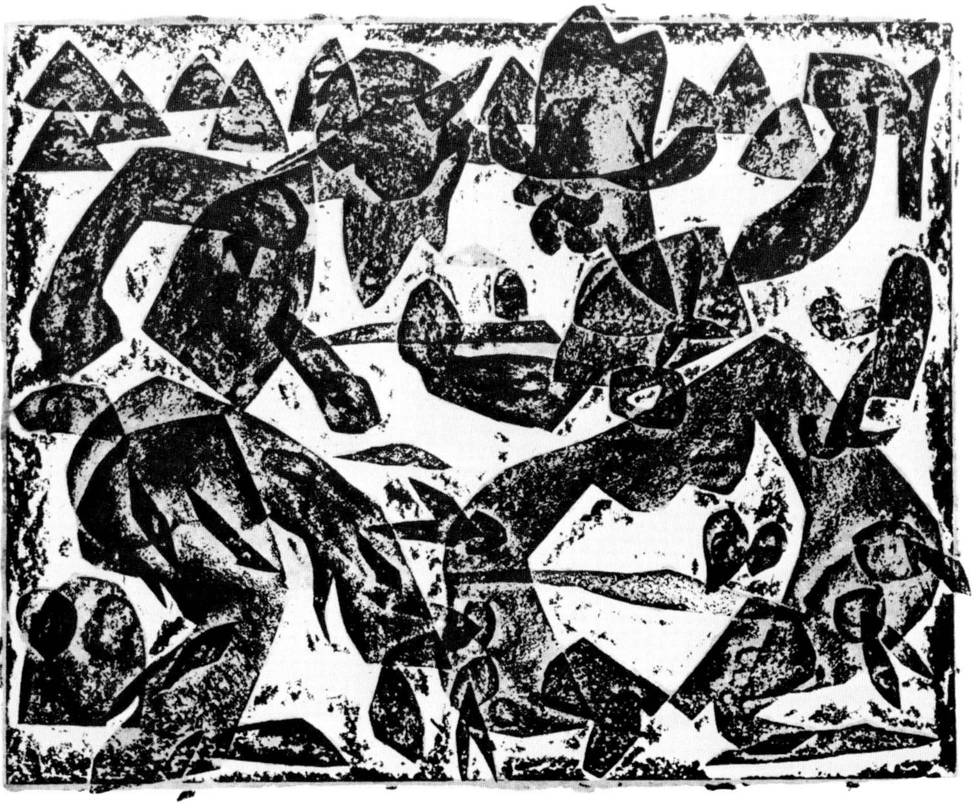

58
Clint Harelson
(b. Baton Rouge, Louisiana, 1947)
Strongman
1978, serigraph, edition: 10
Image: 45.8 x 61.3 (18 x 24⅛)
Sheet: 58.5 x 73.7 (23 x 29)
The Artist

Harelson's *Strongman* presents a richly detailed surface, but color is as much the key to the lively presentation as draughtsmanship. The masklike quality of Harelson's simian weightlifter suggests not only primates but primitives. The sense of the work is iconographic, but funny. The artist worked from eight screens on Strathmore Bristol paper.

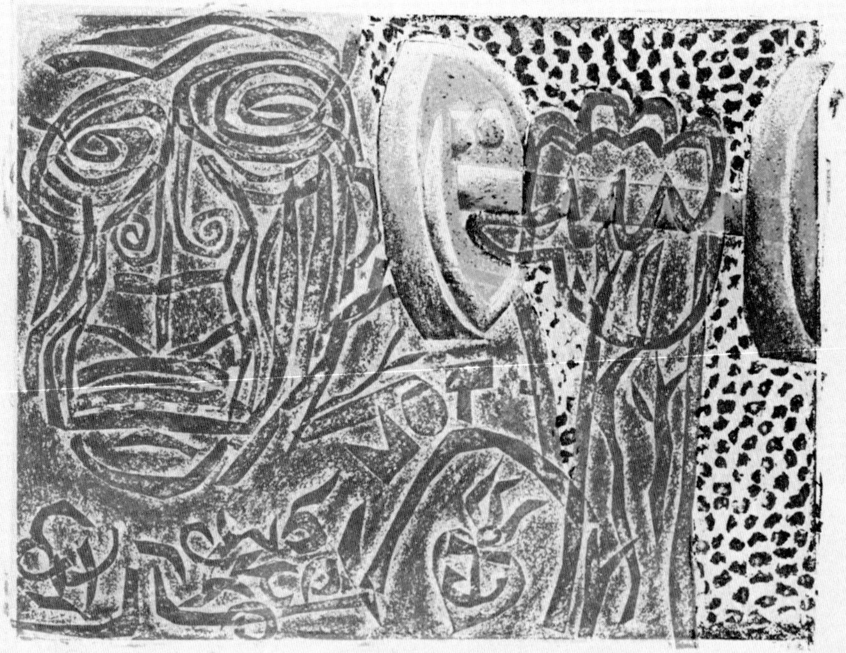

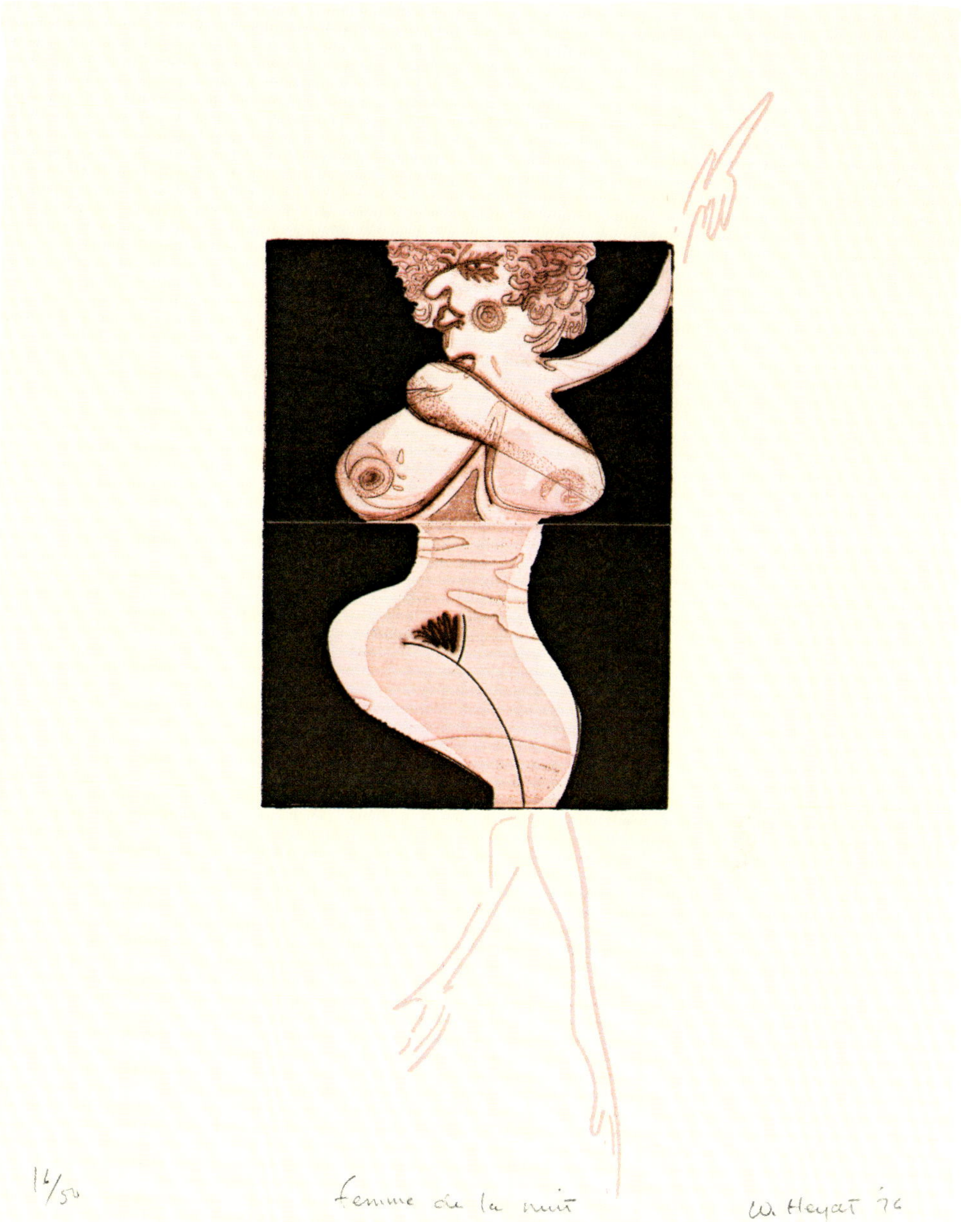
16/50
femme de la nuit

59
William Heydt
(b. New York, New York, 1949)
Femme de la Nuit
1976, etching, aquatint,
and drypoint, edition: 50
Image: 32.4 x 14.9 (12¾ x 5⅞)
Sheet: 35.4 x 28.3 (13 15/16 x 11 ⅛)
Reproduced in color on page 81
The Artist

Heydt's prints are sheerly elegant. I do not mean that his images are necessarily refined, but that he brings to them just the right degree of formality and stylistic verve to make them seem both inevitable and provocative. They have panache. The artist has observed the world closely, is obviously a man of artistic and literary culture, and has something to say. *Femme de la Nuit* succeeds in being as fresh as it is sophisticated, as funny as it is technically assured. The etching was printed by the artist in three runs from two plates on Arches Cover white. The middle panel was made out of two small copper plates that were printed in red-brown ink. The figure was stenciled out, and black was rolled over these two plates. The artist cut a third plate larger than the printing paper (so that its edges would not be visible on the final print); this plate was etched with the figure's legs and hand. This plate was printed intaglio in pink. The two smaller plates were then positioned on the larger plate, and the three were printed together. The artist combined etching, aquatint, and drypoint in the production of the image. The print was one of ten etchings and engravings titled *Mes Amis*.

Illustrated in color on the previous page

Heydt's *The Proposal* suggests a circus scene. Beauty and beast occupy the foreground in a vivid confrontation, and a caged figure is seen in the rear. The drawing is rough and childlike, and the sense of image is enigmatic. But the handling is sure, and one remembers what one sees, a point scored, certainly, in art. The etching is printed in black from a single copper plate on Arches Cover white. The artist used drypoint, engraving, aquatint, and soft-ground in realizing the image.

60
William Heydt
(b. New York, New York, 1949)
The Proposal
1978, drypoint, engraving, aquatint, and soft-ground, edition: 60
Image: 8.9 x 13.7 (3½ x 5⅜)
Sheet: 25.4 x 25.0 (10 x 9⅞)
The Artist

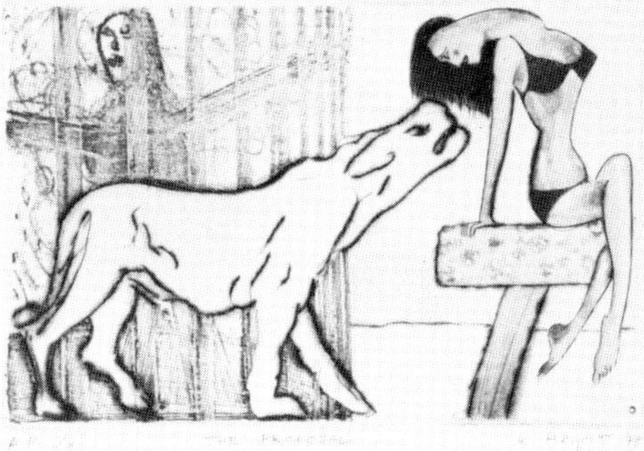

61
Denzil H. Hurley
(b. Barbados, West Indies, 1949)
Other Places #I
1977, engraving, drypoint, etching, and sugar-lift, edition: 10
Image: 30.5 x 45.1 (12 x 17¾)
Sheet: 39.6 x 54.0 (15 9/16 x 21¼)
The Artist

Hurley's prints are full of reminiscent forms, some of them reasonably explicit. Others are suggestive in shape, color, or even in texture of things observed in the natural or the man-made environment. In short, we confront an apparently familiar visual vocabulary that creates a new reality of relationships and energies. The whole surface comes alive with colors, textures, shapes, marks, and blackness. In *Other Places #I* the artist used engraving, drypoint, etching, and sugar-lift in the production of a zinc plate. In some areas he applied color with paper stencils and in others with brush directly. The artist pulled the print on Murillo stock.

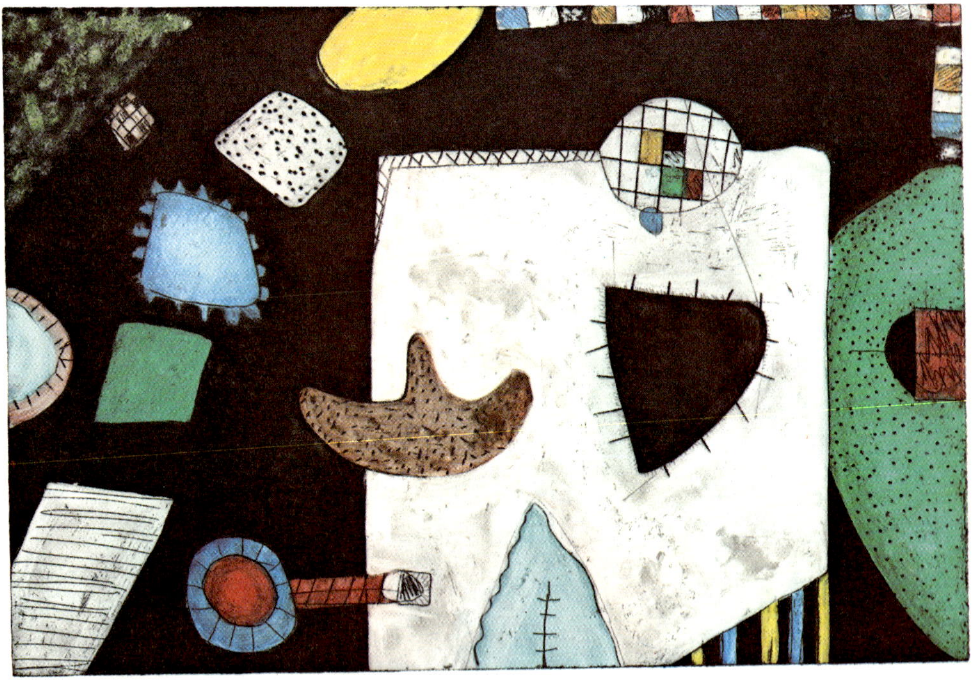

Hurley makes preliminary use of drawing in the production of his prints. The drawing process in relation to the final images may be thought of as a meditative exercise in which the artist discovers the relationships (color, shape, texture, line, and mark) that define his feelings and give them physical and visual location. The artist continues to develop the image during the proofing stage. *Other Places #VIII* involves engraving, drypoint, etching, and sugar-lift. In some areas he applied color with paper stencils and in others with a brush directly. The artist pulled the print on Murillo stock.

62
Denzil H. Hurley
(b. Barbados, West Indies, 1949)
Other Places #VIII
1978, engraving, drypoint, etching, and sugar-lift, edition: 10
Image: 59.7 x 80.3 (23½ x 31⅝)
Sheet: 70.3 x 95.4 (27⅝ x 37 9/16)
The Artist

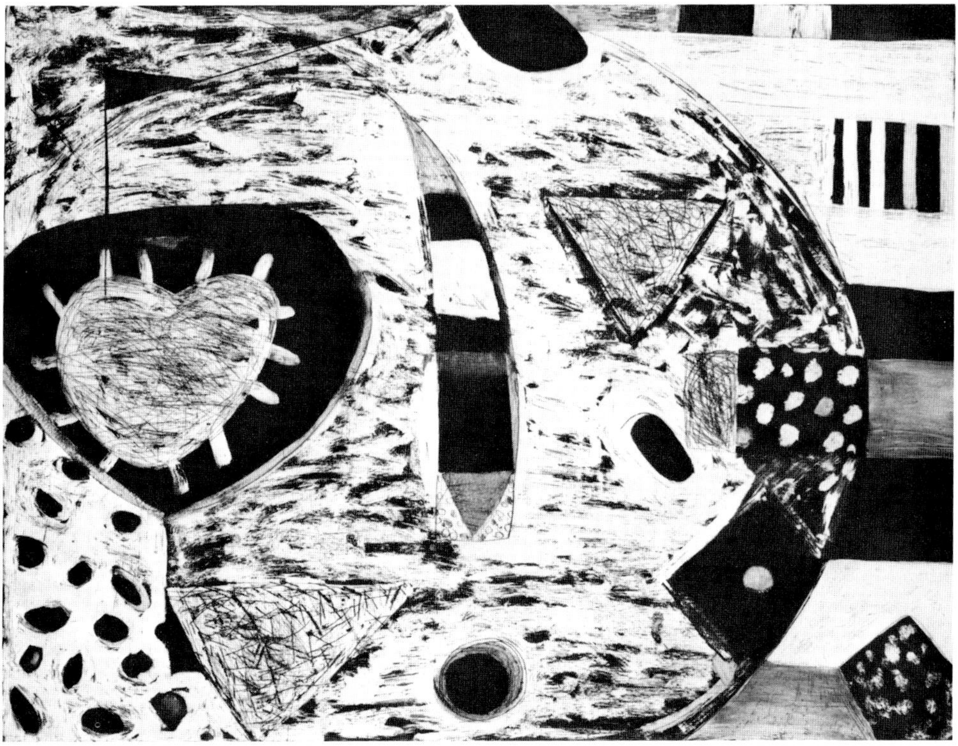

63
Anita Janoff-Katjanelson
(b. Brooklyn, New York, 1925)
Yellow Afterimage
1975, etching, edition: none
Image: 40.0 x 40.0 (15¾ x 15¾)
Sheet: 76.0 x 56.2 (29⅞ x 22⅛)
The Brooklyn Museum *78.56.6*

Janoff-Katjanelson's prints developed originally from her desire to find visual equivalents for the recording of sound patterns. She discusses this in her statement. Gradually, her concern shifted to sheerly visual effects, for instance, to the optical vibration of dots in certain patterns and densities and to the mediating interaction of color with pattern and with color of different hue and intensity. The artist used two etching plates in the production of *Yellow Afterimage* (both have been employed singly or in other combinations in the artist's oeuvre). The plate denominated plate 1 was inked with a mixture of lemon yellow and transparent white base. The plate denominated plate 4 was inked with blue mixed with transparent base. Inks were Lefranc and Bourgeois. The artist printed the yellow plate first and the blue plate second on Arches Cover white.

64
Anita Janoff-Katjanelson
(b. Brooklyn, New York, 1925)
Plates X, II, and I
1978, etching, edition: none
Image: 40.4 x 40.0 (15⅞ x 15¾)
Sheet: 76.0 x 56.3 (29⅞ x 22 3/16)
The Artist

Janoff-Katjanelson's *Plates X, II, and I* is a composite image printed in the indicated sequence by the artist on Arches Cover white. Plate X was inked with one part Graphic Chemical Royal Red and ten parts Inmont's Opaque White to which three parts Inmont's Transparent White Base were added. The artist wiped the plate clean with benzine and surface rolled it in opaque white with minute quantities of royal red, chrome yellow, and peacock blue added. She inked plate II with one part Graphic Chemical Peacock Blue to ten parts Inmont's Opaque White, again adding three parts of Inmont's Transparent White Base. She wiped this plate with benzine until it was free of all surface tone. She inked plate I with one part Flintsink Deep Chrome Yellow to ten parts opaque white and mixed it with three parts transparent white ink. This surface too was wiped clean with benzine, and the plates were printed according to their sequence in the print title.

65
Lucas Johnson
(b. Hartford, Connecticut, 1940)
Velarde II
1978, lithograph, edition: 30
Image: 43.1 x 55.8 (17 x 22)
Sheet: 43.1 x 55.8 (17 x 22)
Moody Gallery

Johnson's draughtsmanship is a strong underpinning both of his paintings and of his prints. He seems equally at home with broad, simplified handling and with delicate linear effects. The particular method chosen is in the service both of observation and of feeling. *Velarde II* is a one-color lithograph drawn in crayon and stick tusche on stone by the artist and printed by David Faulkner at Little Egypt Enterprises, Houston, Texas. The ink is Sinclair and Valentine Stone Neutral Black; the paper German Etching.

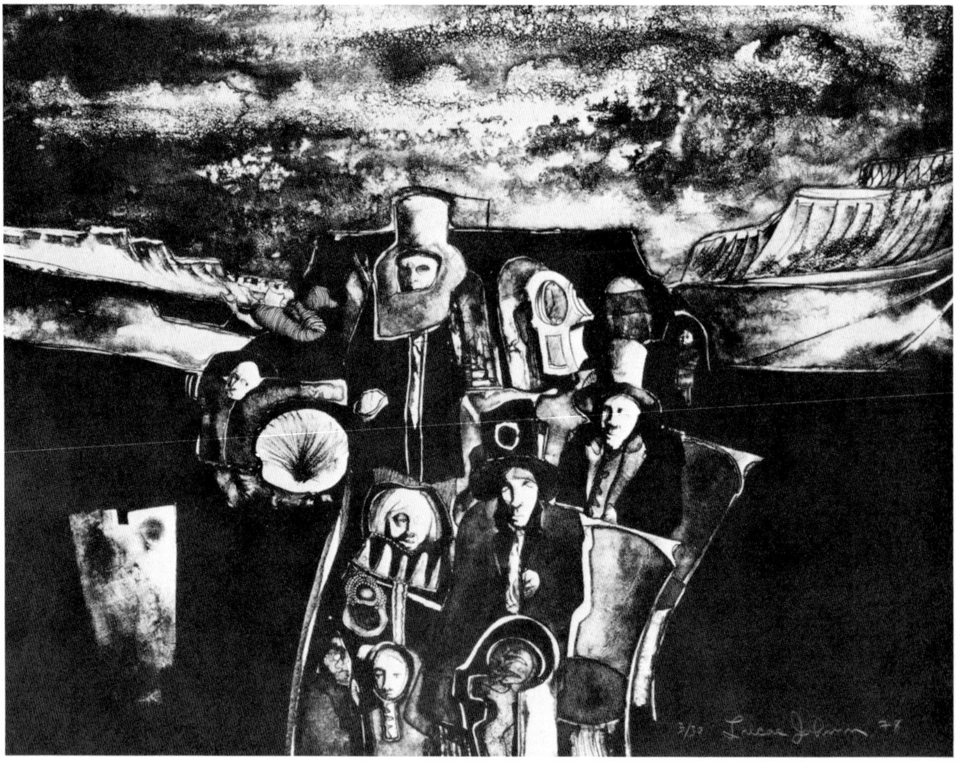

Johnson is at his finest with etching and drypoint. This image was developed on a zinc plate and printed by Rick Leal at Little Egypt Enterprises, Houston, Texas. The ink was Graphic Chemical Vine Black; the paper German Etching.

66
Lucas Johnson
(b. Hartford, Connecticut, 1940)
Homage to Tamayo
1978, etching and drypoint,
edition: 15
Image: 11.1 x 18.0 (4⅜ x 7⅛)
Sheet: 36.9 x 43.5 (14½ x 17⅛)
Moody Gallery

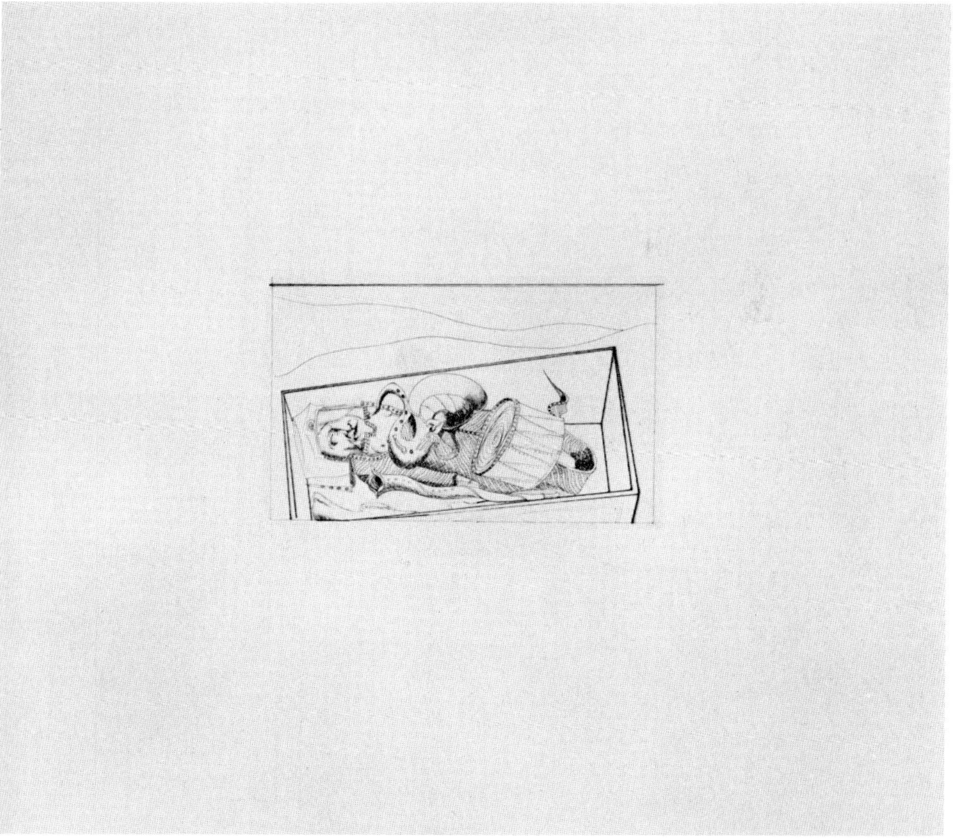

67
Robin Kaneshiro
(b. Honolulu, Hawaii, 1947)
Standing Alligator II
1977, etching, aquatint, spit-bite, and photo-etching, edition: 15
Image: 60.6 x 45.4 (23⅞ x 17⅞)
Sheet: 76.2 x 56.9 (30 x 22⅜)
The Artist

Kaneshiro's *Standing Alligator II* states the fundamentals of the artist's style—delicate personal lines, a created space of floating shapes and marks in varying scales and degrees of flatness, familiar objects and abstract ones, photo-etched passages, velvety blacks and rougher effects in intermediary tones. The artist worked his plates in etching, aquatint, spit-bite, and photo-etching. The work is printed on Arches Cover white.

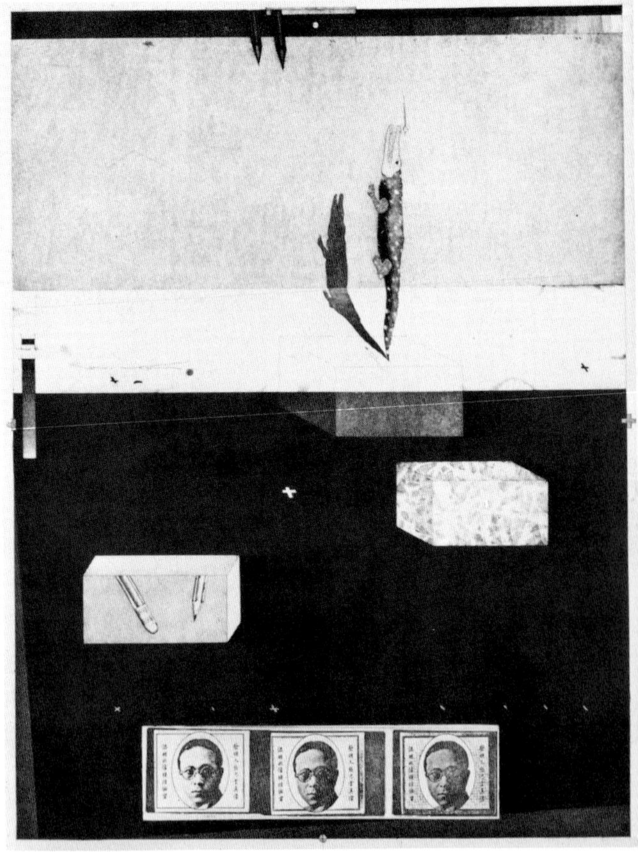

Kaneshiro's etchings reconcile apparently diverse elements and data, drawing them together into a mysterious but effective image. The richness of the plates is a sustaining attraction. In *Untitled* the artist has used etching, aquatint, and engraving and has printed his color both relief and intaglio on Arches Cover white.

68
Robin Kaneshiro
(b. Honolulu, Hawaii, 1947)
Untitled
1977, etching, aquatint,
and engraving, edition: none
Image: 57.0 x 75.9 (22½ x 29⅞)
Sheet: 57.0 x 75.9 (22½ x 29⅞)
The Artist

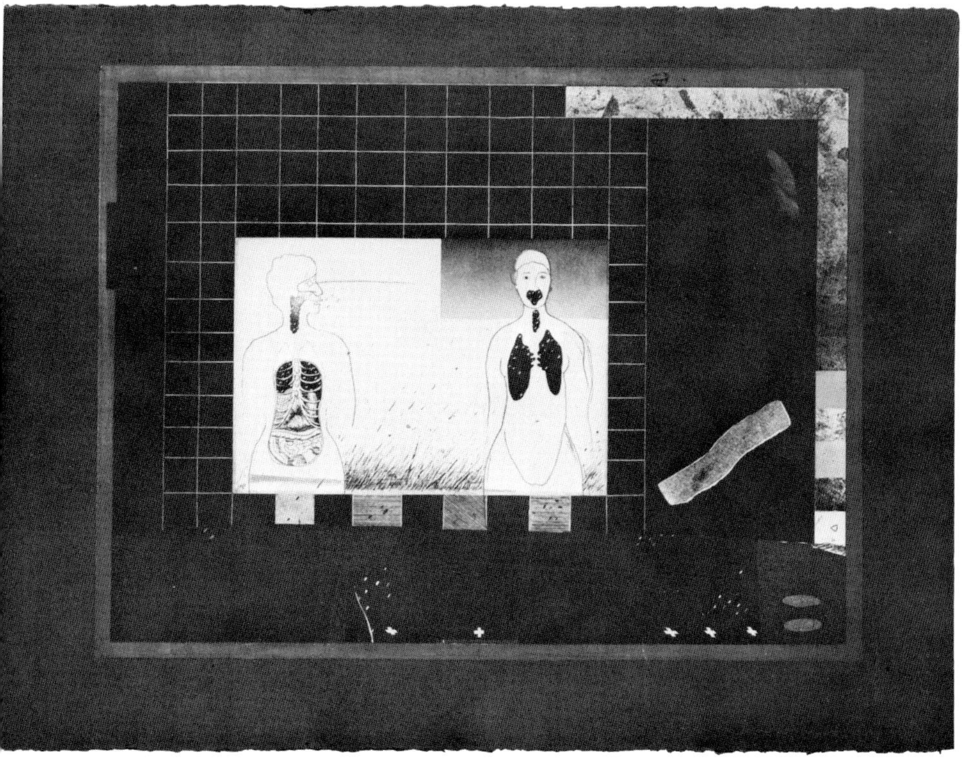

69
Anne Marie Karlsen
(b. Wyandotte, Michigan, 1952)
M.C. Violation (1st state)
1977, lithograph, edition: 6
Image: 49.5 x 73.3 (19½ x 28⅞)
Sheet: 49.5 x 73.3 (19½ x 28⅞)
The Artist

Karlsen's prints suggest activity in progress. No imagery here, but process; the surface is seen in a state of becoming. The metamorphic life of these lithographs is in the artist's sophisticated sense of tone. Colors are there too, of course, but light and dark dominate; they are the theme of a pictorial drama. In *M.C. Violation* the artist airbrushed the key image onto a stone using hand-cut paper stencils. For modulated areas, she airbrushed freehand. Small details were added to the image with a Speedball pen and Korn's autographic ink. Color was printed from a medium gray stone in three separate runs. Colored areas were printed (first printing) using small gelatine rollers in a variety of sizes. Each roller carried a separate rainbow blend, and each color shape was rolled separately so as to change the direction of this blend. In the second printing a single roller was used. And in the third, three separate gelatine rollers each carried a rainbow blend. For the fourth printing, the key image was overprinted on the color shapes. The artist printed on Arches Cover white.

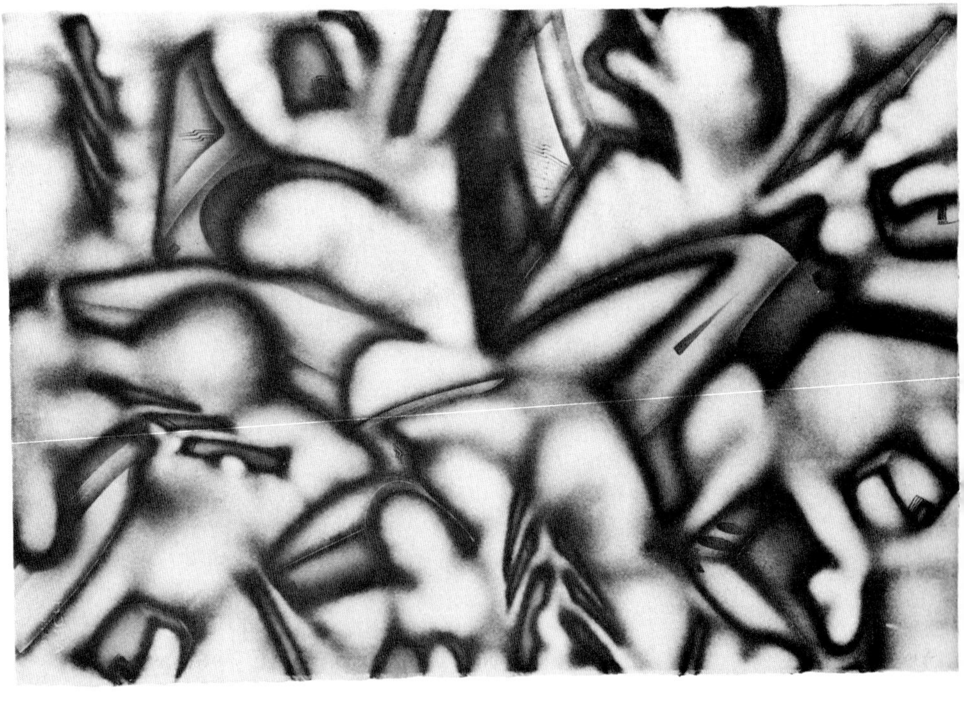

Karlsen's *Violation* in a first state utilized the same stones and images but was printed overall in a pale flesh color. The edition was ten. Prints in both states involved a key image airbrushed onto the stone using hand-cut paper stencils and various found objects. Modulated areas were airbrushed by hand. There were three printings by the artist in various colors rainbow rolled on as a flat over the entire surface of the paper. Then, following this first printing, the artist printed the key image in black. With the third printing, fine line work was added. The artist printed on Arches Cover buff.

70
Anne Marie Karlsen
(b. Wyandotte, Michigan, 1952)
Violation (2nd state)
1977, lithograph, edition: 4
Image: 50.8 x 73.6 (20 x 29)
Sheet: 50.8 x 73.6 (20 x 29)
The Artist

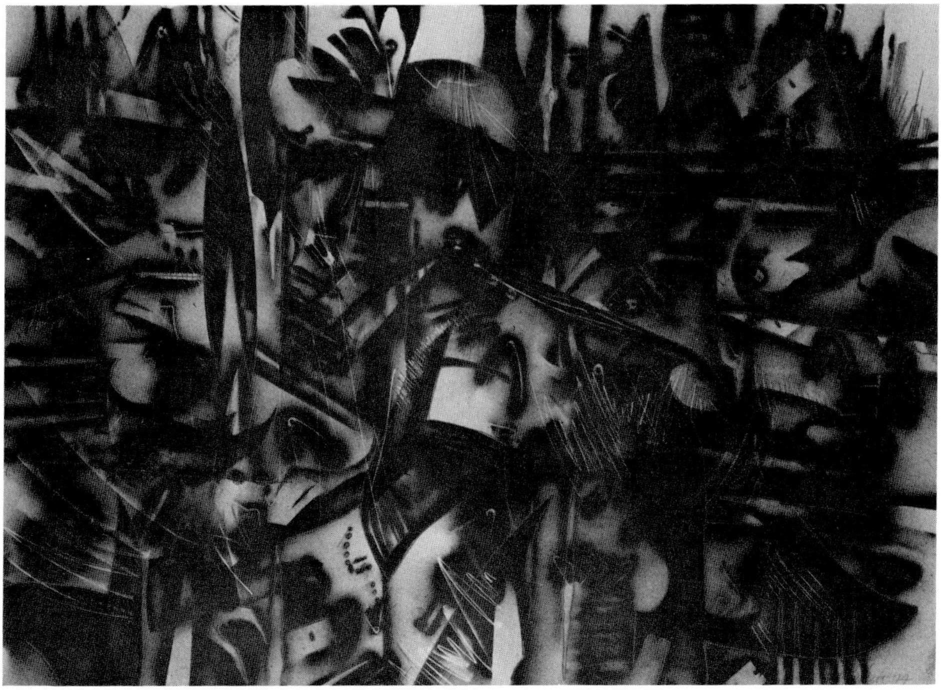

71
David Kessler
(b. Teaneck, New Jersey, 1950)
Shadow Line
1977, lithograph, edition: 100
Image: 44.4 x 65.7 (17½ x 25⅞)
Sheet: 64.2 x 83.8 (25¼ x 33)
The Brooklyn Museum, Gift of Mr. Stephen Foster 78.93.3

Kessler's lithographs have the delicate luminosity of watercolor, a tribute to his airbrush techniques and to the attention he pays to nice shifts of light across his subject matter, not to slight the finesse of the actual printing of the works. For *Shadow Line,* the artist drew the detailed key image on stone. Color was airbrushed on aluminum plates for a total of seven runs as follows: yellow, red-violet, blue-red, brown (on stone), blue, blue-gray, white-blue. Printing was by David Salgado, Master Printer, ADI Graphic Editions, San Francisco, California.

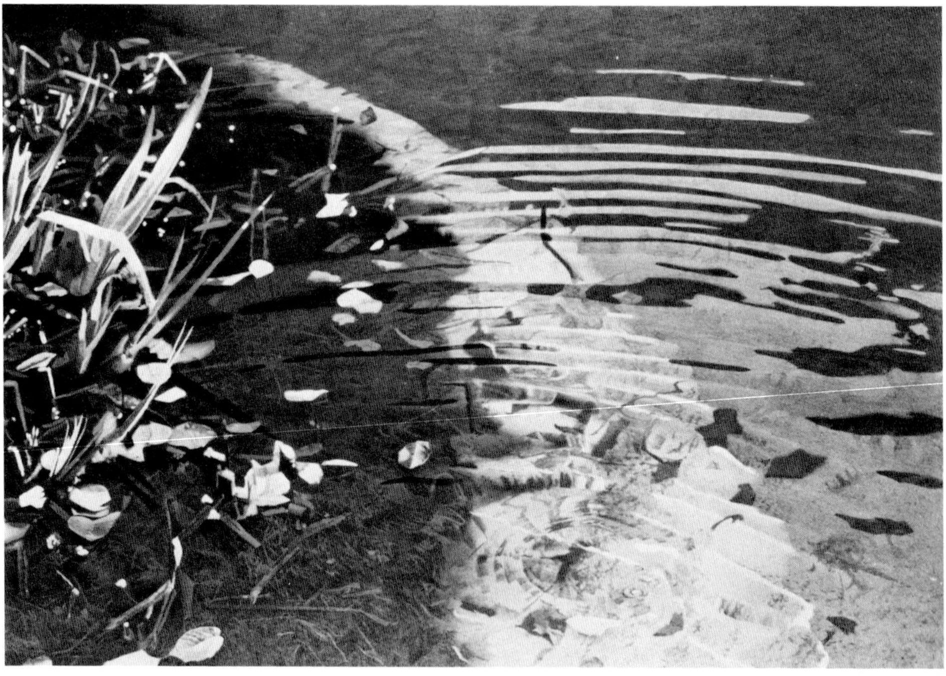

Kessler's *Surface Disturbance,* with its complex incidents of light and variety of forms in light-induced motion, presented formidable technical problems, all expertly managed. This print is an eight-color lithograph printed from one stone and seven aluminum plates. The key image was printed first in black and the plates printed in order as follows: blue, yellow-green, tan, blue, orange, purple, brown. For these aluminum plates, an acrylic solution was sprayed with airbrush through stencils. Printing on Rives BFK was by David Salgado, Master Printer, ADI Graphic Editions, San Francisco, California.

72
David Kessler
(b. Teaneck, New Jersey, 1950)
Surface Disturbance
1978, lithograph, edition: 60
Image: 65.5 x 44.5 (25¾ x 17½)
Sheet: 89.5 x 67.7 (35¼ x 26⅝)
The Brooklyn Museum, Gift of Mr. Stephen Foster *78.93.1*

Illustrated in color on the next page

Cat. 72

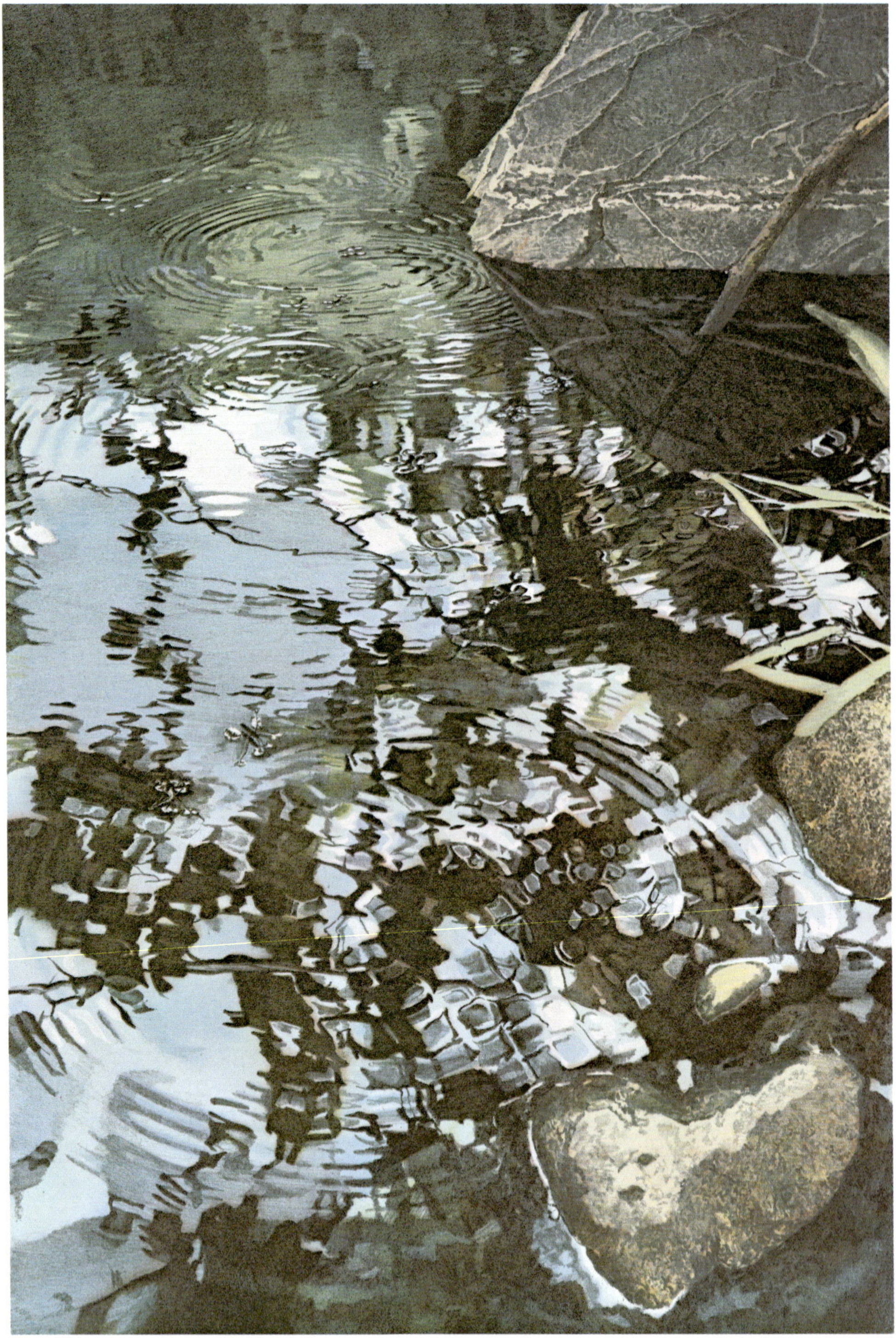

Kimball's lithographs have a persuasive intimacy, as though tiny door to the imagination were opened, and there were uddenly a new world to share, whose familiarity and ddity alike invited close examination. The door might be he covers of a book, for the works, while not seeming to lustrate anything in particular, are nevertheless anecdotal their titles too are literary). And they do present, even ntroduce, a self-conscious personality, someone who vants to be known by these juxtapositions, these images, his manner of presentation. *Properly Mounted Texas Long-orn* is a ten-color lithograph printed by the artist in ten ress runs on German Etching paper.

73
Wayne Kimball
(b. Salt Lake City, Utah, 1943)
Properly Mounted Texas Longhorn
1976, lithograph, edition: 100
Image: 38.2 x 27.9 (15 x 11)
Sheet: 38.2 x 27.9 (15 x 11)
Reproduced in color on page 141
ADI Gallery

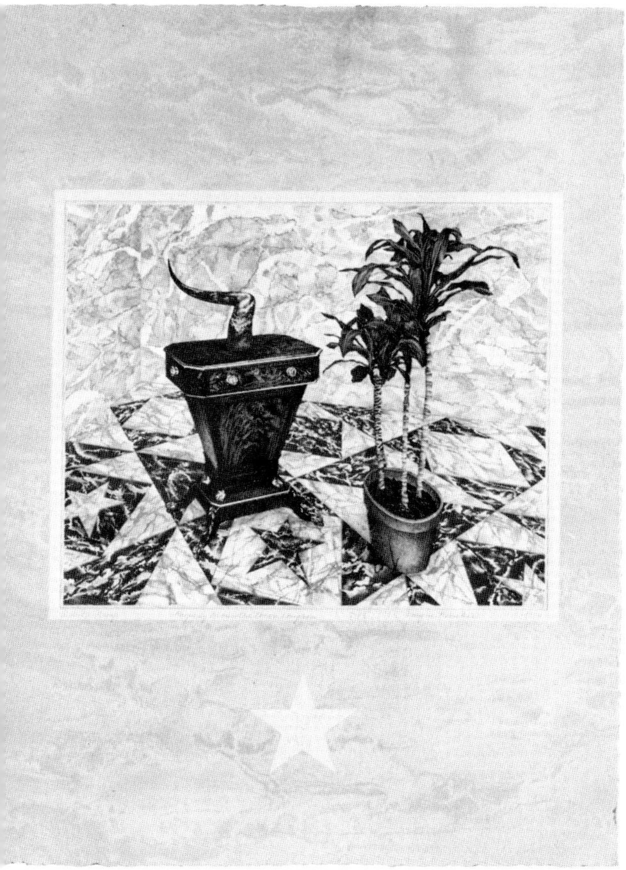

74
Wayne Kimball
(b. Salt Lake City, Utah, 1943)
Longhorn in Sheep's Clothing
1977, lithograph, edition: 100
Image: 37.7 x 28.2 (14⅞ x 11 1/16)
Sheet: 37.7 x 28.2 (14⅞ x 11 1/16)
ADI Gallery

Kimball has written in his artist's statement of his "sense c kinship" with the Islamic and Indian miniaturists. We ca see in his lithographs a like desire to perfect an idiom, t make a style, a manner of telling, the key to the perceive reality. In *Longhorn in Sheep's Clothing,* wit and craftsman ship have come together in a wholly identifiable way though the artist does not have a formidable array of suc works behind him. And this piece, while related to som others of his, manages an individual integrity that overrid association with other work. In Indian and Islamic minia tures, too, idiom does not swamp the personality of th individual variant. This lithograph is in sixteen colors an fifteen press runs, twelve from stone and three fror aluminum plates. The artist was the printer and split th edition 1-60, 61-100 beween, respectively, German Etchin paper and Rives BFK newsprint gray.

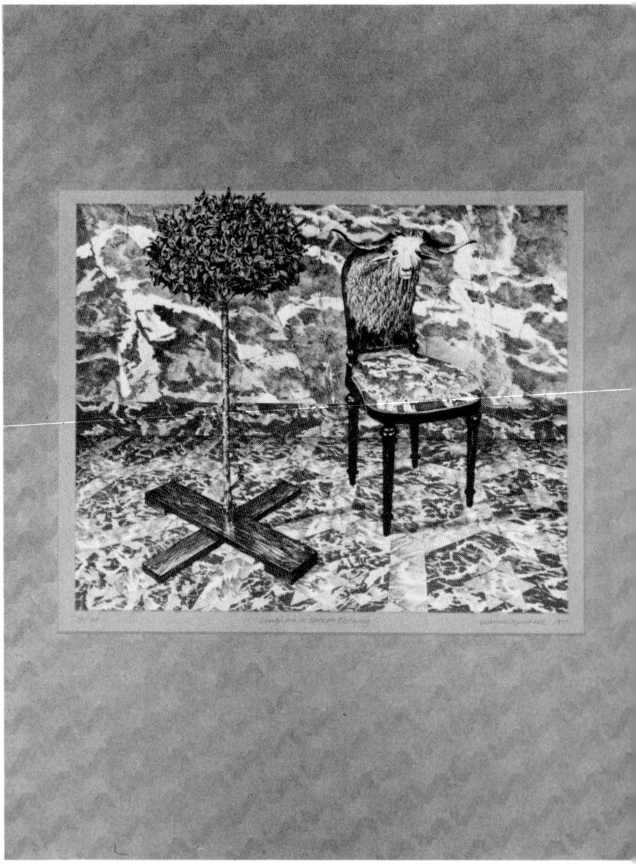

Kirk has devised a cactus series based upon masterworks of art. The present lithograph takes off from Henri Rousseau's *The Sleeping Gypsy.* And after all, is not a cactus more likely to be found in the desert nowadays? The lion seems even more undecided than he does in the original. The lithograph was printed in black from one stone and hand-colored by the artist. The paper is Arches Cover white.

75
Pat Angle Kirk
(b. Metuchen, New Jersey, 1951)
Sleeping Saquaro on a Henri Rousseau Desert
1976, hand-colored lithograph, edition: 7 black and white, 7 hand-colored
Image: 43.3 x 57.7 (17 x 22¾)
Sheet: 56.9 x 70.0 (22⅜ x 27½)
The Brooklyn Museum 78.27

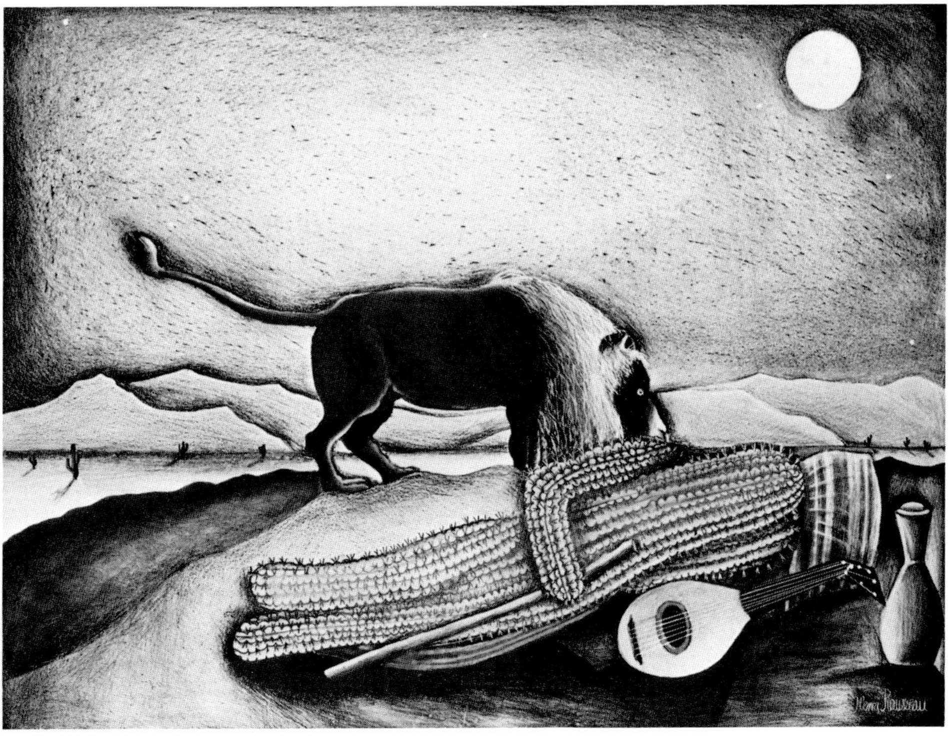

76
Pat Angle Kirk
(b. Metuchen, New Jersey, 1951)
At the Opera
1977, lithograph, edition: 10
Image: 61.0 x 46.1 (24 x 18⅛)
Sheet: 61.0 x 46.1 (24 x 18⅛)
Van Straaten Gallery

Kirk has exalted the cactus in a number of prints that marry pithy social commentary to decorative art. Here, she has elaborated the prickly texture of the plant in a variety of marks and reminiscent shapes to describe the opera house and its prominent patrons. It is a persuasive metaphor of aloofness. *At the Opera* is a twelve-color lithograph printed from stone by the artist in ten runs (two colors were printed simultaneously twice). Paper is Arches Cover white.

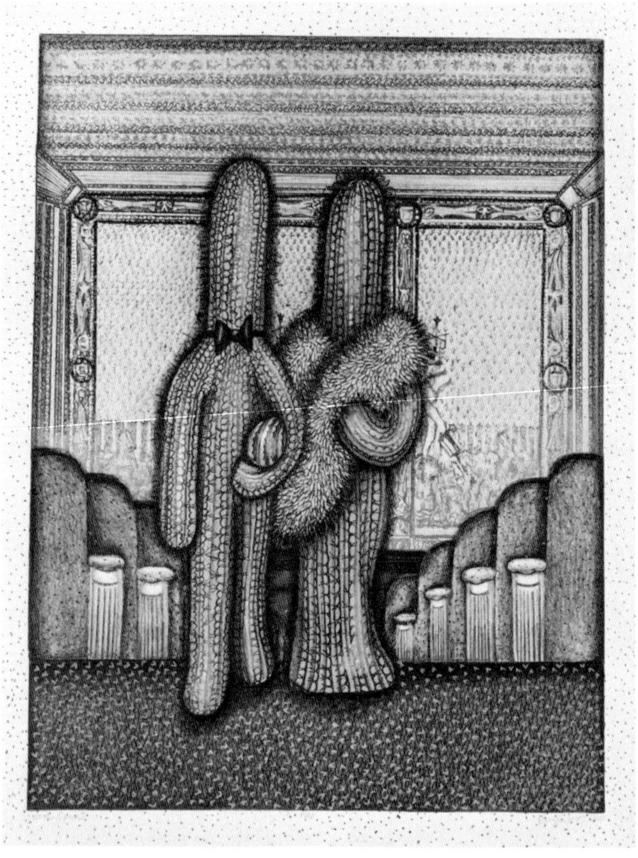

Kmetko's prints are concerned with presenting spatial illusion within the two-dimensional plane of the print surface. In one sense, the print surface is wall-like, and the marks made upon it are, in effect, the incising and marking of the surface. The depth is established literally by the action of a tool and illusionistically by the direction and interrelationship of lines and abraded surfaces. The print is a basic response to the problem of creating a sense of space on a two-dimensional surface. But the richness and the pallor of this artist's aquatint field, into which the lines are let, project a glow that itself seems to signify depth or at least indeterminacy of plane. This particular print is the first of two states. The artist began the plate with an aquatinted field that she then altered with scraping and burnishing. The artist printed with hand-made ink (powdered graphite, plate oil, and varnish) on Arches Cover white.

77
Alison Kmetko
(b. Buffalo, New York, 1953)
Collage Series
1977, aquatint with scraping and burnishing, edition: 5
Image: 22.5 x 22.5 (8⅞ x 8⅞)
Sheet: 53.3 x 53.3 (21 x 21)
The Artist

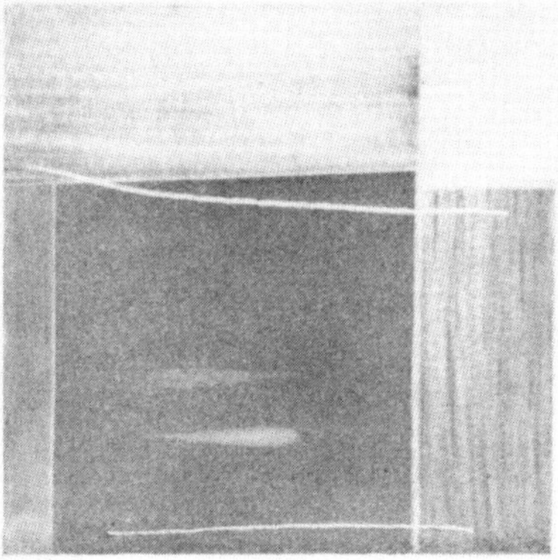

78
Alison Kmetko
(b. Buffalo, New York, 1953)
La Bajada
1978, aquatint and engraving with scraping and burnishing, edition: 10
Image: 28.1 x 28.7 (11 x 11¼)
Sheet: 28.1 x 28.7 (11 x 11¼)
The Artist

Kmetko's *La Bajada* presents a rich aquatint field, so rich that its glow seems to suggest depth in its own right, or at least indeterminacy of plane. This handsome surface is energized through scraping and burnishing. The dark and light linear elements describe space in drawing terms, while their literal quality is enhanced by the grip of the aquatint. The artist printed the image as bled; no plate mark appears. Hence the print is experienced more directly, not merely looked at as episode within a platemark border. The artist printed on Arches Cover buff.

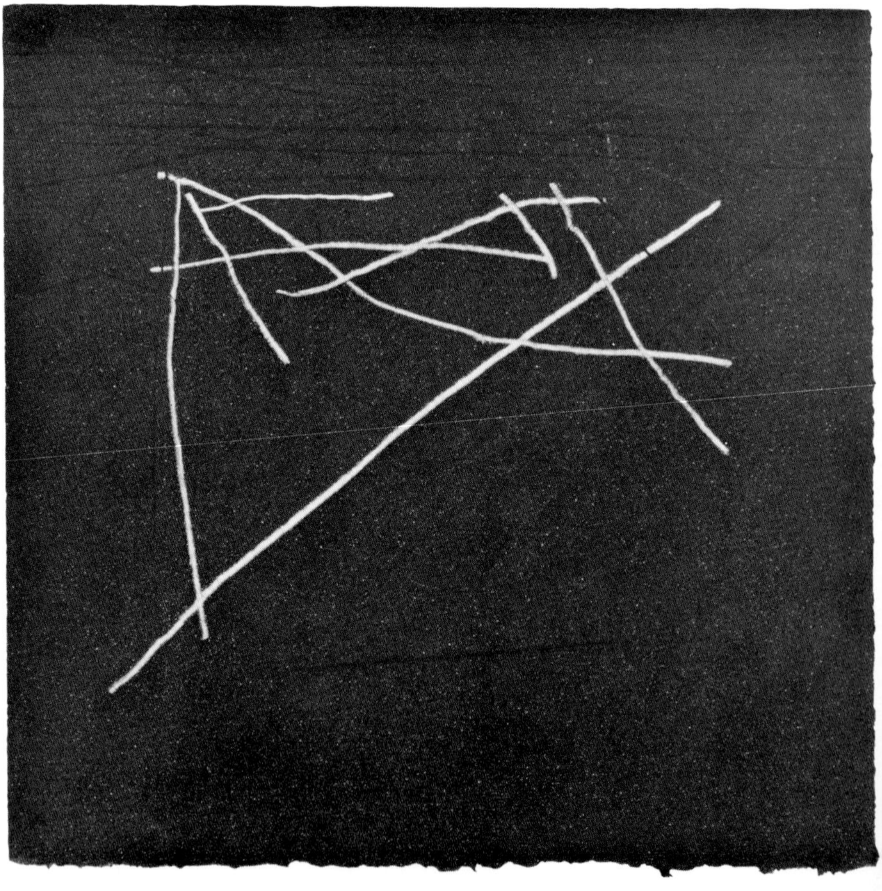

79

Mark Kuchar

(b. Manchester, New Hampshire, 1952)

Line #2

1977, etching, engraving, and aquatint, edition: 10

Image: 20.0 x 14.9 (7⅞ x 5⅞)

Sheet: 48.2 x 37.6 (19 x 14¾)

The Artist

Kuchar's art is evocative. The structure presented in these prints suggests a variety of formal references and equiva-ences, some natural, some man-made. The relationships of the elements one to another can create both form and space and even an instability of positive and negative. Edges can be crucial, as in *Line #2,* one of a suite of ten prints titled *Ten Lines* that the artist printed at the Cranbrook Academy of Art, Bloomfield Hills, Michigan. The "line" is suggestive of landscape, and small engraved lines reinforce this illusion as if the image were an aerial view. The print was made with etching, engraving, and aquatint; the paper is Copperplate.

80
Mark Kuchar
(b. Manchester, New Hampshire, 1952)
Perimeter Series #1
1978, etching, soft-ground, aquatint, and engraving, edition: 10
Image: 45.4 x 37.8 (17⅞ x 14⅞)
Sheet: 73.2 x 63.3 (28¾ x 24⅞)
The Artist

Kuchar's *Perimeter Series #1* deals with suggestions of structures and their relationships to interior space. The artist incorporated line etching with soft-ground, aquatint, and engraving in the making of this plate. He encouraged foul-biting in the etching process so as to add to an overall plate tone. He printed on Rives BFK newsprint gray.

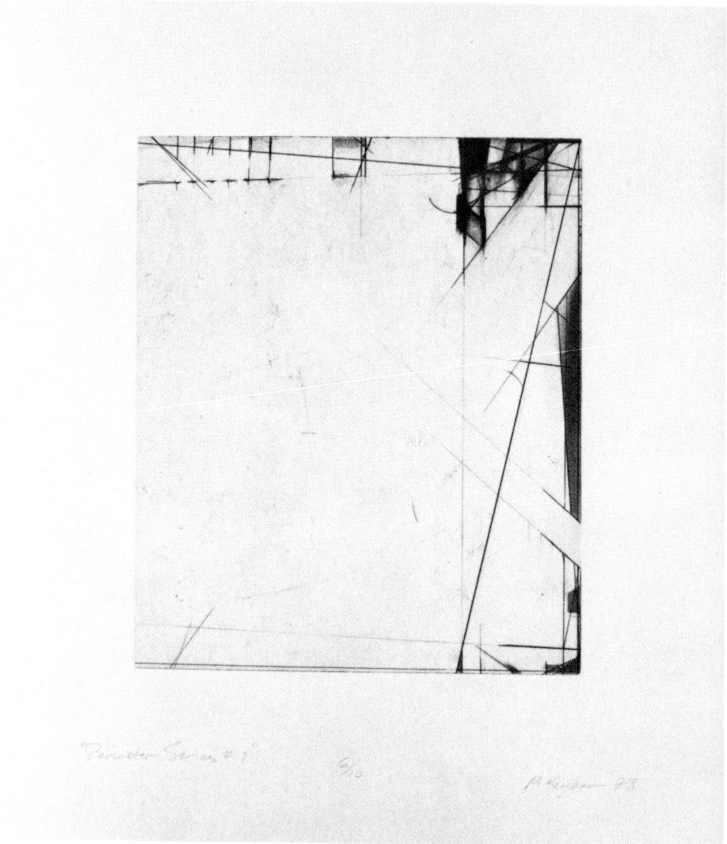

81

Leonardo Lasansky

(b. Iowa City, Iowa, 1946)

Orientalia

1976, soft-ground, etching, engraving, drypoint, and roulette, edition: 70

Image: 69.5 x 45.1 (27⅜ x 17¾)

Sheet: 77.8 x 52.0 (30⅝ x 20½)

The Brooklyn Museum 78.114.5

Lasansky's security as a draughtsman and his grasp of printmaking techniques have allowed him to experiment successfully with an essentially conservative vocabulary so as to extend the expressive range and personality of his images, which relate to portraiture. In *Orientalia,* the artist used soft-ground, engraving, drypoint, and roulette in the production of one master plate and three color plates. His dominant means was soft-ground etching, a technique he handled with uncommon skill and inventiveness, but the integration of elements supporting intaglio techniques are also notable for refinement of handling. Consistency of mood, harmony of image, reflect in this instance the rightness of technical choice. The first of four plates was printed with silver metallic ink. The second and third plates carried nearly a dozen colors with individual color areas wiped to prevent color bleeding. The inks used are transparent and delicate in color range, a result achieved by the use of ink extender base and white in most ink mixtures. The final plate was printed with hand-made black ink. Paper is Nideggen, and printing was by Dale Schwictenberg and Fred Hagstrom under the artist's supervision at his studio.

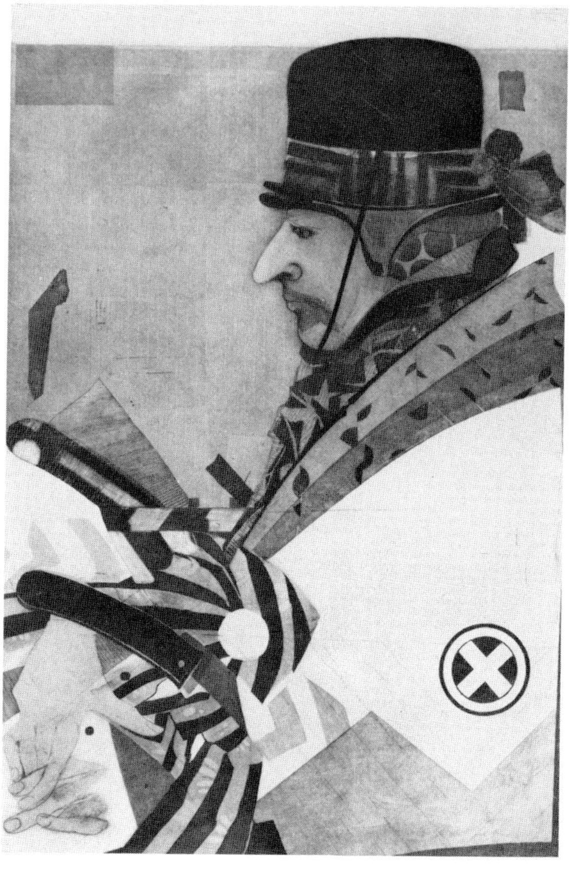

82
Leonardo Lasansky
(b. Iowa City, Iowa, 1946)
Tomás
1978, soft-ground with etching, sugar-lift, and engraving, edition: 70
Image: 60.7 x 50.2 (23⅞ x 19¾)
Sheet: 69.5 x 56.5 (27⅜ x 22¼)
The Brooklyn Museum *78.114.1*

Lasansky's *Tomás* was developed from four copper plates primarily in soft-ground with additions of line etching, sugar-lift, and engraving. Important, too, are scraping and burnishing for tonal modification and the softening of edges. Lasansky manages color with great interest to create watercolor transparency and beguiling tints. It is the printing of the master plate in hand-made ink (ground and milled by the artist with no modifiers added) that brings harmony to the whole through exact modulation of tone. The grays seen in the final image are both strong and lovely. The first plate was a gray background. Two and three were carefully inked and wiped color plates. The final plate was painted black as described above. Printing was done in the artist's studio under his supervision by Dale Schwictenberg with the assistance of Nick Swearer and Fred Hagstrom.

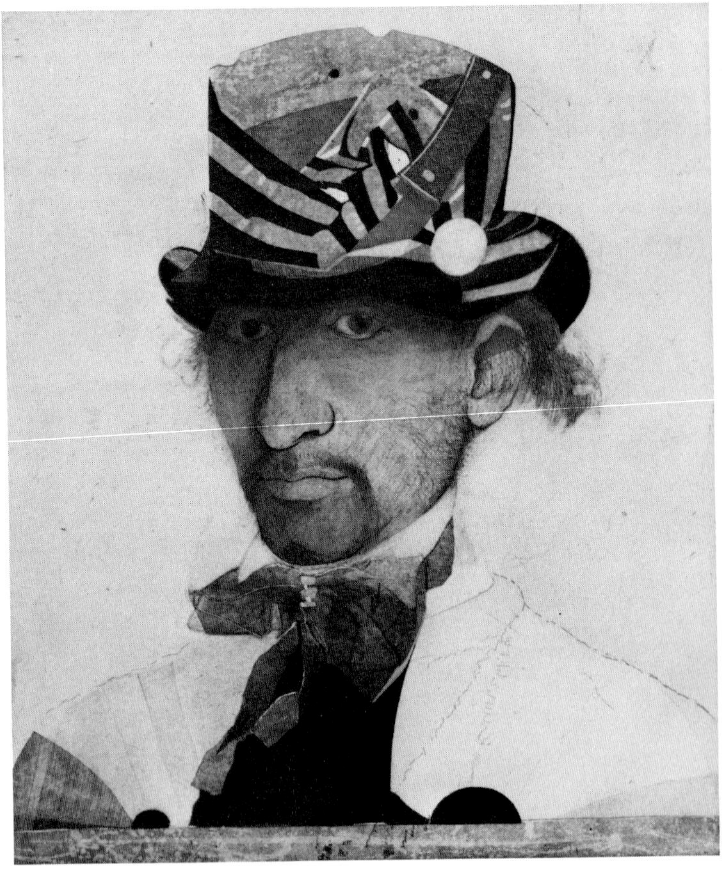

Lasuchin's prints are metaphoric and hold for the artist a metaphysical meaning, which he discusses in his statement. Seen merely as color geometrics with areas of interaction within configurations and with configuration in relation to a declared space, they convey a vibrant, positive life. Scale is an important issue in establishing the personality of these works and their upbeat character. In the serigraph *Trans,* the artist printed nine colors as follows: midnight blue, blue, cobalt blue, radiant ultra-blue, opaque white, silver, brilliant light orange, bright cerise, raw umber, and emerald green. Inks were Nazdar. Paper is Arjomari (Arches) silkscreen paper.

83
Michael Lasuchin
(b. Kramatorsk, U.S.S.R., 1923)
Trans
1976, serigraph, edition: 50
Image: 44.4 x 32.7 (17¼ x 12⅞)
Sheet: 52.3 x 37.1 (20⅝ x 14⅝)
Associated American Artists, Philadelphia

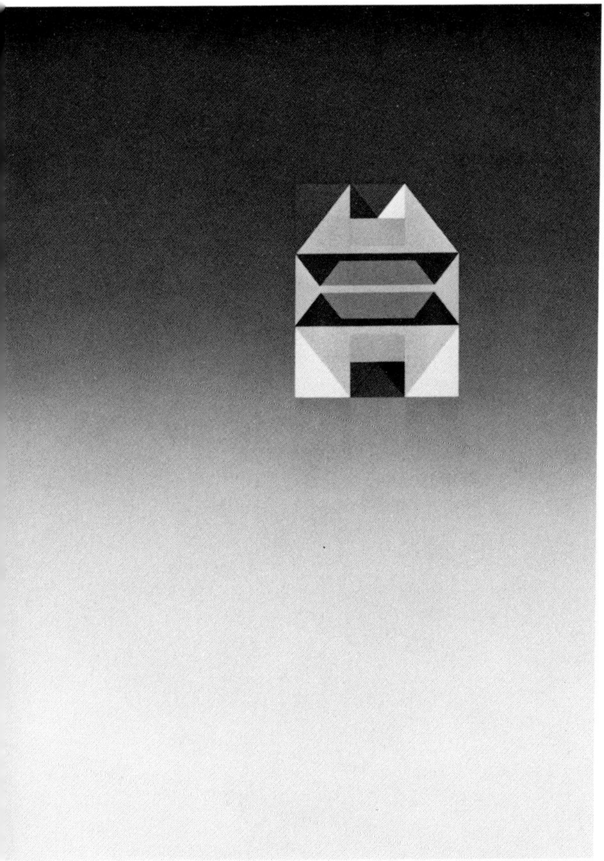

84
Michael Lasuchin
(b. Kramatorsk, U.S.S.R., 1923)
Triad
1976, serigraph, edition: 50
Image: 31.3 x 31.1 (12⅜ x 12¼)
Sheet: 52.4 x 37.2 (20⅝ x 14⅝)
Associated American Artists, Philadelphia

Lasuchin's *Triad* required fourteen screens. The artist printed jet black, glossy black, opaque white, light chrome yellow, brilliant light orange, light gray, dark royal purple, midnight blue, cerulean blue, radiant ultra-blue, dark peacock blue, emerald green, and bright cerise. Inks were Nazdar. Paper is Arjomari (Arches) silkscreen paper.

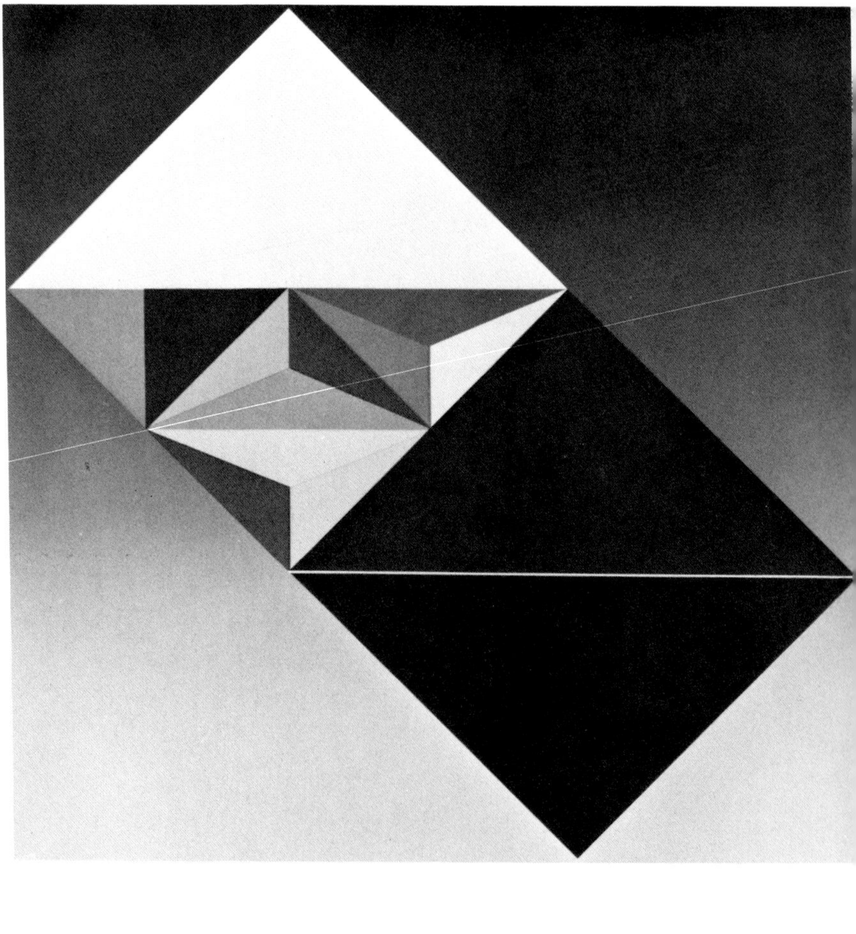

Lerner's prints are episodic, a dozen images in varied mediums and from varied viewpoints. The subjects are arranged in a grid, and elements within single images are, so to speak, in dialogue all across the board. Color, shape, pattern, opacity, degree of modeling, overlays—you name it—all these as well as individual images interact rhythmically, creating a variety of visual tempos and syncopated notes. Printing by the artist involved serigraph, monoprint, color Xerox, Dupont Chromolin process, photo-montage, and solvent transfer. Papers are various.

85
Allan Jay Lerner
(b. Brooklyn, New York, 1951)
Laughing Cow
1978, Xerox, serigraph, monotype, Dupont chromolin, photo-montage, and transfer, edition: unique
Image: 29.7 x 29.9 (11 11/16 x 11 3/4)
Sheet: 29.7 x 29.9 (11 11/16 x 11 3/4)
The Artist

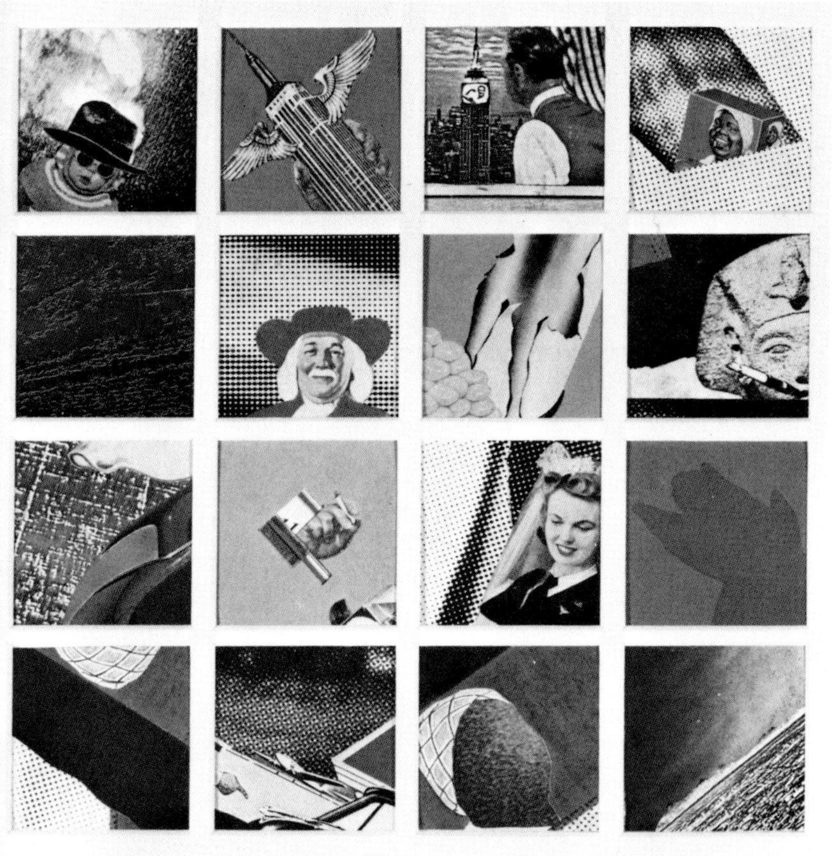

86
Allan Jay Lerner
(b. Brooklyn, New York, 1951)
Laughing Gas
1978, Xerox, serigraph, monotype, Dupont chromolin, photo-montage, and transfer, edition: unique
Image: 30.0 x 30.0 ($11\frac{3}{4}$ x $11\frac{3}{4}$)
Sheet: 30.0 x 30.0 ($11\frac{3}{4}$ x $11\frac{3}{4}$)
The Artist

Lerner's method of work for *Laughing Gas* is the same as that for *Laughing Cow* (Cat. 85). Different combinations of technique and image give these pictures different energies singly and in combination. *Laughing Gas* presents a more vibrant and active surface overall than *Laughing Cow*.

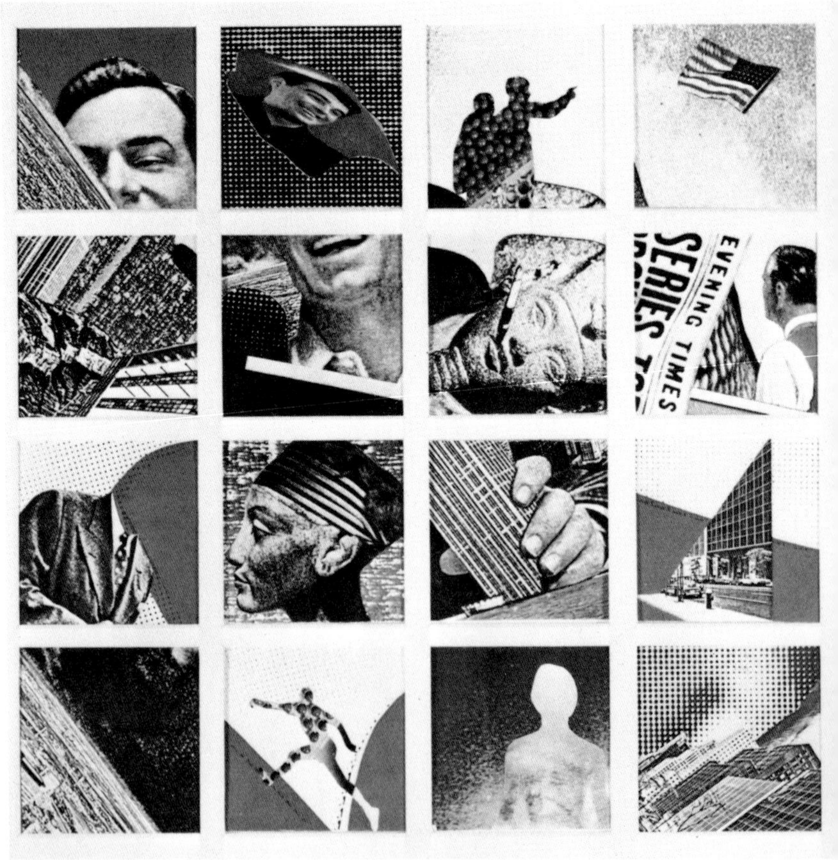

McCoy's jellyfish trail their tentacles not only within the central rectangle of her image but outside of it as well. The invasion of the border by the dome of the creature establishes the looming, menacing life of the image. The lithograph was printed from an aluminum plate in blue-black by Maurice Sanchez, New York, on Lana paper and was hand-colored by the artist. The publisher is Brooke Alexander, Inc., New York.

87
Ann McCoy
(b. Boulder, Colorado, 1946)
Meduse
1978, lithograph, hand-colored with color pencils, edition: 30
Image: 57.1 x 44.1 (27½ x 17⅜)
Sheet: 76.1 x 56.8 (30 x 22⅜)
Brooke Alexander, Inc.

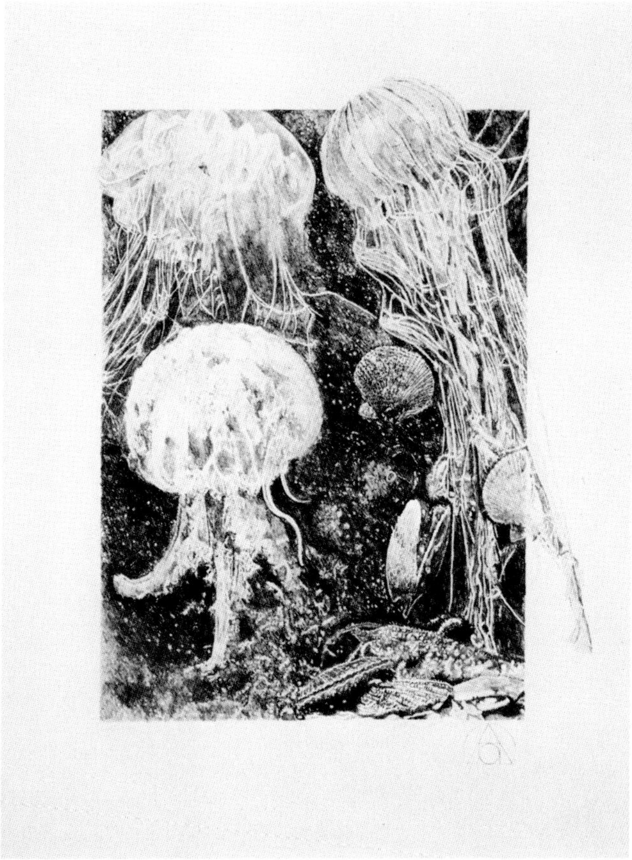

88
Ann McCoy
(b. Boulder, Colorado, 1946)
Night Sea (diptych)
1978, lithograph, hand-colored with color pencils, edition: 30
Each:
Image: 165.7 x 87.0 (65¼ x 34¼)
Sheet: 165.7 x 87.0 (65¼ x 34¼)
Brooke Alexander, Inc.

McCoy's undersea imagery is intended to have the force of metaphor. The artist invokes the psyche by way of a number of mythological references discussed in her statement. Whether one carries this apparatus to the prints or not, the imagery beguiles. A mysterious floating life is presented, insufficiently exact in its rendering to suggest illustration; or to put it more positively, the work reveals personality in draughtsmanship. The diptych was printed in blue-black by Maurice Sanchez on Arches Roll paper, and was hand-colored by the artist with pencils. An aluminum plate was used. The publisher is Brooke Alexander, Inc., New York.

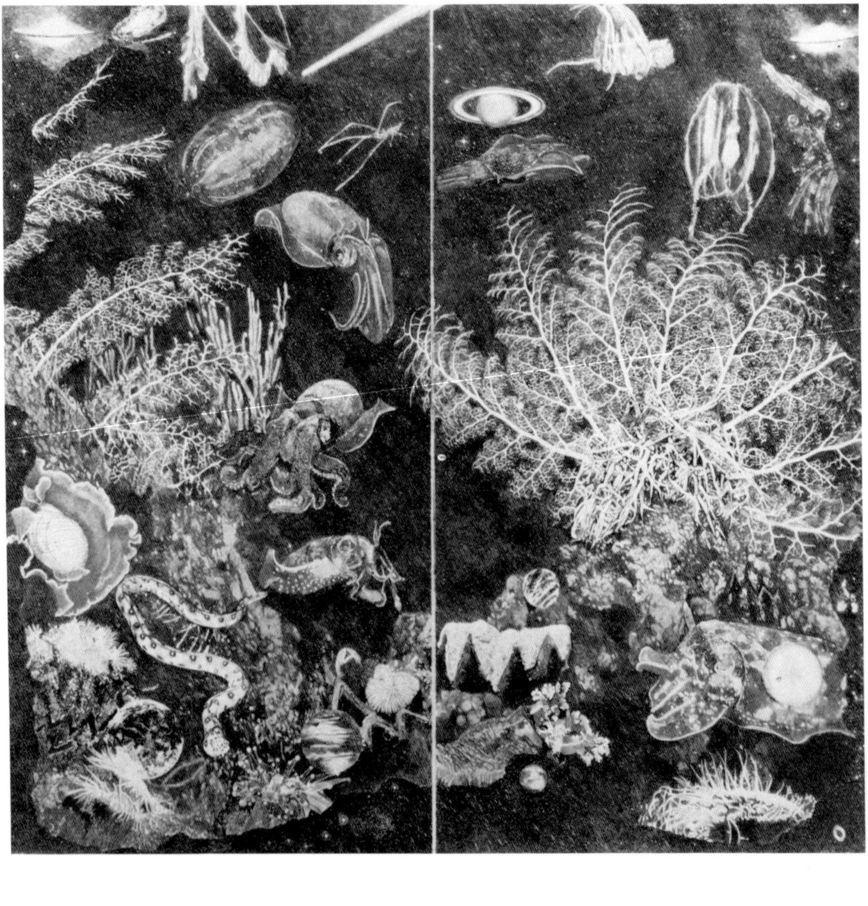

McGowen's etchings have great surface vitality, an exuber-nt overall activity that takes off from a variety of marking ystems in uneasy concourse. But all is held in balance. The nergies favor tension. These prints are as interesting to xamine as they are to look at, for the small incidents are ften as intriguing as the full image. The artist printed from copper plate on hand-made paper and bled his image.

89
Michael McGowan
(b. Brooklyn, New York, 1952)
Untitled
1977, etching, edition: 16
Image: 57.3 x 52.1 (22½ x 20½)
Sheet: 57.3 x 52.1 (22½ x 20½)
The Artist

90
Michael McGowan
(b. Brooklyn, New York, 1952)
Untitled
1978, etching and aquatint,
edition: 20
Image: 42.9 x 30.2 (16⅞ x 11⅞)
Sheet: 58.7 x 46.4 (23⅛ x 18¼)
The Artist

McGowen's draughtsmanship is the substance of his fan-tasy. He needs hardly more than a few kinds of marks t[o] create the sense of a world in flux. This print carries som[e] explicitly descriptive drawing, but not much. Most of it[s] memorable presence is made from squiggles, lines, an[d] dots. The artist printed from a zinc plate on hand-mad[e] paper.

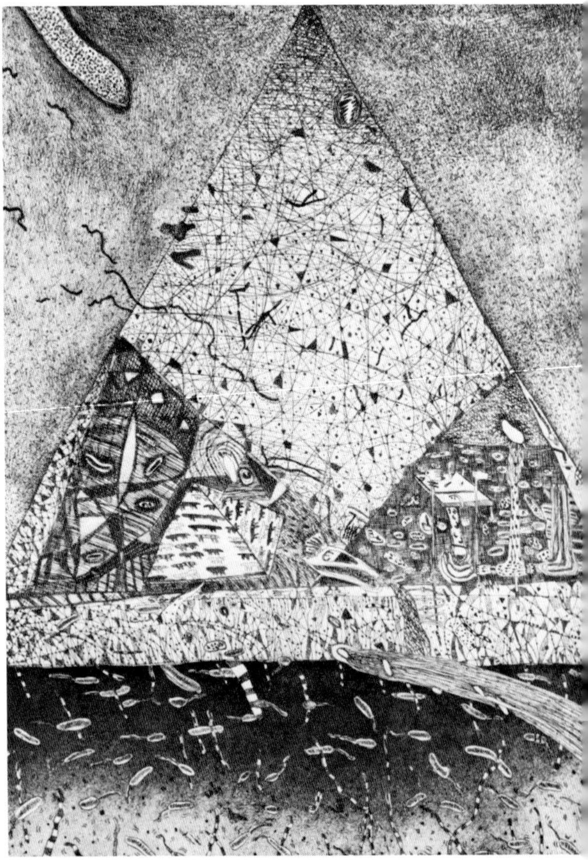

McMillan uses the technique of progressive aquatint etch-ng. When his plate drawing is done, he paints out the ightest areas and etches them, painting out areas of successively deeper tonal range with appropriate etching. Often he artist will re-aquatint in order to darken the tones and to nhance textural richness. He may use as many as three quatints on a plate with the coarsest grained aquatint laid lown first. The artist printed *Papyrus and Fern* on Lana aper.

91
Stephen McMillan
(b. Berkeley, California, 1949)
Papyrus and Fern
1978, aquatint, edition: 120
Image: 49.5 x 70.5 (19½ x 27¾)
Sheet: 56.5 x 73.7 (22¼ x 29)
ADI Gallery

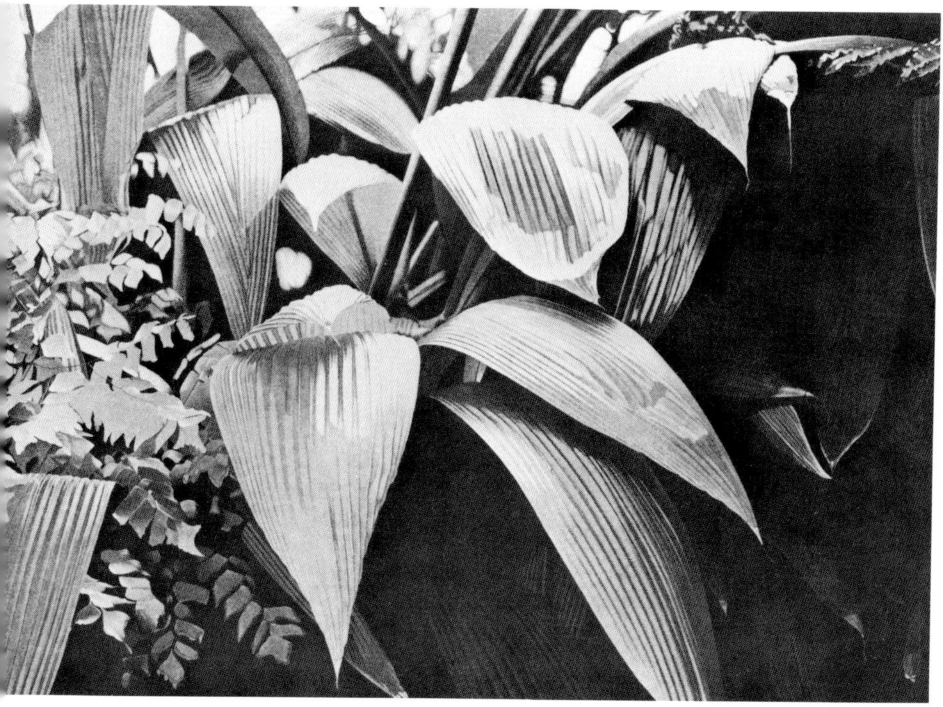

92
Stephen McMillan
(b. Berkeley, California, 1949)
Reflections and Carp
1978, hand-colored aquatint,
edition: XV
Image: 22.3 x 19.7 (8¾ x 7¾)
Sheet: 45.7 x 37.8 (18 x 14⅞)
ADI Gallery

McMillan uses photographs as sources of information fo his prints, but the prints in no way involve photo-etching process. The artist works directly on an aquatinted coppe plate painting freehand with asphaltum. His photographi source may be modified radically during this drawing phas with elements subtracted or added. The artist printed thi aquatint on Lana paper and hand-colored it with water color. The publisher is ADI Graphic Editions, San Fran cisco, California.

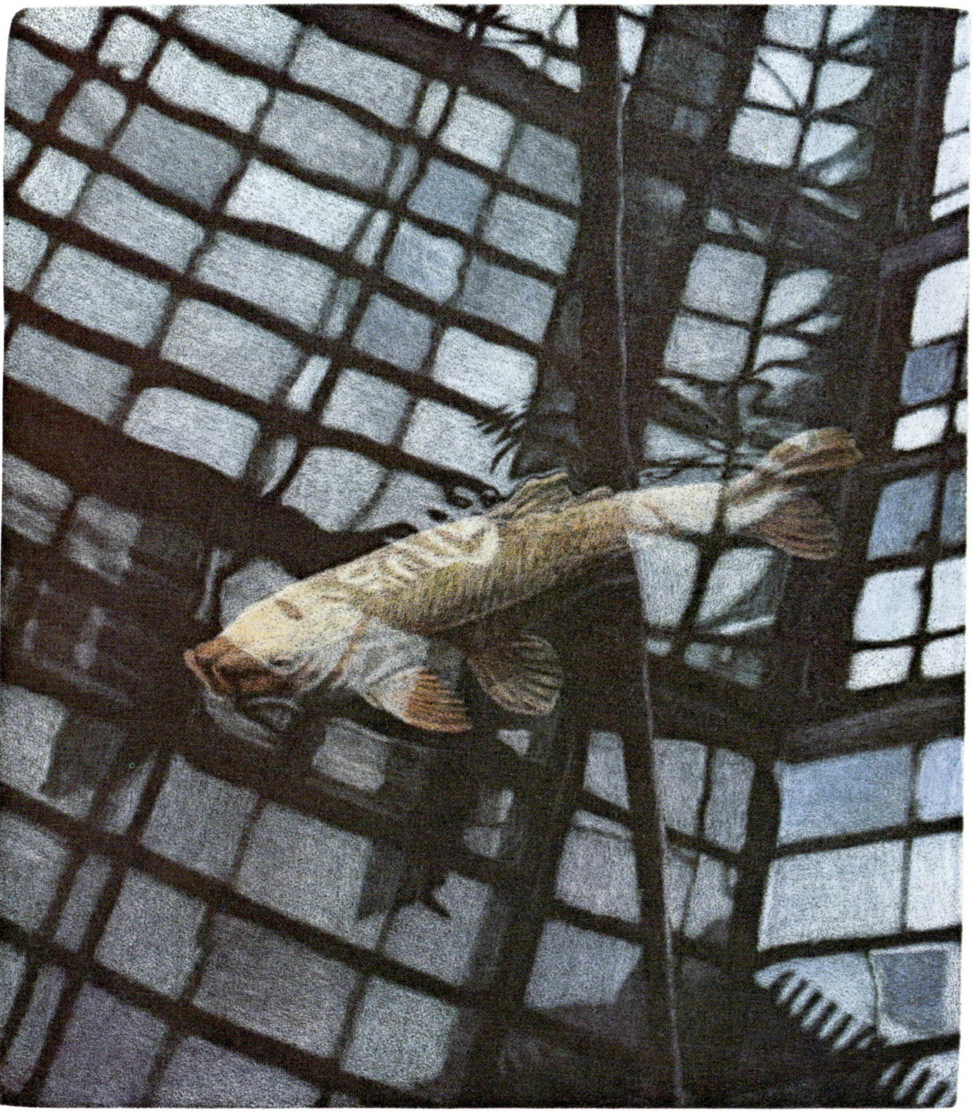

93

Deng Ming-Dao

(b. San Francisco, California, 1954)

Rain Basin

1978, woodcut, edition: 25

Image: 61.0 x 45.1 (24 x 17¾)

Sheet: 80.3 x 61.2 (31⅝ x 24⅛)

ADI Gallery

Deng Ming-Dao's woodcuts are extraordinary evocations of the spirit of landscape conveyed through the balancing of idiosyncratic shapes whose spatial allusion is augmented by color. In *Rain Basin* there is rather more linearity than in any of the artist's other prints, but the straight lines play against the curved ones, adding to our sense of depth, to the sensation of viewing landscape from a height. The artist's prints are made by reduction cutting. He uses a single block of solid birch core plywood. The artist makes a series of cuts for the first color and prints the entire edition. He then cuts the block further for the second color and prints the entire edition. With each successive color, the block is further reduced until all colors are printed, and the print is completed. *Rain Basin* was printed by the artist in four color runs on Hosho paper. The publisher is ADI Graphic Editions, San Francisco, California.

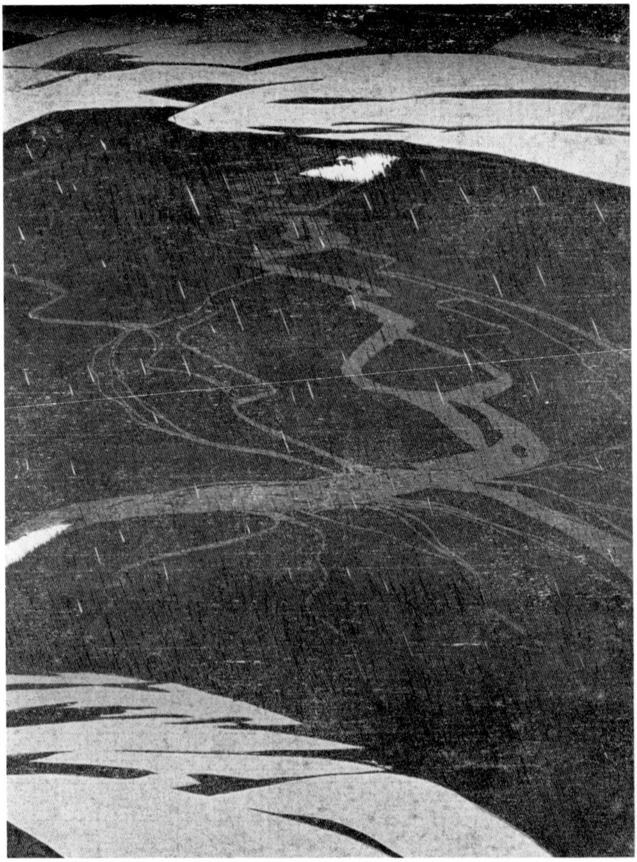

Deng Ming-Dao's *Cloud Shadows* is remarkable in its woodblock cutting. The rationalization of shapes and colors achieved in this landscape is highly individual and bold. The artist used reduction block process, cutting for color, printing, recutting, printing a second color, and so forth. For *Cloud Shadows,* he printed four color runs in all, some runs employing split-fountain rolls. The artist printed with oil-based inks on Hosho paper with pressure applied by hand using a baren of the Japanese type made of a coil of rope wrapped in a bamboo leaf.

94
Deng Ming-Dao
(b. San Francisco, California, 1954)
Cloud Shadows
1978, woodcut, edition: 25
Image: 60.4 x 45.7 (23¾ x 18)
Sheet: 80.0 x 62.2 (31½ x 24½)
ADI Gallery

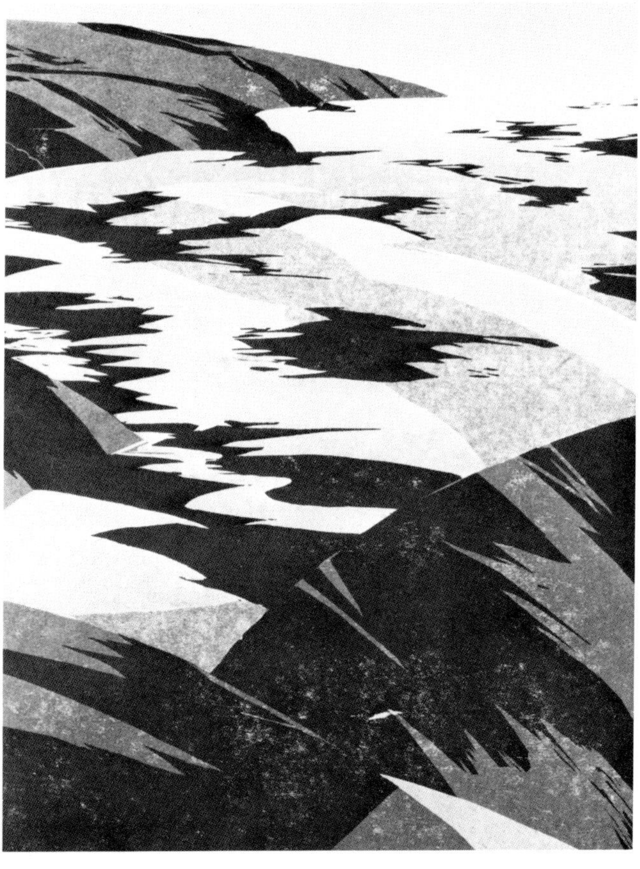

95
Philip E. Mullen
(b. Akron, Ohio, 1942)
Kathmandu Eccentric
1977, serigraph, edition: 34
Image: 76.2 x 51.5 (30 x 20¼)
Sheet: 76.2 x 51.5 (30 x 20¼)
The Brooklyn Museum 78.23.2

Mullen's prints are built up with overprinting to create a glowing, painterly surface. The combination of an implied grid format with broken, overprinted color gives an autographic feeling to the print. In the case of *Kathmandu Eccentric,* printed on a laminated Nepalese paper, each sheet has highly individual characteristics.

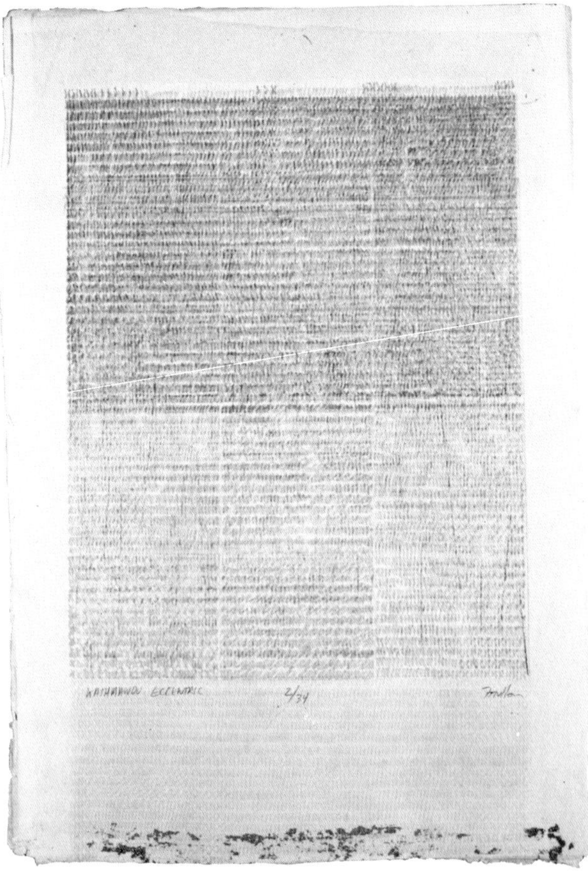

96
Philip E. Mullen
(b. Akron, Ohio, 1942)
ADI Blue
1977, serigraph, edition: 28
Image: 60.4 x 41.6 (23¾ x 16⅜)
Sheet: 71.1 x 46.7 (28 x 18⅜)
Reproduced in color on page 18
The Artist

Mullen's *ADI Blue* was printed on a paper made by Don Farnsworth from a design suggested by the artist based on a paper made by Nancy Albertson. The paper was air-dried for a rough texture and has a large silk content and an extra rough deckle edge. Mullen gives collaborator credit to artist-printer Susan Heath, who was serving an apprenticeship with him at the time he made this print. He reported that "she had such feeling for the work that she suggested many of the colors." For this project, Mullen also had a printing consultant, Steve Nevitt, who stood by to assist with technical problems. Nineteen colors were printed. Orange, blue, and maroon were printed as thin lines and subsequently overprinted. They are now only partially to be seen in the final print. Subsequent colors printed included yellow, earth-green, brown, red-brown, and various blues and pinks. These colors were printed in the shape of small brush marks and in varying degrees of transparency so that overlaying colors would form additional colors. The final colors printed were off-white and creams, also in the form of small brush marks and of relative transparency so that the brighter underlying colors would show through.

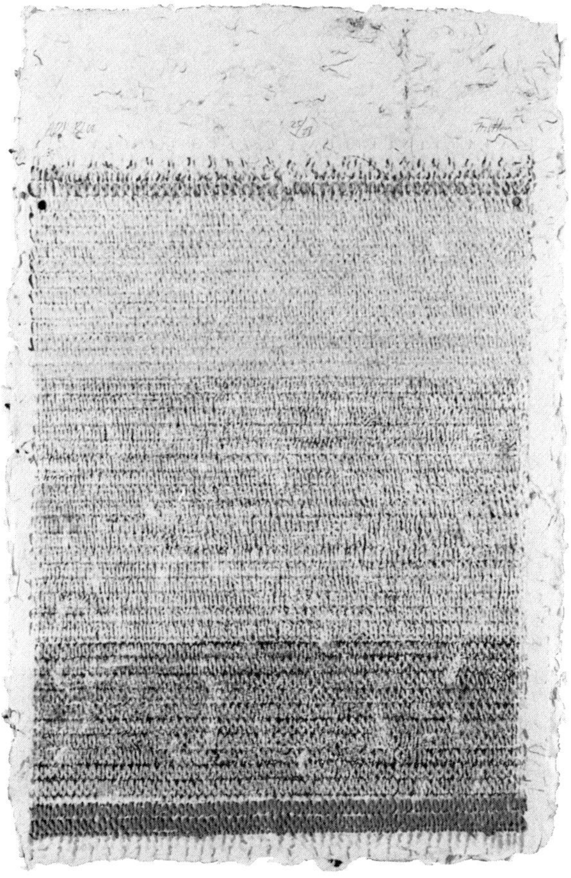

97
Mark A. Nelson
(b. Winnipeg, Canada, 1953)
Remains B^3
1977, lithograph, edition: 15
Image: 56.5 x 76.2 (22¼ x 30)
Sheet: 56.5 x 76.2 (22¼ x 30)
The Artist

Nelson's imagery suggests breakdown, decay, the reduction of forms, the accretion of remains. The sense of his prints is a consistent restructuring, a living process of matter dissolving into its constituents. *Remains B^3* was printed by the artist from aluminum plates, first in flat dark green, then in a silver gray image. Paper was Arches Cover buff.

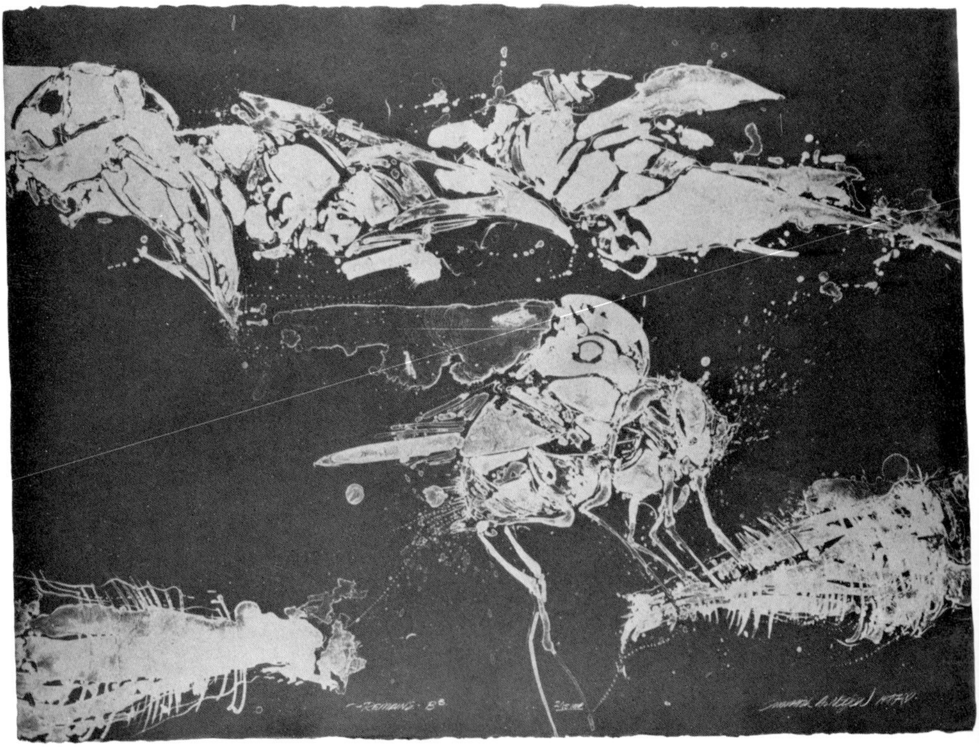

Nelson's *Deathmask* was produced through an acid-tinting method that the artist stumbled upon. Later, he discovered the Tamarind Lithography Workshop's notes on acid tinting, but he considers that procedure to be more complicated than the one he himself developed. He works with very strong mixtures of nitric acid and gum arabic painted on lithographic stone over a flat black ink layer. The mixture is allowed to bubble on this covering. The artist then works in the reduction method, taking out some of the image, printing, removing more, printing again, until he considers the image complete. The strength of the gum arabic mixture determines the texture of the tint. In *Deathmask* a number of textures were arrived at through this method of acid tinting. *Deathmask* was printed in six colors from stone by the artist in four press runs on Arches Cover buff.

98
Mark A. Nelson
(b. Winnipeg, Canada, 1953)
Deathmask
1978, lithograph, edition: 8
Image: 73.6 x 52.9 (29 x $20\frac{7}{8}$)
Sheet: 76.2 x 57.1 (30 x $22\frac{1}{2}$)
The Artist

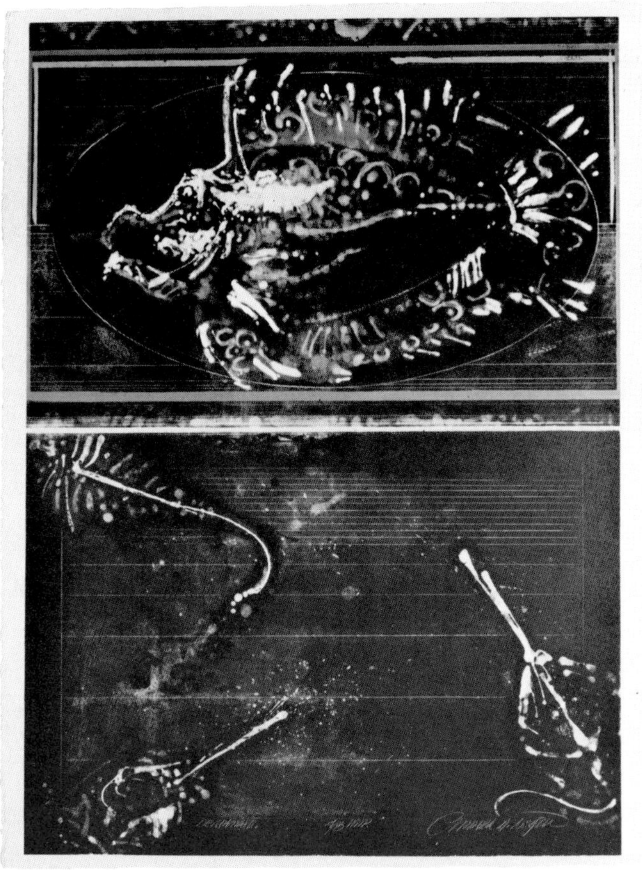

99
Thomas Wilson Northington
(b. Seattle, Washington, 1947)
University Bridge
1976, collagraph,
edition (varied): 10
Image: 38.2 x 50.6 (15 x 19⅞)
Sheet: 44.5 x 57.3 (17½ x 22⅝)
Davidson Galleries

Northington's prints have a painterly richness and a beguiling surface. *University Bridge* is one of ten printed variations of a single image taken from the videotape *Interstate Five,* directed and recorded by the artist in 1975. Still photographs were taken from the studio monitor. Two were selected and enlarged to the matrix size, mounted on upsom board, and covered with plastic screen mesh. Gloss lacquer was then painted into the desired relief areas on the plates. Various overprintings combined intaglio and relief inking of both plates. Each of the print variations required many passes through the press. This printing approach and the fragile construction of the plates allowed just ten prints to reach completion before the plates broke down. The artist printed the collagraph by offset in metallic ink with carborundum on Arches Cover white.

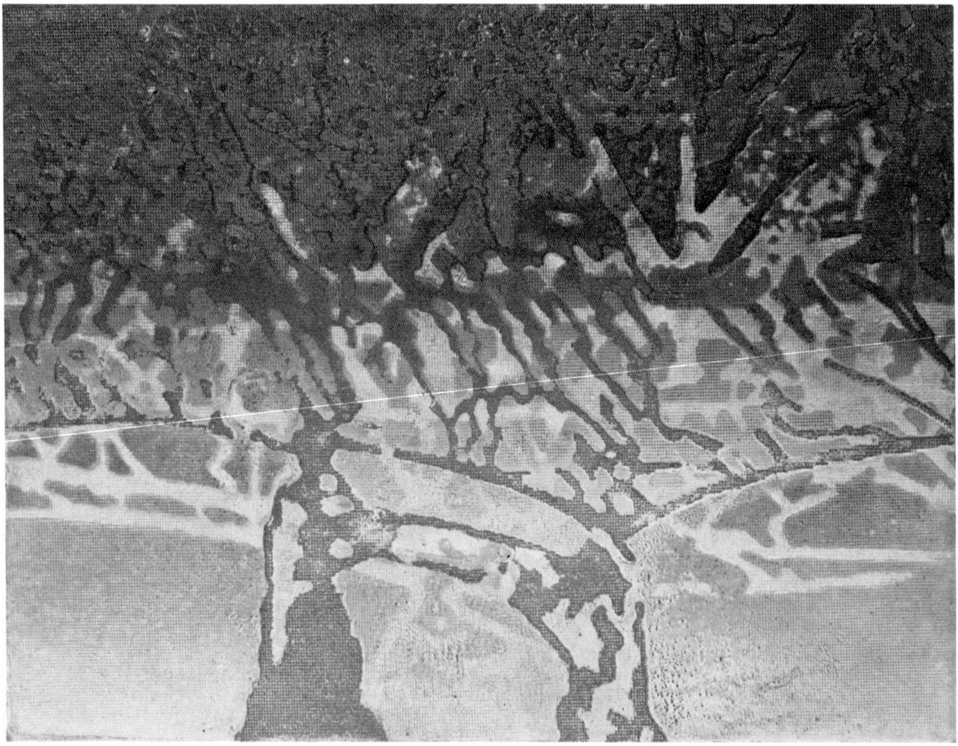

Northington's *Encroaching on the Continent* is the unique printing of a single image from the artist's current series, *The Championship USLTA Collagraph Series.* It combines two collagraph plates and one photo-etched zinc plate. Plates were printed and overprinted by the artist as many as twenty times, inked both intaglio and relief. The paper is Arches Cover white.

100
Thomas Wilson Northington
(b. Seattle, Washington, 1947)
Encroaching on the Continent
1977, collagraph and
photo-etching, edition (varied): 6
Image: 29.2 x 44.9 (11½ x 17⅝)
Sheet: 29.2 x 44.9 (11½ x 17⅝)
Davidson Galleries

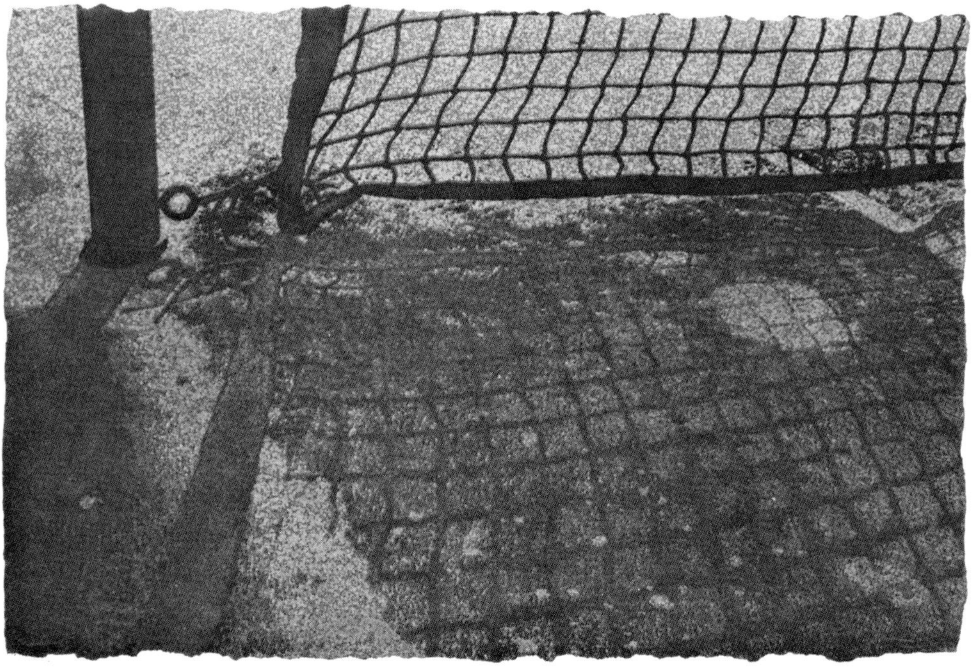

101
Michael Nushawg
(b. Dayton, Ohio, 1944)
RE-4
1977, etching, relief, lithograph, and chine collé with collage, edition: 10
Image: 148.1 x 85.3 (97 ½ x 33⅝)
Sheet: 148.1 x 85.3 (97 ½ x 33⅝)
ADI Gallery

Nushawg's prints have their source in color relationships. Nevertheless, the artist's manipulation of shape and his use of a variety of printmaking techniques, including chine collé and collage, assist in the creation of spatially dynamic works. The expansive scale, space, and energy in these works suggest the spatial vocabulary of contemporary American paintings in the past few decades. This print, employing intaglio, relief, lithography, and chine collé in ten colors, was printed and collaged on Rives BFK by the artist and Jack McCaslin.

102
Michael Nushawg
(b. Dayton, Ohio, 1944)
(Dové Te) Destiny Kinnel
1978, lithograph, etching,
relief, and serigraph
with collage, edition: 18
Image: 72.1 x 177.2 (28⅜ x 69¾)
Sheet: 91.4 x 193.3 (36 x 76)
ADI Gallery

Nushawg printed thirteen colors for this image involving lithography, intaglio, relief, silkscreen, and chine collé collaged onto Rives BFK paper.

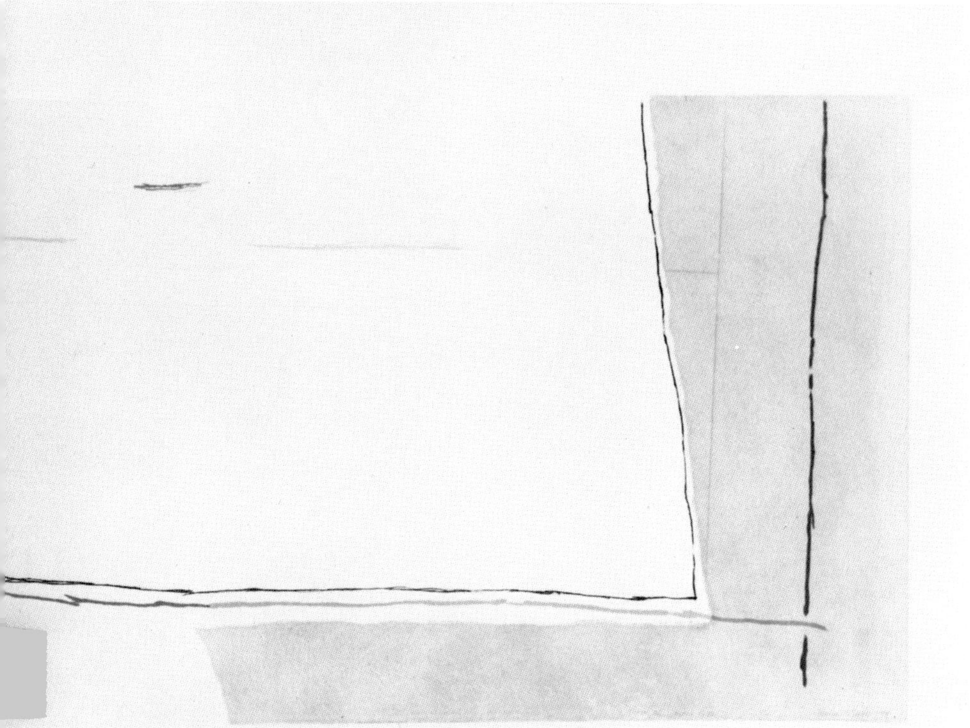

103
Eva Pokorny
(b. Turnov, Czechoslovakia, 1949)
My Life
1978, monotype, edition: unique
Image: 18.1 x 12.7 (7⅛ x 5)
Sheet: 25.4 x 20.1 (10 x 7⅞)
Reproduced in color on page 14
The Artist

Pokorny's monotypes are rich in color and intensely personal and evocative in handling. Her statement in this volume is of particular interest in delineating her artistic and literary sources. *My Life* is a single image taken by the artist from glass. Speedball oil-based ink for black printing was applied by brayer to the glass surface. Dry Arches paper was placed on this inked surface, and a sheet of rice paper was then placed over the Arches for protection before the reverse drawing was made in pencil. The process was repeated for each color. Registration was by the Japanese method.

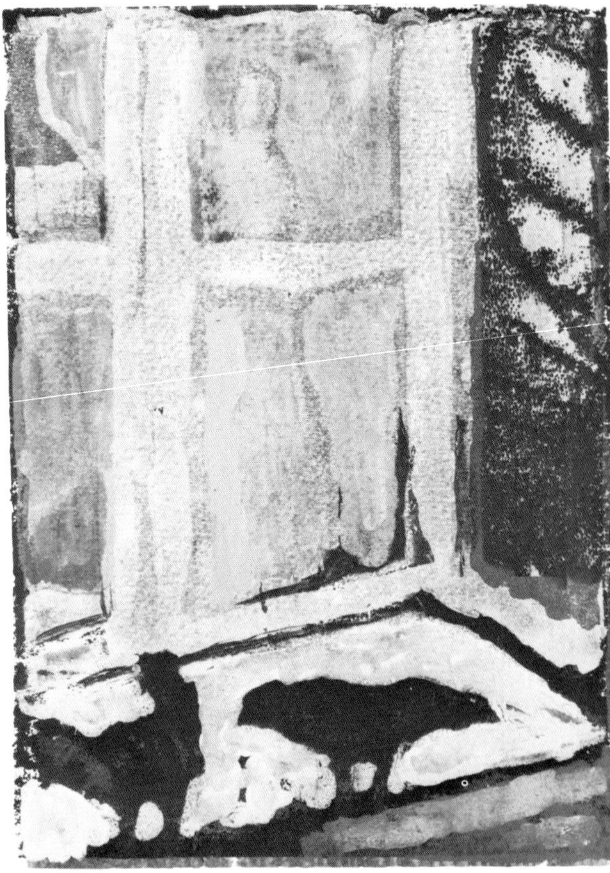

Pokorny's *In the Ravine* presents a lush surface, rather in the mood of Expressionism, for the evocation of landscape. The print was produced in the same way as *My Life* (Cat. 103). It was printed on Arches Cover white.

104
Eva Pokorny
(b. Turnov, Czechoslovakia, 1949)
In the Ravine
1978, monotype, edition: unique
Image: 17.8 x 12.7 (7 x 5)
Sheet: 25.7 x 20.3 (10⅛ x 8)
Reproduced in color on page 14
The Artist

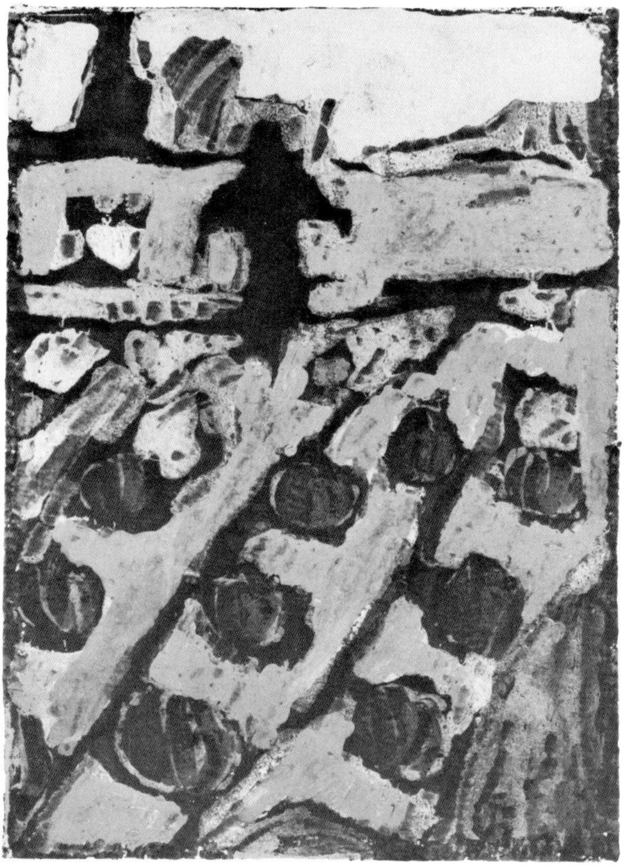

105
Madeline Poster
(b. Chicago, Illinois, 1948)
Rockefeller Center
1976, serigraph, edition: 50
Image: 71.4 x 45.0 (28⅛ x 17¾)
Sheet: 88.6 x 63.4 (34⅞ x 25)
The Brooklyn Museum *78.25.5*

Poster's prints ought to stimulate a special affection in New York. Her treatment of scenes and events around town are delightfully witty and have a personality as distinct as the subjects pictured. Their charm conceals great technical skill and serious artistic underpinnings. *Rockefeller Center* began as an etching on a small plate. When this etching was finished, the artist had the image photographed and blown up, and both positive and negative Kodaliths were made. The artist used the negative Kodalith on the screen, an easy method for transferring the image as a line drawing. This negative was used to print the solid areas of color. A blue stencil was used for each color; fifteen in all were made from the negative. The artist then removed the negative image and replaced it on the screen with the positive. The positive was used for printing the sixteenth color, the black line. The artist does not use color studies for her prints, but works intuitively while making the stencils and mixing the inks. In this instance, she printed on Arches Cover white.

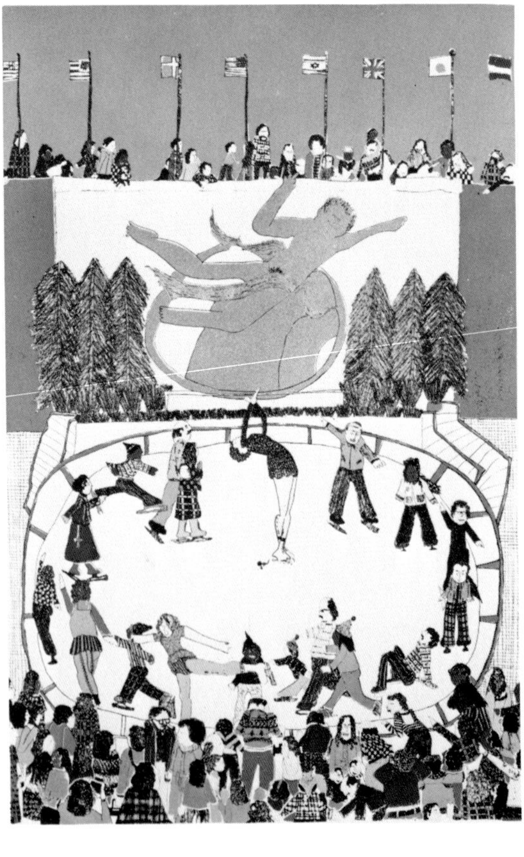

106
Madeline Poster
(b. Chicago, Illinois, 1948)
Festival of San Gennaro —Mulberry St.
1978, etching, edition: 50
Image: 60.7 x 34.6 (23⅞ x 13⅝)
Sheet: 75.8 x 56.5 (29⅞ x 22¼)
The Brooklyn Museum *78.25.1*

Poster's *Festival of San Gennaro—Mulberry Street* developed from a rough drawing on newsprint in which the artist found "bones of the composition." She overlaid this drawing with tracing paper and made a rough study of figure movement in dark and light. She transferred only the essential lines of the composition to a copper plate covered with hard-ground. Characteristically, she began drawing the plate in the lower left corner and moved to the right, her composition growing to the top of the plate. She then added textures and darks. No aquatint was used. The plate was bitten three times, first in Dutch Mordant and twice in ferric chloride. Printing by the artist was on Arches Cover buff.

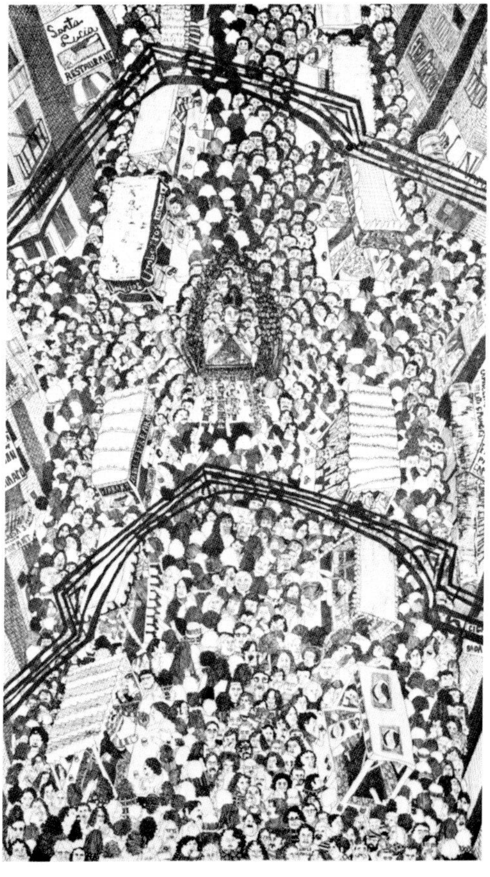

107
Scott Reeds
(b. Sioux City, Iowa, 1953)
End of the Reel
1977, aquatint and drypoint,
edition: 5
Image: 22.3 x 22.5 (8⅝ x 8⅞)
Sheet: 70.1 x 51.1 (27⅝ x 20⅛)
The Artist

Reeds's *End of the Reel* was first printed on a single sheet as three plates of identical size and title. Now Reeds prints the plates separately. The title and composition refer to what may be seen at the end of a movie reel. The artist printed the plate colored à la poupée in one press run on Murillo paper.

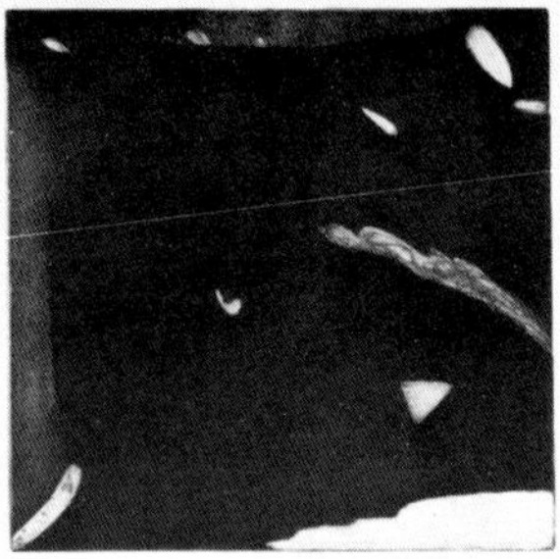

Reeds's *Side Arm* is developed from the sense of natural gesture in throwing a ball. The treatment reflects metaphysical sensation. In the case of the print, the "throw" was made with the etching needle. Spontaneity and playfulness are important elements, both of the situation alluded to and of the visual metaphor. The plate is essentially aquatint and drypoint. The artist applied color à la poupée and printed the plate once on Murillo paper.

108
Scott Reeds
(b. Sioux City, Iowa, 1953)
Side Arm
1978, aquatint and drypoint, edition: 5
Image: 45.1 x 45.1 (17¾ x 17¾)
Sheet: 62.6 x 57.2 (24⅝ x 22½)
The Artist

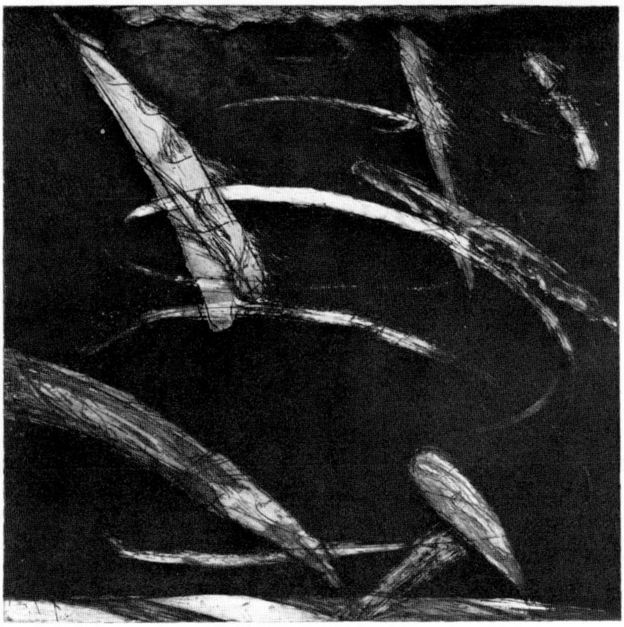

109
Minna Resnick
(b. New York, New York, 1946)
Entrance
1977, lithograph, edition: 20
Image: 48.3 x 37.8 (19 x 14⅞)
Sheet: 48.3 x 37.8 (19 x 14⅞)
The Brooklyn Museum 78.67

Resnick's mysterious and elegant lithographs play nude female figures against an abstract or simplified setting—a kind of timeless space where they perform, either individually or in pairs, simple physical gestures: bending, sitting, walking. Her treatment takes on the solemnity of ritual. The artist draws from photographs that she has taken over several years of a single model. Incorporated into these drawings are partial rubbings from half-tones on aluminum plates. She uses a stylus, a comb, or her thumbnail to transfer a part of the image onto the stone or plate. Often she draws with an etching needle through carbon paper, which enables her to get a very crisp, fine line. The carbon paper is covered with a sheet of Mylar to protect it from tearing. Frequently areas are airbrushed. The artist printed seven colors on Arches Cover white for *Entrance*. The first run was light to medium blue with a diagonal blend in the figure. The artist then printed transparent yellow, transparent orange, and dark green. The fifth run from a stone was in purple and carried the key drawing. The sixth and seventh runs were respectively transparent white and navy blue.

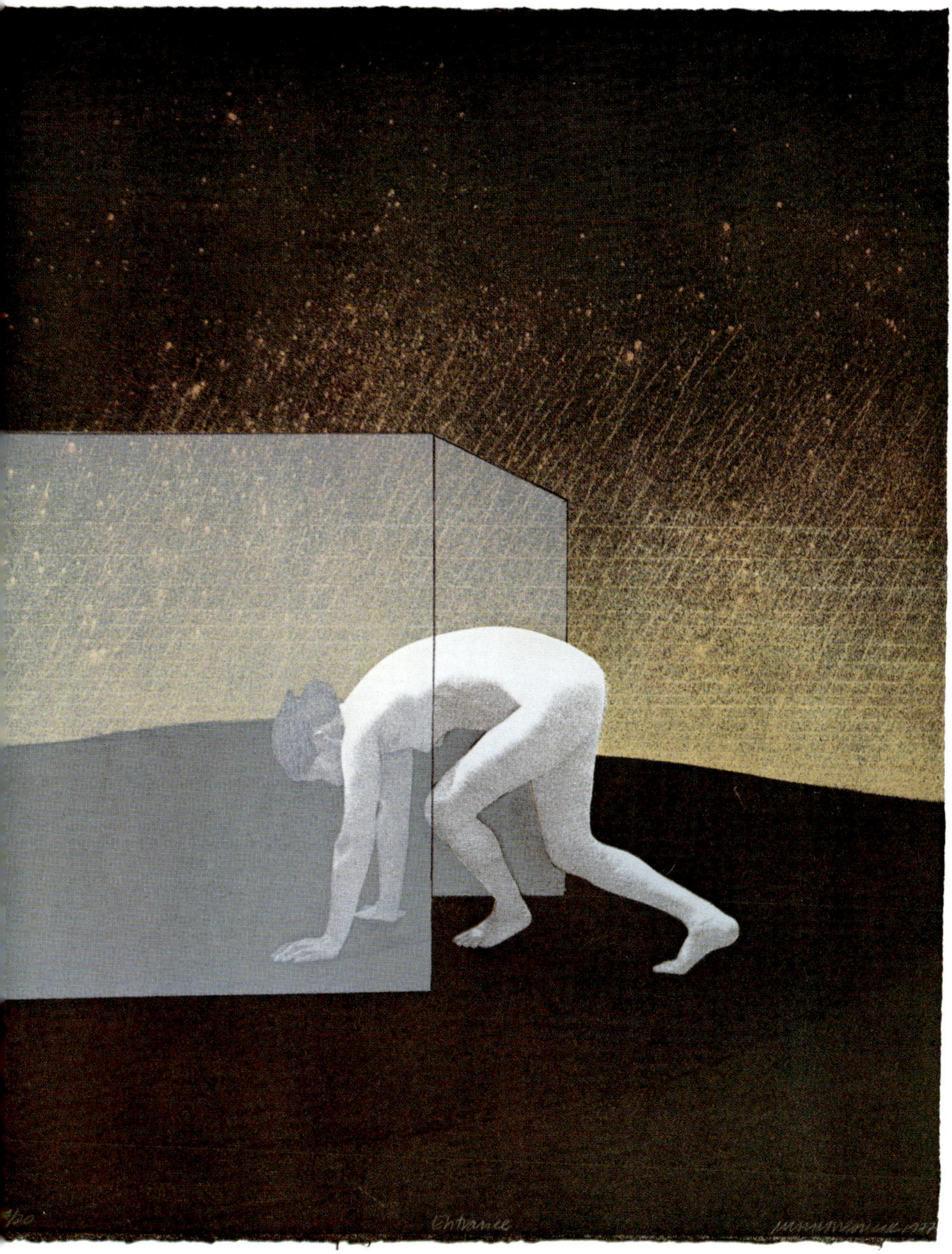

Entrance

110
Minna Resnick
(b. New York, New York, 1946)
Stage Spirits II
1978, lithograph, edition: 20
Image: 38.2 x 56.9 (15 x 22⅜)
Sheet: 38.2 x 56.9 (15 x 22⅜)
The Artist

Resnick's *Stage Spirits II* suggests a relationship, a dramatic connection, if you will, between two figures, one seated and one walking. But the two are in fact the same figure. The artist printed on Arches Cover white in five runs from one stone and four aluminum plates. The first run involved a peach-gray rainbow; the second, left to right, a rainbow of transparent light blue-gray and medium green-gray. The third run was in transparent mauve; the fourth dark mauve. The final run was the stone drawn in brown.

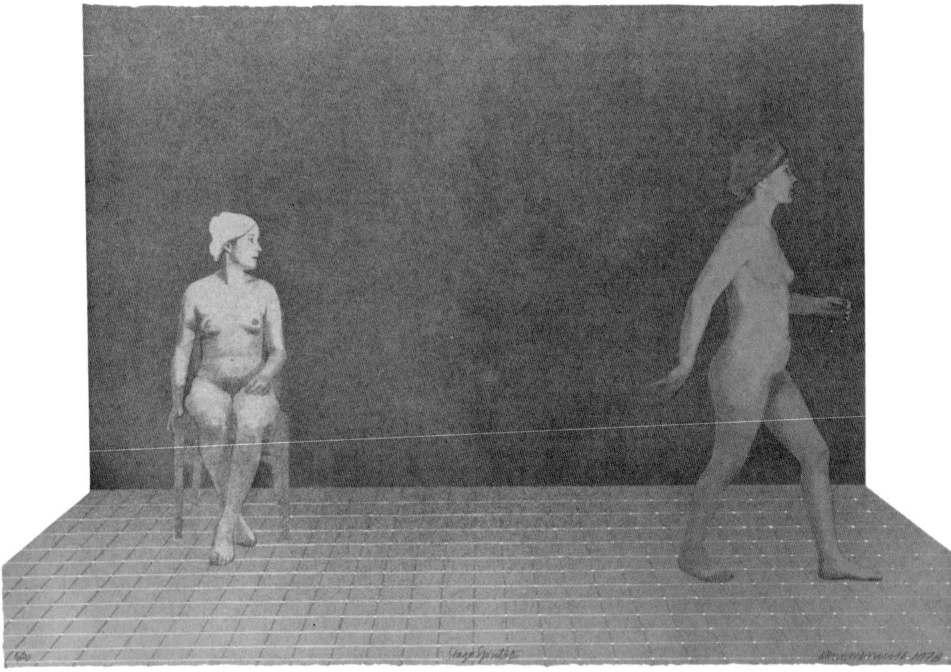

Ruble has described the evolution of his imagery in his statement in this volume. Interestingly, his meditated works have the impact and staying power of dreams. They are evolutions, resolutions of things. They are more than mere arrangements. *Dying Rhino* derives from a drawing the artist made on acetate. He exposed it photographically and reworked the plate by hand. Dennis McWilliams printed on Murillo paper.

111
Ronald L. Ruble
(b. St. Louis, Missouri, 1935)
Dying Rhino
1978, etching, edition: 150
Image: 41.6 x 61.3 (16⅜ x 24⅛)
Sheet: 55.9 x 75.9 (22 x 29⅞)
Associated American Artists, New York

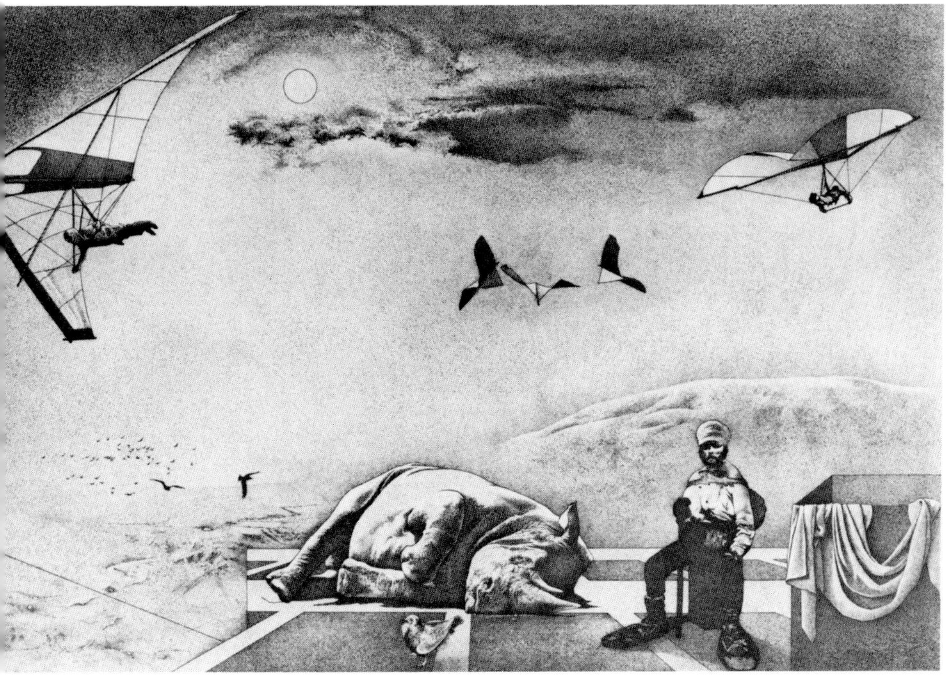

112
Ronald L. Ruble
(b. St. Louis, Missouri, 1935)
She Who Controls Dreams (Violet Haze)
1978, screenprint, edition: 150
Image: 36.5 x 36.5 (14⅜ x 14⅜)
Sheet: 53.3 x 53.0 (21 x 20⅞)
Associated American Artists, New York

Ruble's *She Who Controls Dreams (Violet Haze)* is one of hi most persuasive images. Repetition of rounds and volumes the sensation of balance and floating, create a trance-lik insistence and visual pulse. Here, management of the imag and exploitation of its cultural and psychic association create a highly effective unity. The screenprint was printe by Robert Danner on Arches Cover white in seventee colors.

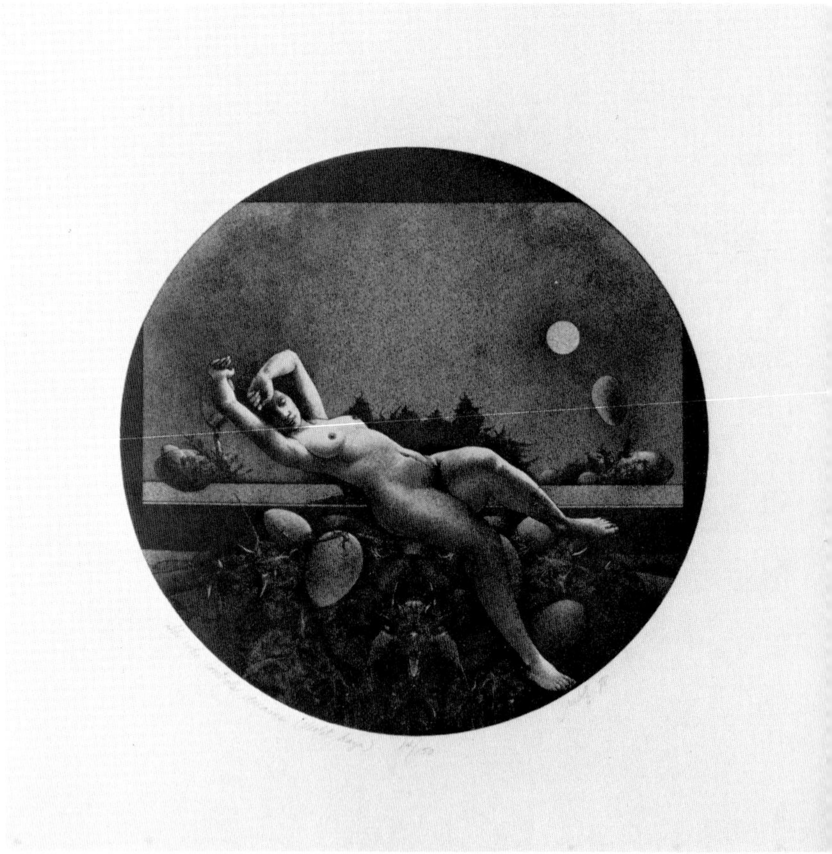

Cat. 73

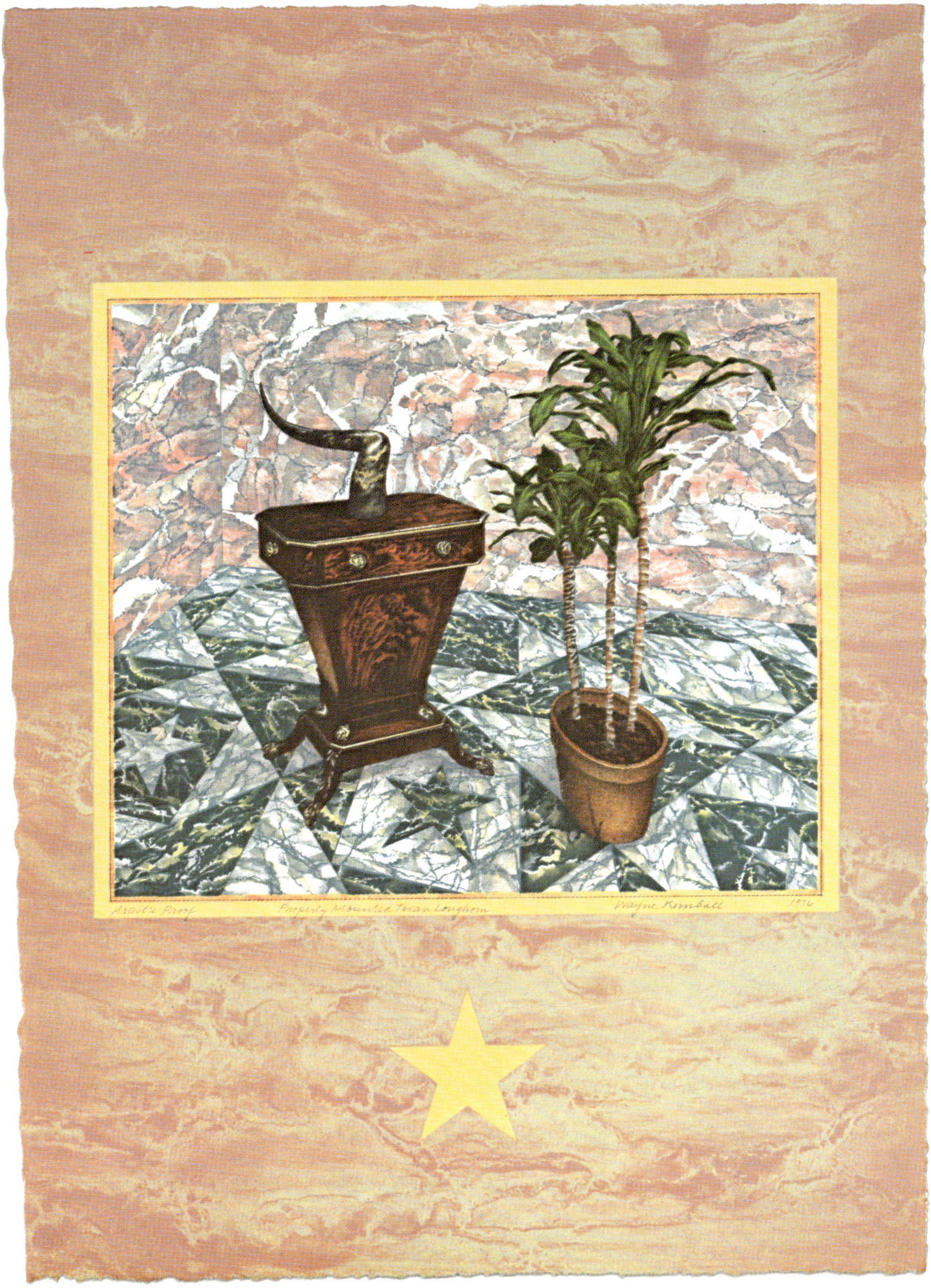
Artist's Proof
Properly Mounted Texan Longhorn
Wayne Kimball
1976

113
Shunji Sakuyama
(b. Tokyo, Japan, 1940)
A House in Brooklyn
1978, lithograph, edition: 15
Image: 65.7 x 50.8 (25⅞ x 20)
Sheet: 76.2 x 56.8 (30 x 22⅜)
The Brooklyn Museum *78.68.2*

Sakuyama's prints often deal with architectural subjects in the area of Brooklyn where he lives. His treatment of buildings not only has descriptive accuracy but gives a sense of the character of place which, in essence, is his manner of handling his theme. *A House in Brooklyn* is a lithograph from one aluminum plate with the drawing developed by spray and painting in ink and by crayon. It was printed by the artist on Arches Cover white.

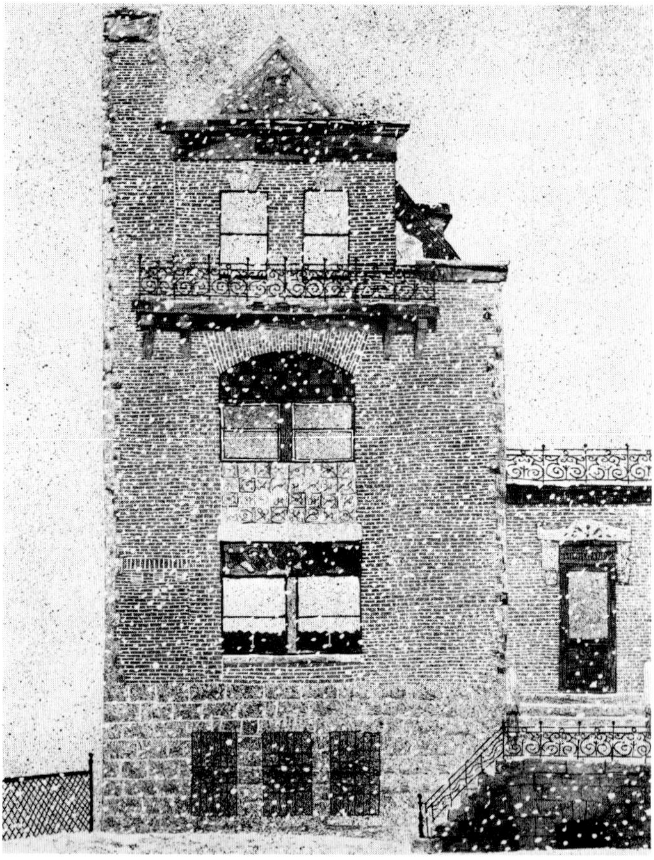

Sakuyama's *Prospect Park West* is apparently a view of the building of the Brooklyn Society for Ethical Culture through a window stenciled with lettering. The image is given unusual spirit and intensity by placement, scale, detail, cleanness of approach, and color. The artist printed this lithograph from seven aluminum plates in eight runs on Arches Cover white.

114
Shunji Sakuyama
(b. Tokyo, Japan, 1940)
Prospect Park West
1978, lithograph, edition: 20
Image: 66.0 x 50.8 (26 x 20)
Sheet: 76.2 x 56.8 (30 x 22⅜)
Reproduced in color on the back cover
The Brooklyn Museum 78.68.3

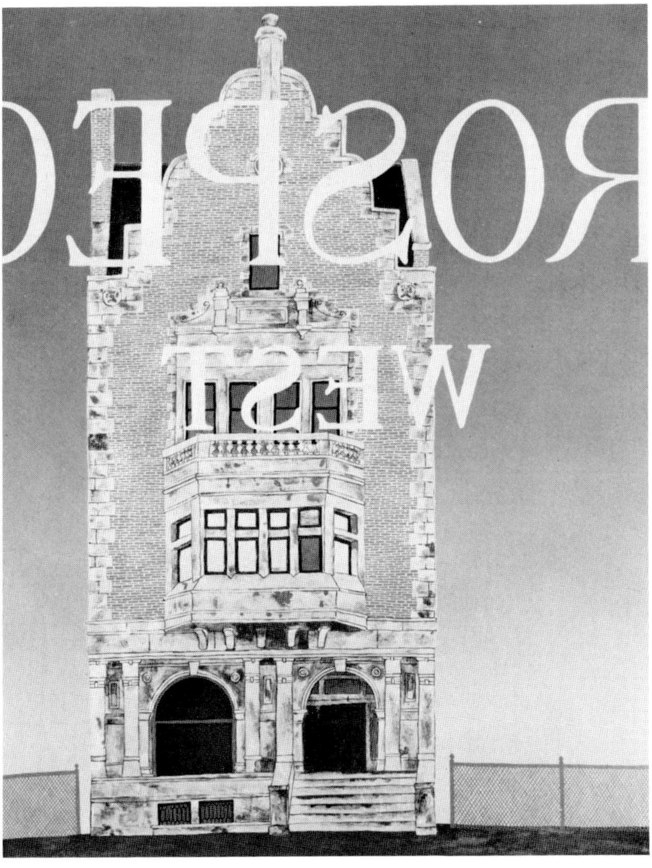

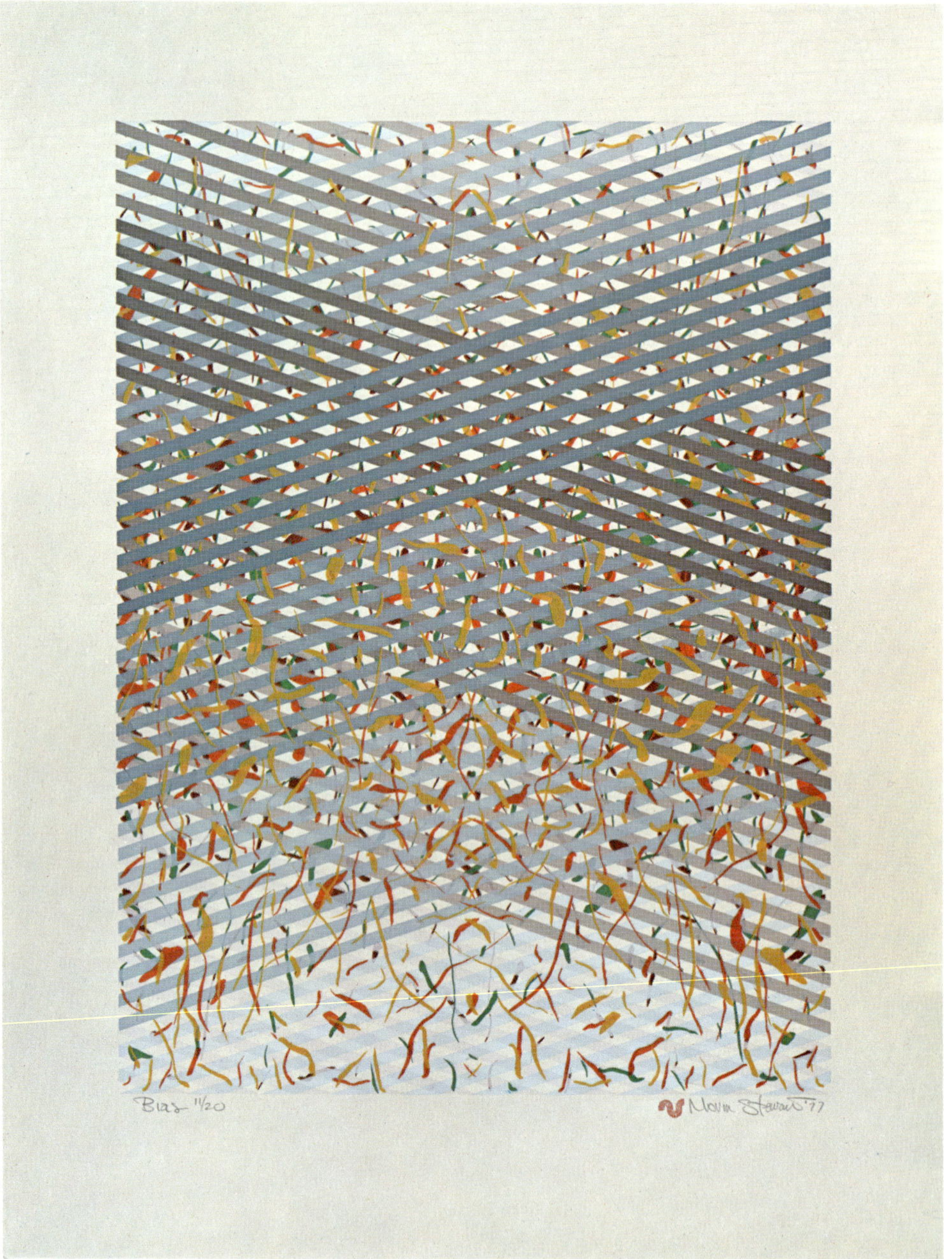
Bias 11/20

Semivan's prints suggest passage, a movement through pace. They have delicacy but are nevertheless strong, a efinement in the service of clarity. *Receiver II* was printed by the artist from three wood blocks, cherry for the black ink, birch for the color. He applied Windsor and Newton gouache with brushes and used Japanese stick sumi, water-based ink. The paper is Torinoko. The publisher is Estampe Works of Art on Paper, Detroit, Michigan.

115
Douglas K. Semivan
(b. Detroit, Michigan, 1949)
Receiver II
1977, woodcut (sosaku hanga), edition: 7
Image: 41.3 x 26.7 (16¼ x 10½)
Sheet: 52.0 x 36.8 (20½ x 14½)
The Artist

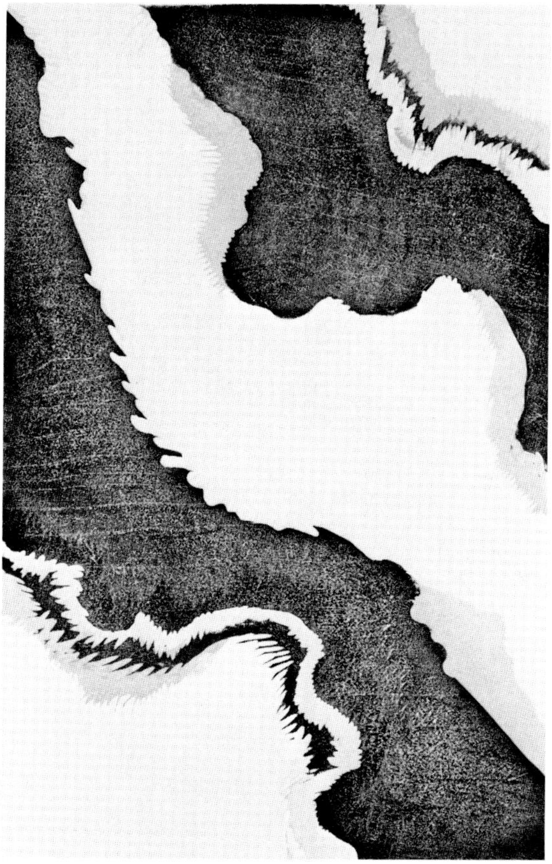

116
Douglas K. Semivan
(b. Detroit, Michigan, 1949)
Black Maru (liner maru)
1978, drypoint, etching, mezzotint, and roulette, edition: 7
Image: 34.9 x 27.0 ($13\frac{3}{4}$ x $10\frac{5}{8}$)
Sheet: 55.9 x 45.7 (22 x 18)
The Artist

Semivan's *Black Maru (liner maru)* brings together allusion and description. The artist worked a single zinc plate with mezzotint, roulette, etching, and drypoint. He printed in Smith's Vine Black no. 41 on Zaan (Holland) paper. The publisher is Estampe Works of Art on Paper, Detroit, Michigan.

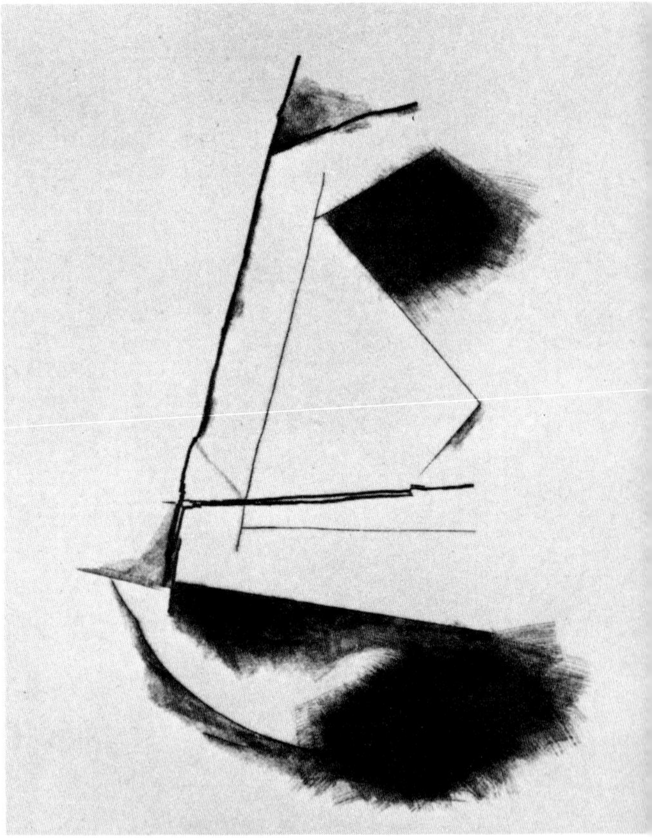

117
Carl F. Smith
(b. Leavenworth, Kansas, 1955)
Numbered Chair
1978, aquatint and relief,
edition: 5
Image: 29.6 x 25.8 (11⅝ x 10)
Sheet: 36.8 x 30.5 (14½ x 12)
The Artist

Carl Smith's prints are informed with printmaking process. They express their techniques elegantly and succinctly. But beyond their aptness to printmaking, they have wit and personality that declares itself as style. *Numbered Chair* combines aquatint with relief. The artist printed the aquatint first on a single plate using four gray gradations and black, and then the plate was printed in brown. The artist produced the border by subtraction and printed it in relief. First, the whole solid border was printed in a yellow-white mixture approximately two to one. Later, a run of red was laid down. The third run was a green-white mixture approximately one to three. The fourth run was a green-brown mixture approximately three to one and the fifth and final run was in blue. Runs were allowed to dry before the next printing. Paper is Arches Cover white.

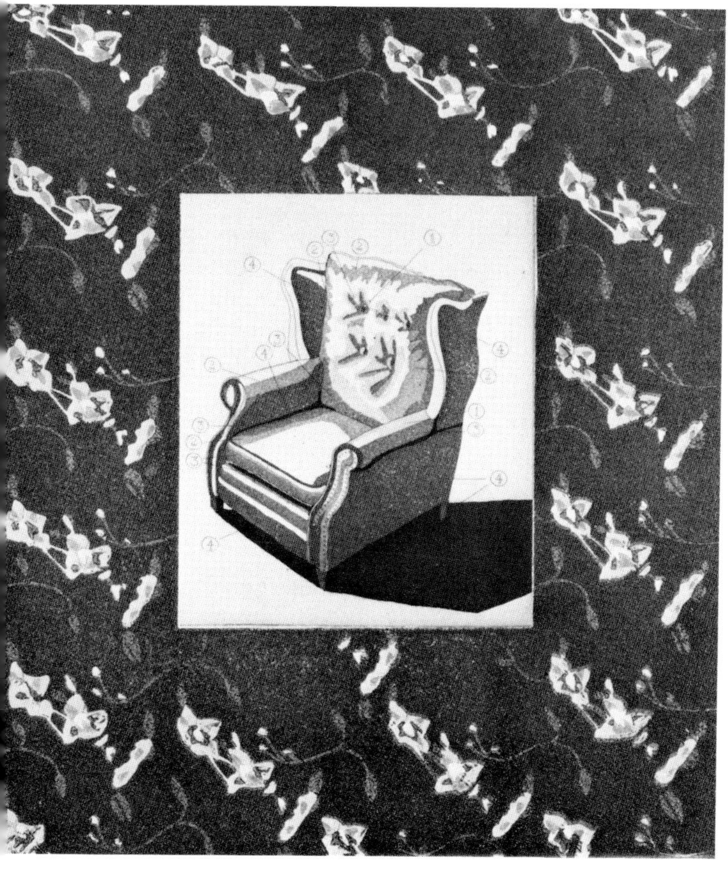

118
Carl F. Smith
(b. Leavenworth, Kansas, 1955)
Daydream
1978, aquatint with relief,
edition: 20
Image: 21.6 x 25.4 (8½ x 10)
Sheet: 26.8 x 31.7 (10½ x 12½)
The Artist

Carl Smith's *Daydream* is another of his attractive combination prints. The aquatint image was printed first by the artist with two zinc plates respectively inked in orange and in brown. The relief border was cut from $^1/_{16}$-inch linoleum and was printed in black by being run through a press. The paper is Arches Cover white.

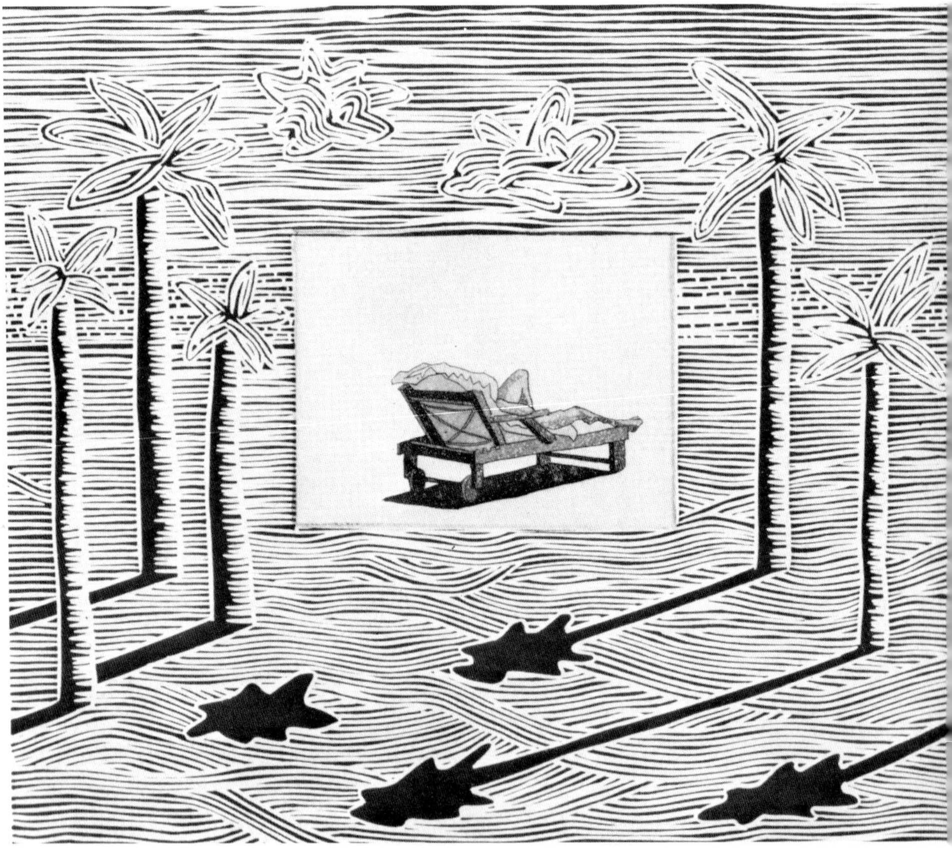

D.G. Smith's lithographs present familiar elements reordered in a personal iconography. In deciphering these prints it is important to absorb them, to feel them, to respond to their energetic surface and vivid interplay of color. *Prickly Pear Cactus* was printed by the artist from seven aluminum plates with eleven colors on Van Gelderzonon paper. His signature is drawn in gold leaf at the bottom.

119
D.G. Smith
(b. Lansing, Michigan, 1946)
Prickly Pear Cactus
1977, lithograph, edition: 7
Image: 50.2 x 65.2 (19$\frac{3}{4}$ x 25$\frac{5}{8}$)
Sheet: 50.2 x 65.2 (19$\frac{3}{4}$ x 25$\frac{5}{8}$)
The Artist

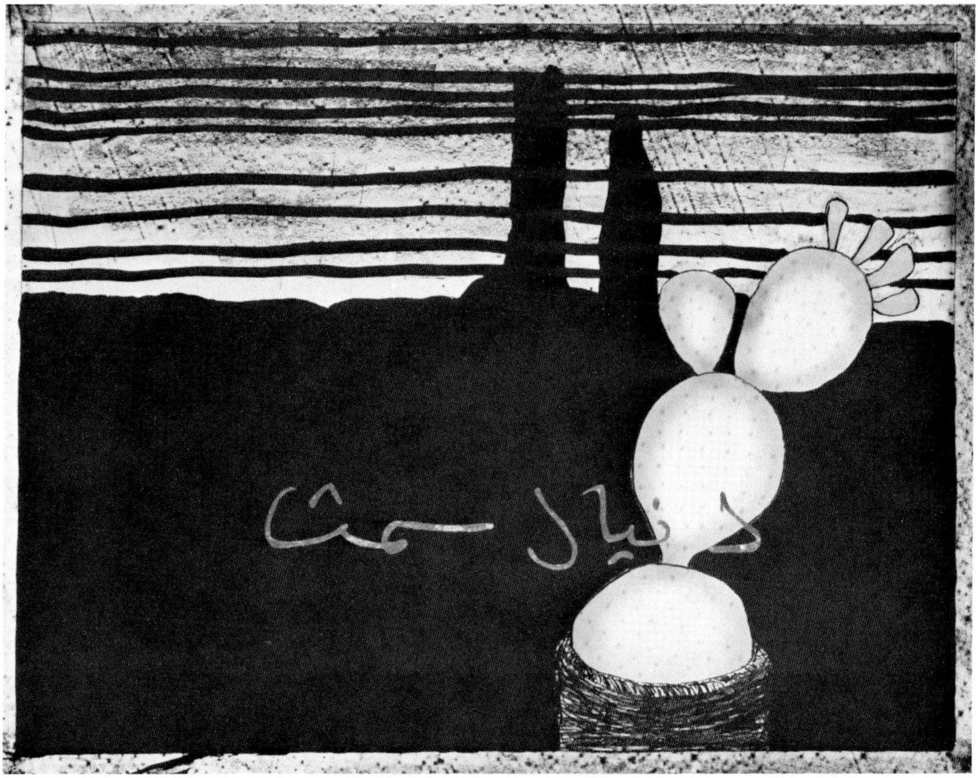

120
D.G. Smith
(b. Lansing, Michigan, 1946)
Sweet Memories
1978, lithograph, edition: 60
Image: 46.6 x 63.3 ($18\frac{3}{8}$ x $24\frac{7}{8}$)
Sheet: 46.6 x 63.3 ($18\frac{3}{8}$ x $24\frac{7}{8}$)
The Artist

D.G. Smith's *Sweet Memories* was printed on an offset press from eighteen aluminum plates with multiple printings from each plate to enhance the coloration. Arabic lettering was photographically exposed onto the plate, which was printed by David Bethlamy on Italia paper. The publisher is Atomic Press, Seattle, Washington.

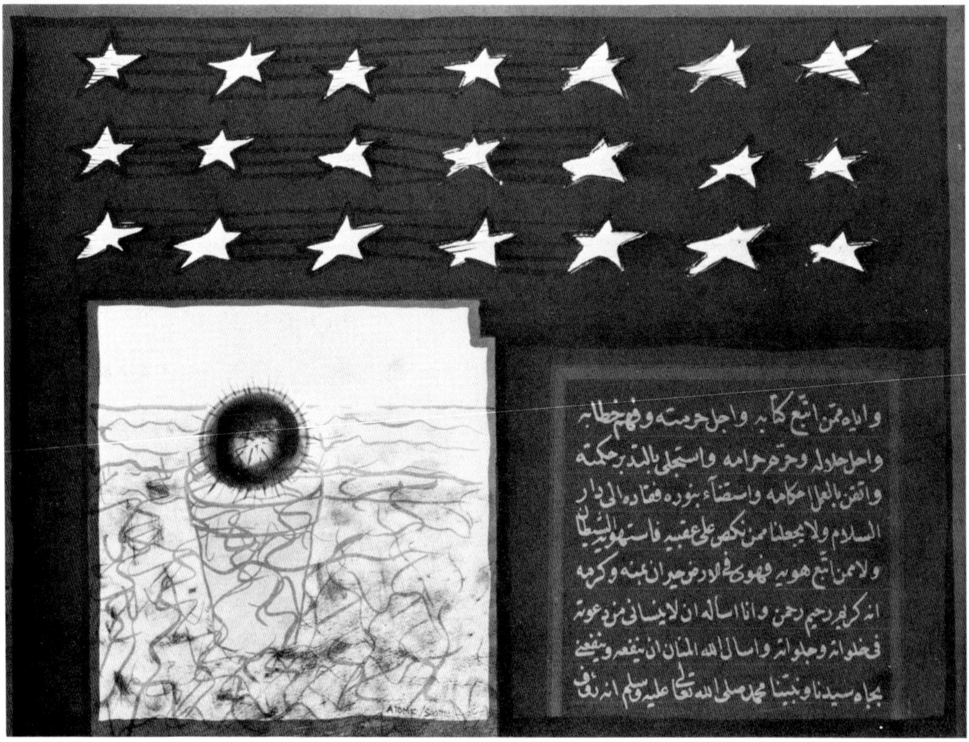

Scott Smith's *Friday Night* is a fine example of the artist's engraving technique. He is able to get very deep, varied black lines from his Plexiglas surface that would be difficult to achieve from a metal plate. He printed this image on Arches Cover buff.

121
Scott Smith
(b. Spokane, Washington, 1951)
Friday Night
1977, engraving on Plexiglas, edition: 10
Image: 32.8 x 42.8 (12⅞ x 16⅞)
Sheet: 41.9 x 51.8 (16½ x 20⅜)
The Artist

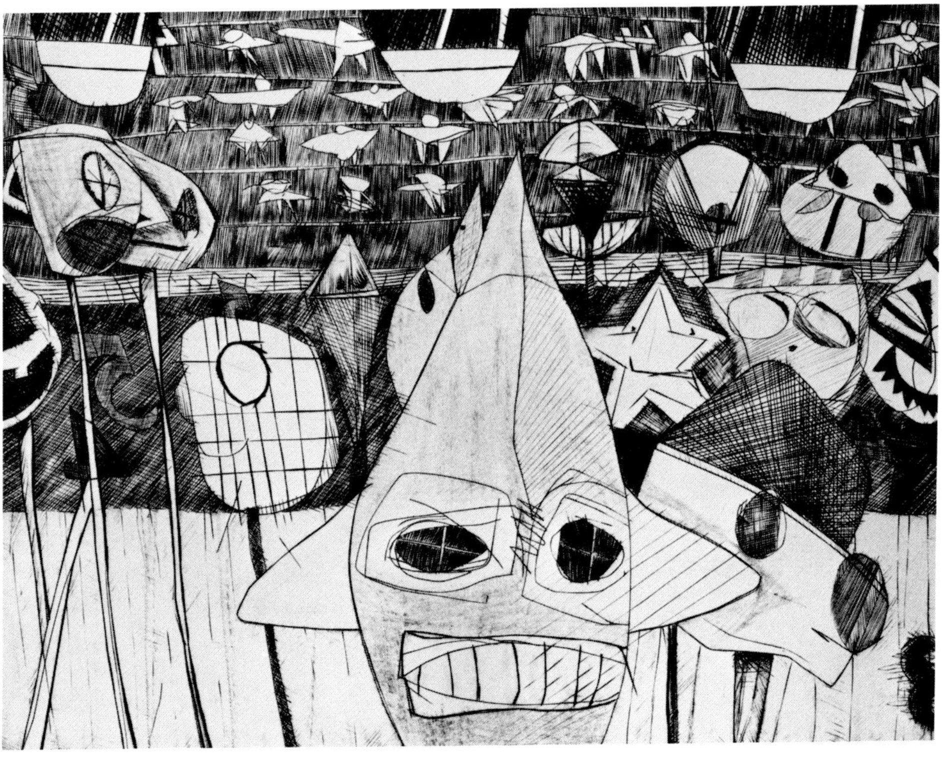

122
Scott Smith
(b. Spokane, Washington, 1951)
House on the Hill
1977, engraving on Plexiglas, edition: 10
Image: 45.4 x 35.0 (17⅞ x 13¾)
Sheet: 54.5 x 44.4 (21½ x 17½)
The Artist

Scott Smith's engravings on Plexiglas have a marvelous freedom and fluency and imaginative verve to match. The artist began engraving on this material and on other plastic sheets in 1975. He was "desperate for material" and began to experiment with a few sheets of plastic that he "picked up off the street." He has since found that engraving on plastic with either a burin or steel point is very reliable and is physically much easier than engraving on copper. The artist reports that he has yet to find a chemical that will attack the plastic surface so as to get a fine aquatint. For *House on the Hill* he printed on Arches Cover buff.

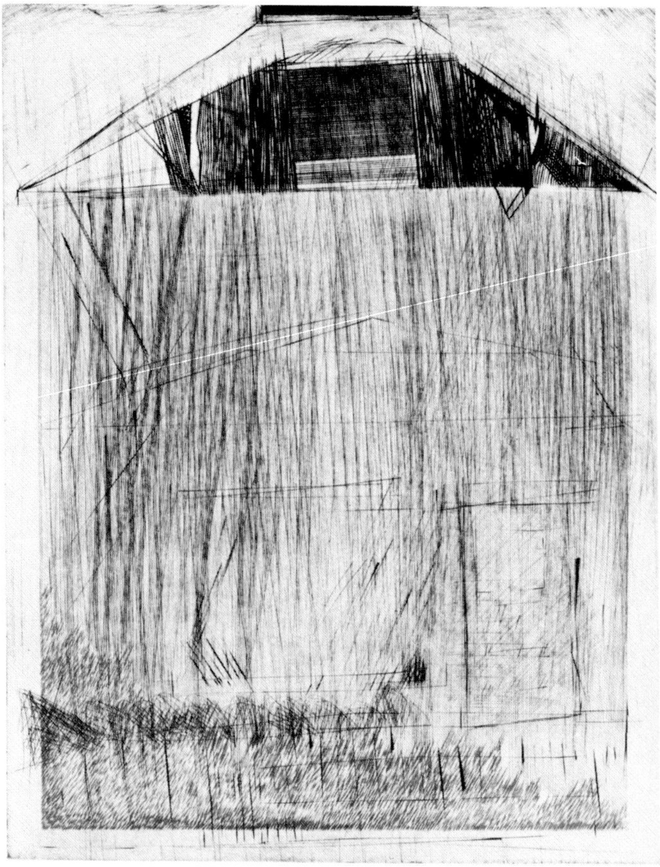

William Kane Smith's prints are revelations of a personal sensibility intimately connected with an understanding of printmaking technique. Method and image are one in structure and expressiveness. For *Houses in the Rain,* the artist prepared a zinc plate with soft-ground lines and etched it. He then made a cardboard relief stencil cut to correspond to the soft-ground lines on the zinc plate. Both plates were then inked, the zinc plate inked in black and wiped almost clean, the cardboard stencil inked in gray relief. The artist laid the zinc plate face up and the inked cardboard stencil face down on the zinc plate. He covered the plates with felts and ran them through the press and printed the cardboard stencil onto the surface of the zinc plate. He then printed the zinc plate on Rives BFK paper, producing black soft-ground lines along with the offset image of the cardboard stencil.

123
William Kane Smith
(b. Cleveland, Ohio, 1955)
Houses in the Rain
1977, soft-ground
and relief, edition: unique
Image: 45.4 x 40.1 (17⅞ x 15¾)
Sheet: 65.2 x 48.0 (25⅝ x 18⅞)
The Artist

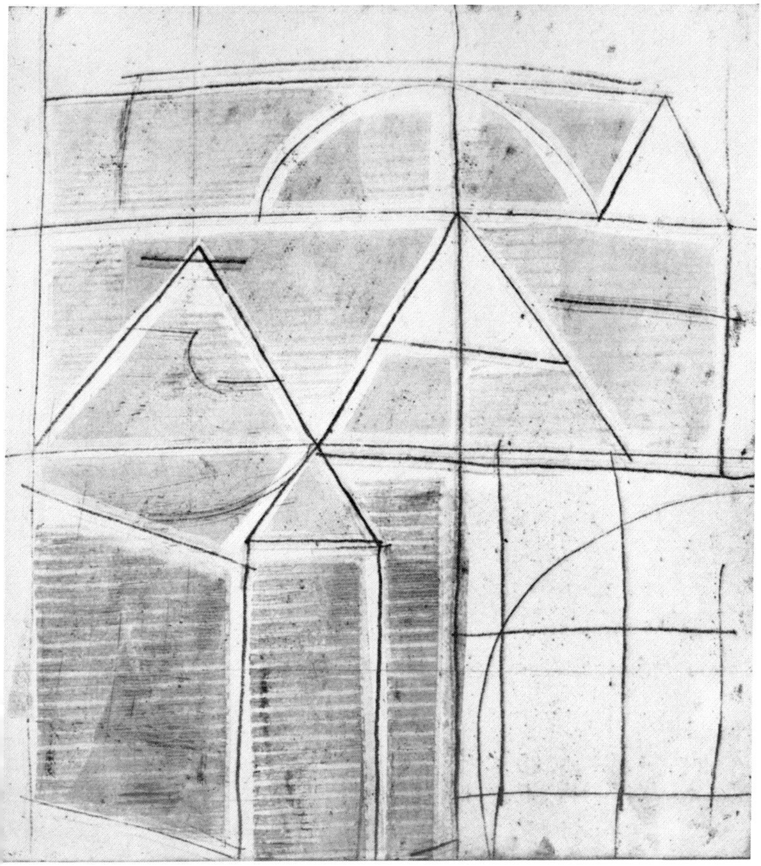

124
William Kane Smith
(b. Cleveland, Ohio, 1955)
Mono Bath
1978, monotype, edition: unique
Image: 35.8 x 29.8 (14⅛ x 11¾)
Sheet: 60.4 x 45.4 (23¾ x 17⅞)
The Artist

William Kane Smith's *Monobath*, a delicate and beautifully articulated work, was managed by the simplest means. The artist inked a zinc plate and covered it with paper, on the back of which he drew the image. He took away this paper and replaced it with a fresh sheet that he then ran through the press. Sad to say, the artist used newsprint for his support.

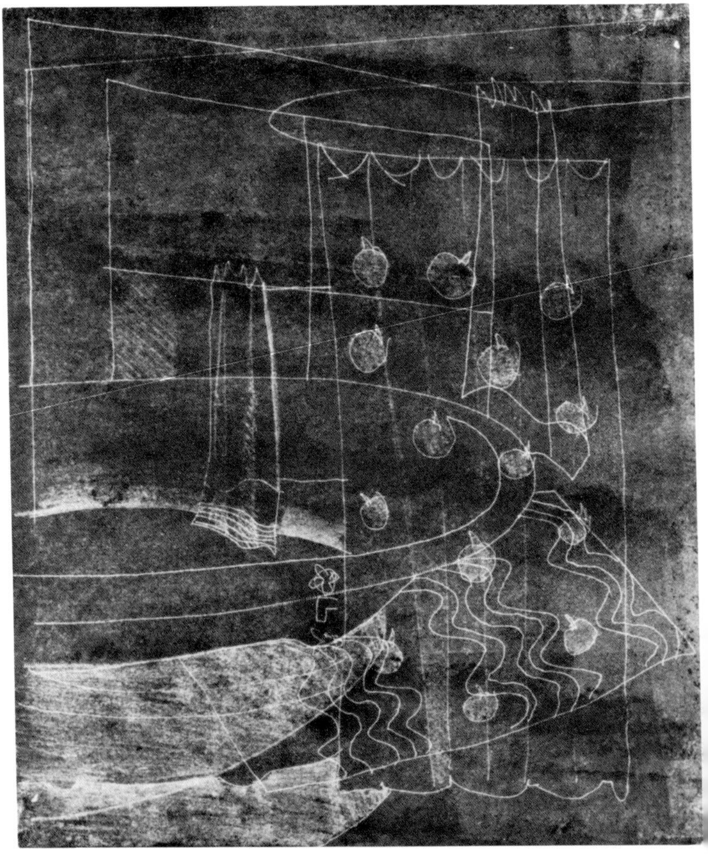

125
John Sommers
(b. Cassopolis, Michigan, 1927)
Alaskan Postcard
1978, lithograph, edition: 16
Image: 39.7 x 51.5 (15⅝ x 20¼)
Sheet: 39.7 x 51.5 (15⅝ x 20¼)
The Artist

Sommers is Master Printer in Charge of the Printer Training Program of Tamarind Institute, Albuquerque, New Mexico, and holds the position of Technical Director of the Institute. He is also an artist in his own right whose images are extrapolated from the natural world. They project a lyrical intensity and formal dynamism that can be visually compelling. *Alaskan Postcard* was printed by the artist in nine colors on six aluminum plates in six press runs on Arches Cover buff. The image is bled. The publisher is San Juan Studio, Albuquerque, New Mexico.

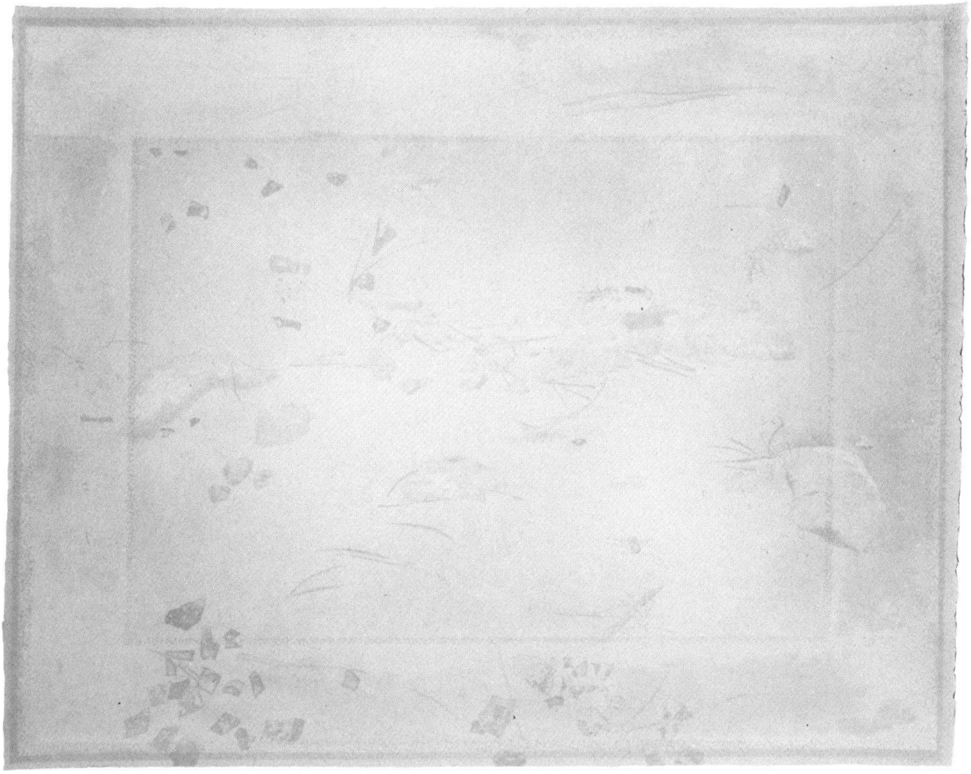

126
John Sommers
(b. Cassopolis, Michigan, 1927)
Dawn
1978, lithograph, edition: 15
Image: 49.5 x 66.7 (19½ x 26¼)
Sheet: 49.5 x 66.7 (19½ x 26¼)
The Artist

Sommers's lithographs engage the medium fully. It is fair to say that part of the energy of these works comes from the artist's engagement with the processes of his art. In *Dawn* the artist printed fourteen colors on six aluminum plates and one stone. He printed on Arches Cover buff with the assistance of Margaret May. The image is bled. The publisher is San Juan Studio, Albuquerque, New Mexico.

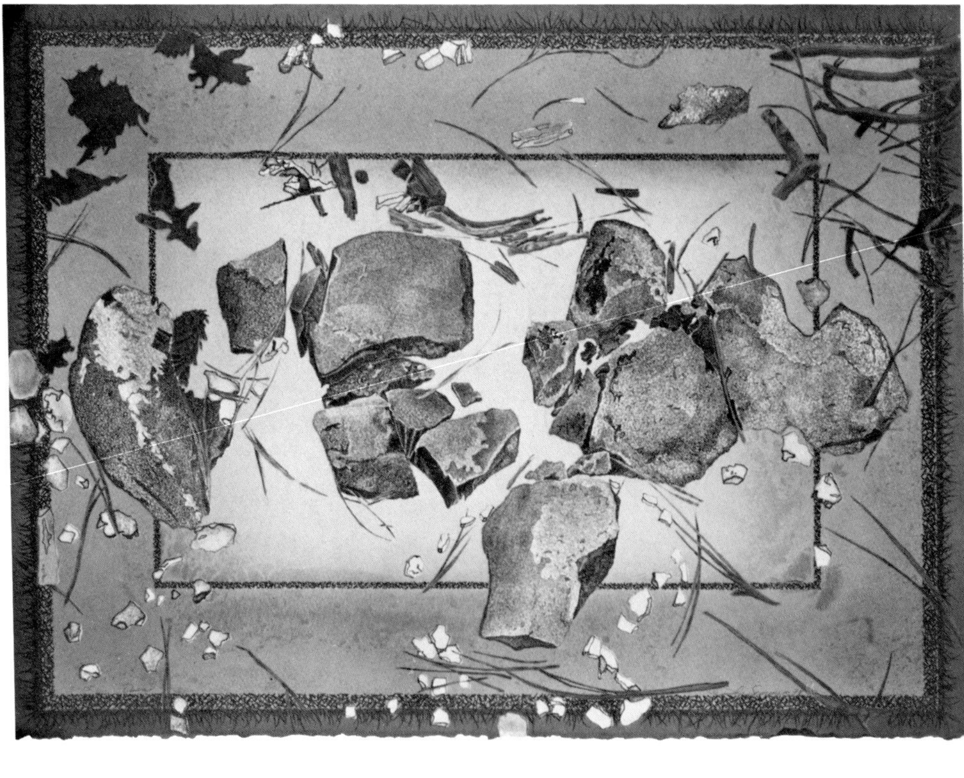

Sorman's prints run counter to mechanical process in the feelings they convey. Printing itself seems absorbed into the image, as if the lyrical statement with its personal and cultural references evolved rather than was made. This lithograph is a two-color triptych printed from one stone and one aluminum plate on Japan Shibugami Persimmon Bitter paper by Master Printer Steven Anderson, assisted by Philip Barbar at Vermillion Editions, Ltd., Minneapolis, Minnesota. The left and right panels were hand-cut and collaged. Publisher is Bird Island Publishing, Minneapolis, Minnesota.

127
Steven Sorman
(b. Minneapolis, Minnesota, 1948)
Spaces between Words/ A Deaf Man Sees
1978, lithograph, edition: 27
Image: 50.5 x 96.8 (19⅞ x 38¼)
Sheet: 50.5 x 96.8 (19⅞ x 38¼)
Vermillion Editions, Ltd.

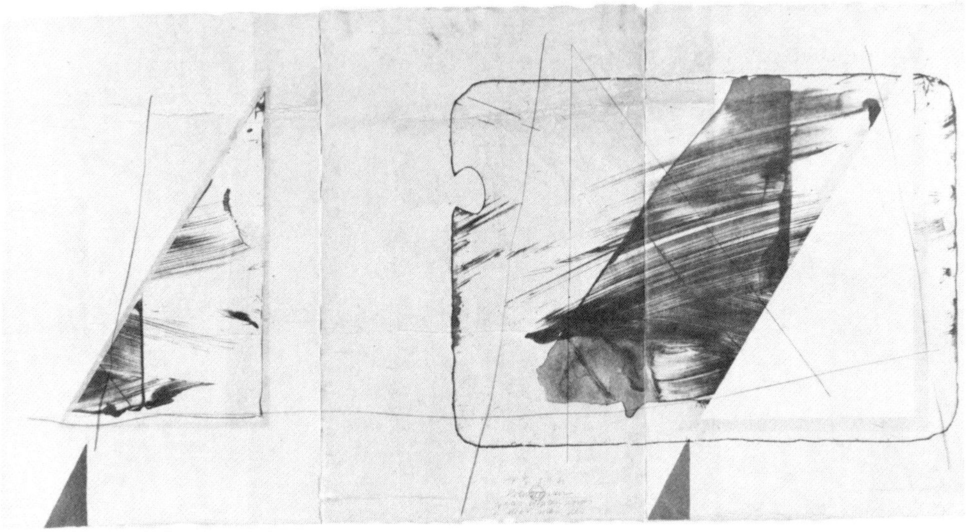

128

Steven Sorman

(b. Minneapolis, Minnesota, 1948)

The Letter to Matisse

1978, lithograph with gouache and collage, edition: 25

Image: 79.7 x 69.9 (31 3/8 x 27 1/8)

Sheet: 79.7 x 69.9 (31 3/8 x 27 1/8)

Vermillion Editions, Ltd.

Sorman's *The Letter to Matisse* has the feeling of a classical hanging. This lithograph with gouache and collage was printed at Vermillion Editions, Ltd., Minneapolis, Minnesota, by Philip Barbar and Gregory Page under the direction of Master Printer Steven Anderson. Japan Shibugami Persimmon Bitter paper was wood-stamped using stamp pad ink. On the same paper, yellow was lithographed from stone and dusted with Radiance Gold powder. This sheet was then collaged. A second sheet of the same paper was placed with the first on the press with DeWint watercolor paper that had been hand-painted by the artist with red gouache. A lithograph from stone was then printed over these three sheets in American Green. Triangles hand-painted by the artist in gouache were collaged onto the Shibugami and DeWint papers.

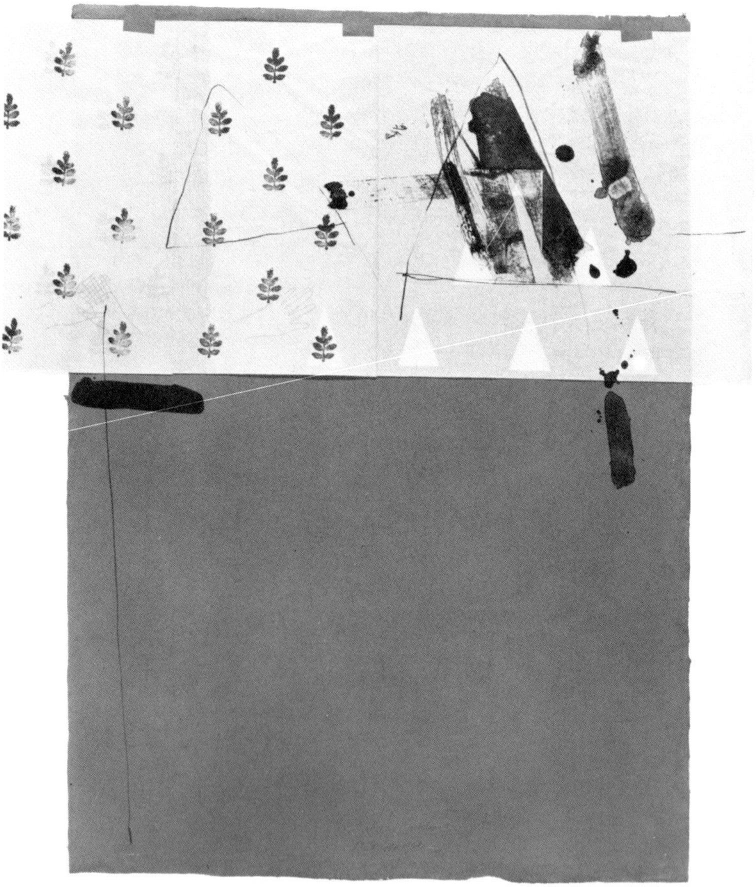

129
Norman Stewart
(b. Detroit, Michigan, 1947)
Cranbrook Suite: Gossamer
1977, serigraph, edition: 20
Image: 51.4 x 38.7 (20¼ x 15¼)
Sheet: 66.1 x 50.9 (26 x 20)
The Artist

Stewart's color concerns find vivid expression in the serigraphic process, where he can deal with the interaction of apparently random and regular incidents of color, the whole activity tempered by the color of the paper support. *Cranbrook Suite,* of which *Gossamer* is a part, is a cooperative collection of ten prints plus a title page and a colophon produced by the Printmaking Workshop at Cranbrook Academy of Art, Bloomfield Hills, Michigan, during the spring of 1977. The contributing artists were Master of Fine Arts degree candidates in their final year at the Academy. The artist printed from twelve colors on Rives BFK newsprint gray. All color separations were printed through monofilament polyester screens utilizing a polyvinylchloride direct photographic emulsion sensitized with a bichromate.

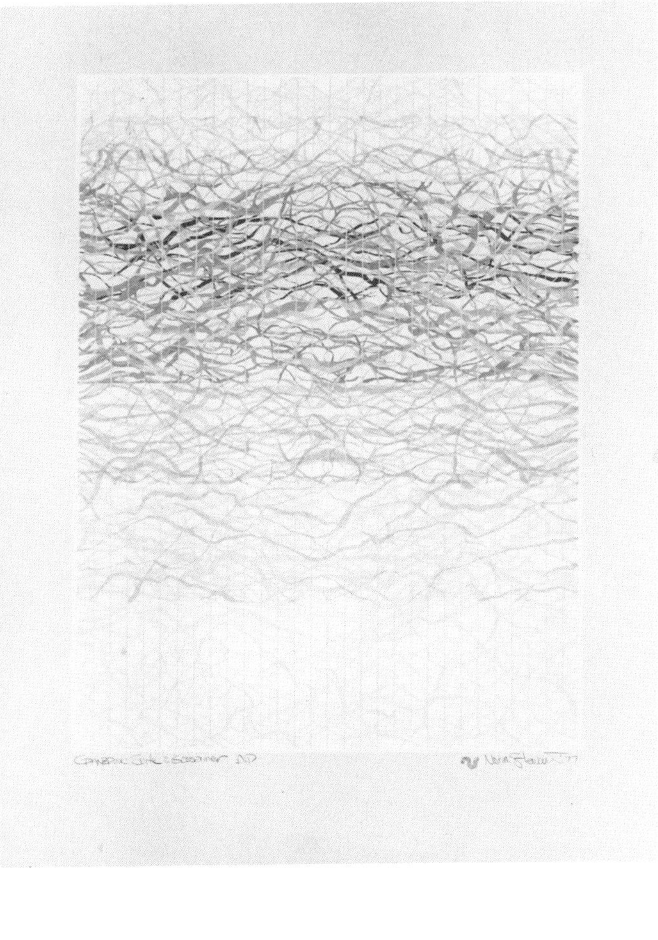

130
Norman Stewart
(b. Detroit, Michigan, 1947)
Bias
1977, serigraph, edition: 20
Image: 50.7 x 38.0 (20 x 15)
Sheet: 66.0 x 50.7 (26 x 19 $^{15}/_{16}$)
Reproduced in color on page 144
The Artist

Stewart's *Bias* was hand-printed by the artist on Rives BFK newsprint gray. All color separations were printed through monofilament polyester screens utilizing a polyvinylchloride photographic emulsion sensitized with a bichromate.

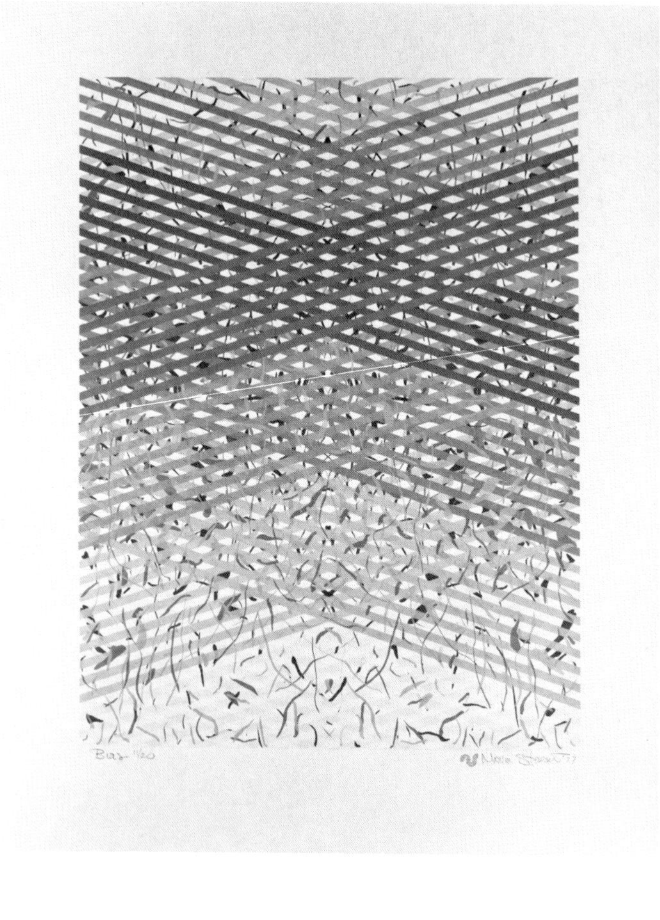

131
David Sullivan
(b. Boston, Massachusetts, 1941)
Facade
1977, serigraph, edition: 100
Image: 51.0 x 79.0 (20⅛ x 30⅛)
Sheet: 70.8 x 93.2 (27⅝ x 36⅝)
Associated American Artists, New York

Sullivan's vision gets beyond illustration and into his feelings for the subjects he depicts so clearly. His devotion to serigraphy of the immaculate and luminous sort sharpens our focus upon the subject in view. For *Facade,* the artist printed thirty-two colors from twenty-eight screens hand-cut by him in lacquer film. Paper is Arches 88.

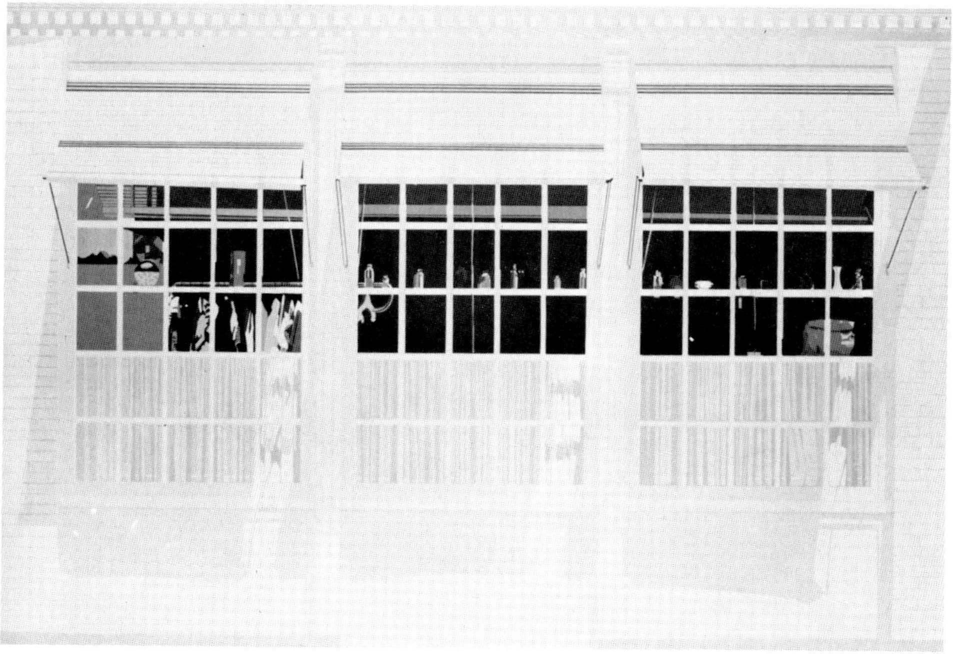

132
David Sullivan
(b. Boston, Massachusetts, 1941)
Asymmetry
1978, serigraph, edition: 100
Image: 50.8 x 76.2 (20 x 30)
Sheet: 70.4 x 95.9 (27 11/16 x 37 3/4)
Associated American Artists, New York

Sullivan's *Asymmetry* captures the gestural quality of static forms. He rediscovers for us the visual interest in the subject considered to be without aesthetic appeal, in objects unnoticed except when the gas tank needs filling. The artist printed thirty-one colors from as many screens, hand-cut by him from lacquer film. The paper is Arches 88.

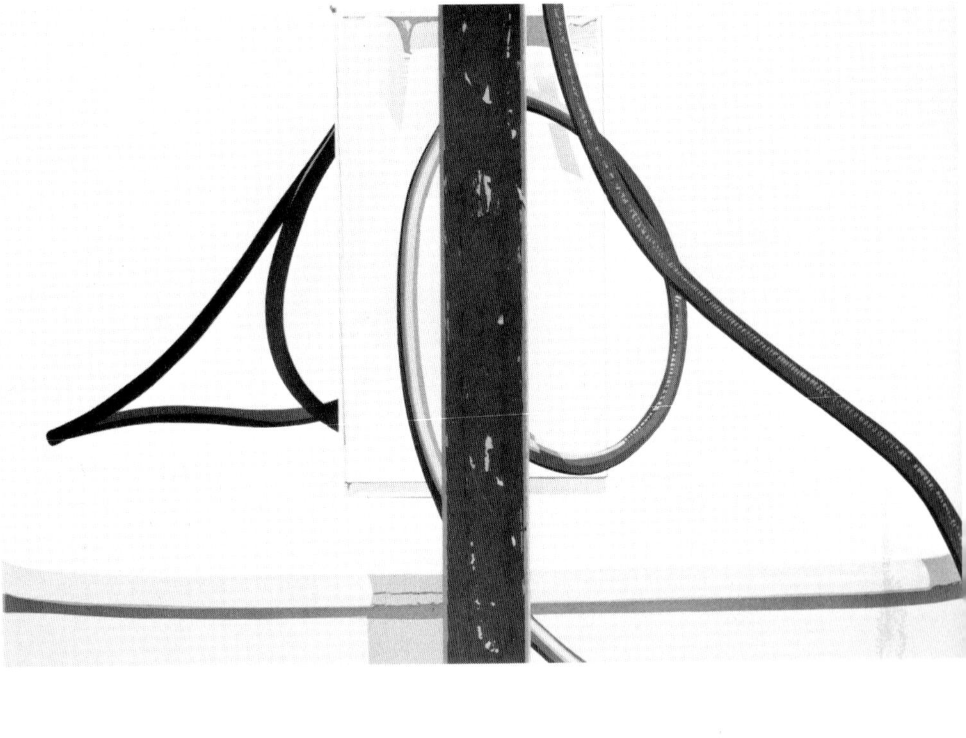

Summer's collagraph *Dream from a Majestic Past III* is the more directly pictorial and conventionally descriptive of his two images in the *Twenty-first National.* Yet here the sense of change and loss seems even sharper for being familiar, a room that can be suggested by other rooms. Again, the printmaking means lent themselves to the artist's insight. The built-up surface of the collagraphic plate is erosion in reverse. The artist made the plate with paper, carborundum, and acetate adhered to a cardboard base. He used polymer medium (gloss and gel) to make the plate impervious to inks and solvents and reduced some of the plate's surface texture. Printing was in blue-black ink (Graphic Chemical 327) on Arches Cover white.

133
Evan Summer
(b. Buffalo, New York, 1948)
Dream from a Majestic Past III
1976, collagraph, edition: 25
Image: 72.7 x 59.7 (28⅝ x 23½)
Sheet: 81.0 x 67.7 (31⅞ x 26⅝)
The Artist

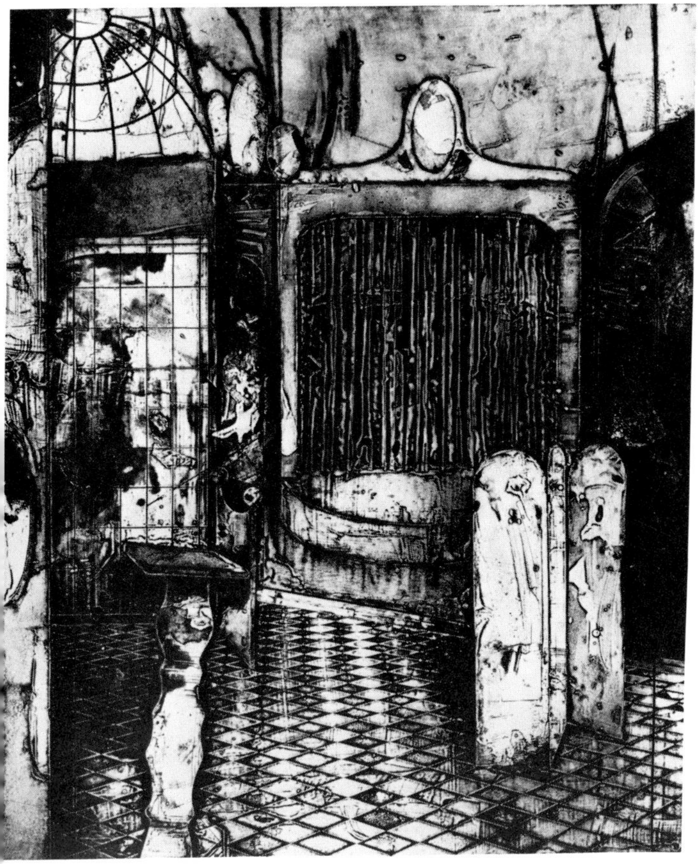

134
Evan Summer
(b. Buffalo, New York, 1948)
Untitled
1978, etching and drypoint,
edition: 25
Image: 59.4 x 55.3 (23⅜ x 21¾)
Sheet: 75.0 x 71.2 (29½ x 28)
The Artist

Summer's imagery, with its insistence on change, is close to the nature of the etching plate itself, to the bitten and eroded surface of metal worn down. Here, too, tonal incidents are of great importance, the inflections of surface that give physical texture to his forms and involve them with light. Beyond the drawing, there is the activity of surface, which may express itself as atmosphere or as substance. The artist's metaphor is intrinsic to his means. This etching and drypoint on copper was printed by the artist in Charbonnel no. 55981 black ink on Rives BFK paper.

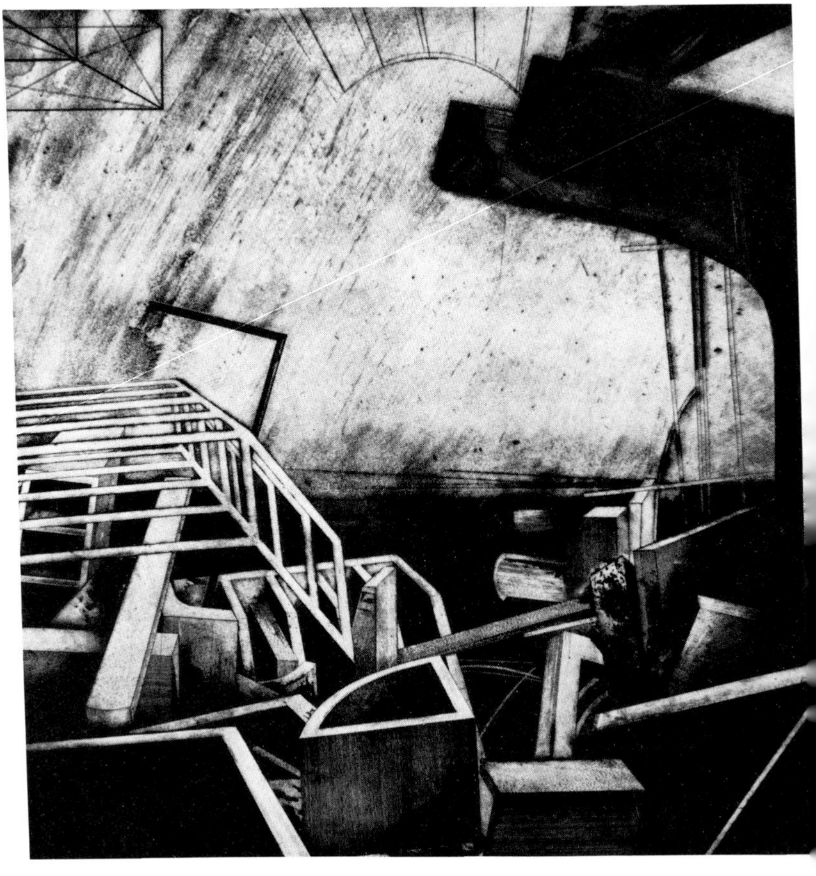

Thorn's serigraphs involve the disposition of linear elements so as to create the sense of color mass, an equivalent to the development in etching of a tone by the closeness and overlay of lines. But the interest in the artist's work gets well beyond procedures into the realm of feeling. A pleasure to analyze, the print still wins its point as image. The print is on Arches Cover.

135
Robert Thorn
(b. Quincy, Massachusetts, 1953)
160 Lines
1976, serigraph, edition: 15
Image: 30.5 x 41.2 (12 x 16¼)
Sheet: 56.2 x 73.4 (22⅛ x 28⅞)
Impressions Workshop, Inc.

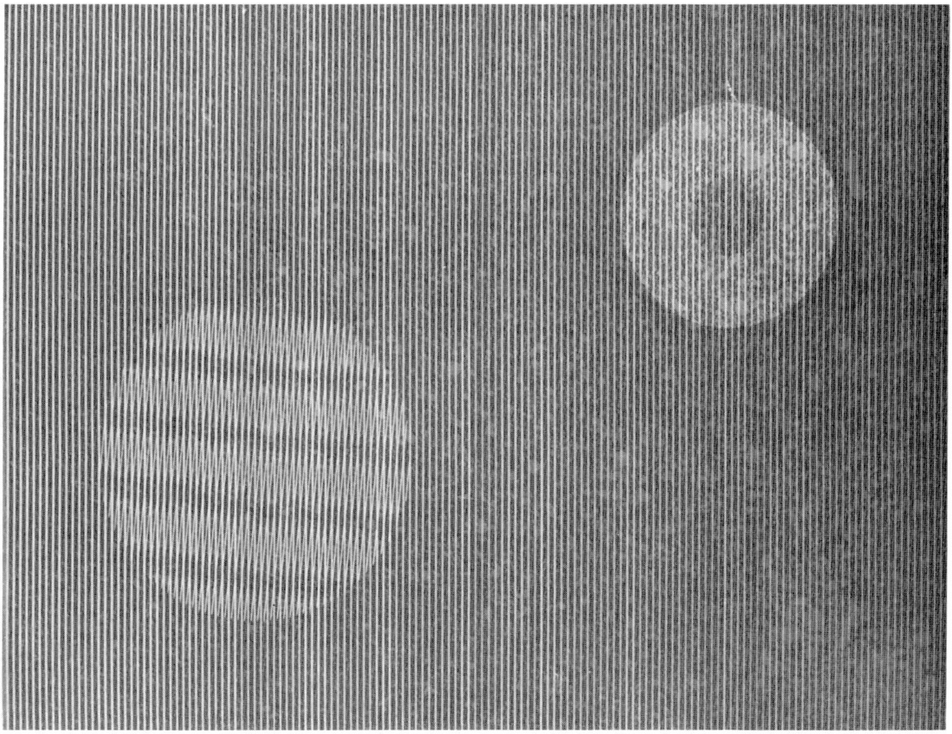

136
Robert Thorn
(b. Quincy, Massachusetts, 1953)
It's All the Same
1978, serigraph, edition: 20
Image: 35.9 x 35.9 (14⅛ x 14⅛)
Sheet: 50.9 x 51.8 (20 x 20⅜)
Impressions Workshop, Inc.

Thorn's *It's All the Same* proposes a richly inflected space made up of the energetic interactions of color strokes in combination with lines and grids. This print represents a free approach to serigraphy and to artistry. The artist printed on Stonehenge paper.

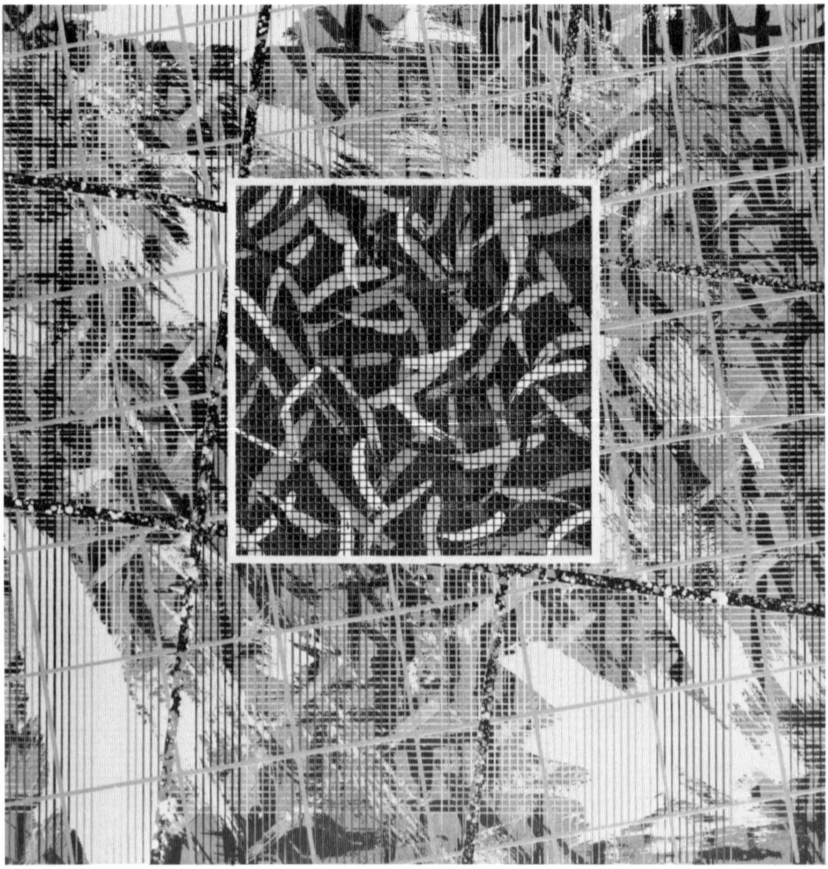

Torre-Whitesell's *Mosaic Vision* treats a grid format with varied color intensities to give a lively center block. Spatial suggestion and energy of surface are powerful. The artist printed two plates, a soft-ground texture printed twice, first in Hanco Benezide Yellow and second in Hanco Transparent Red. The second plate, an aquatint of a geometric pattern, was printed in Hanco Policy Green with toner removed to highlight the central square. Paper is Arches Cover white.

137
Marilyn Torre-Whitesell
(b. Glenridge, New Jersey, 1950)
Mosaic Vision
1976, soft-ground and aquatint, edition: 6
Image: 55.3 x 55.6 (21¾ x 21⅞)
Sheet: 69.2 x 69.2 (27¼ x 27¼)
The Artist

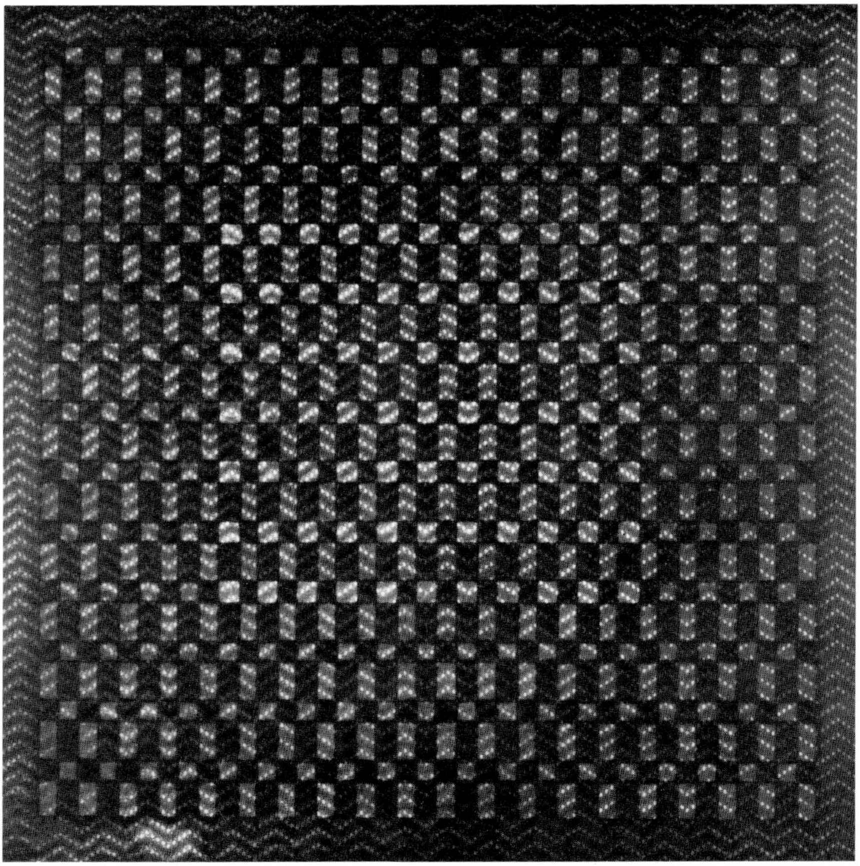

138
Marilyn Torre-Whitesell
(b. Glenridge, New Jersey, 1950)
Ziggy
1976, etching, edition: 5
Image: 55.2 x 54.6 (21¾ x 21½)
Sheet: 69.2 x 68.5 (27¼ x 27)
The Artist

Torre-Whitesell's prints have a painterly richness of surface. Her glowing color densities are achieved by overprinting. For *Ziggy,* she used a single plate etched with lines, which she relief rolled and printed three times, turning the plate to overlap the lines in the second and third printings. The first printing in relief was in Hanco Process Magenta, Opaque White, and Transparent Yellow. The second plate, also relief rolled, was printed in Hanco Thalo Blue-Green. The last printing was inked in intaglio in Hanco Process Magenta and Opaque White. The paper is Arches Cover white.

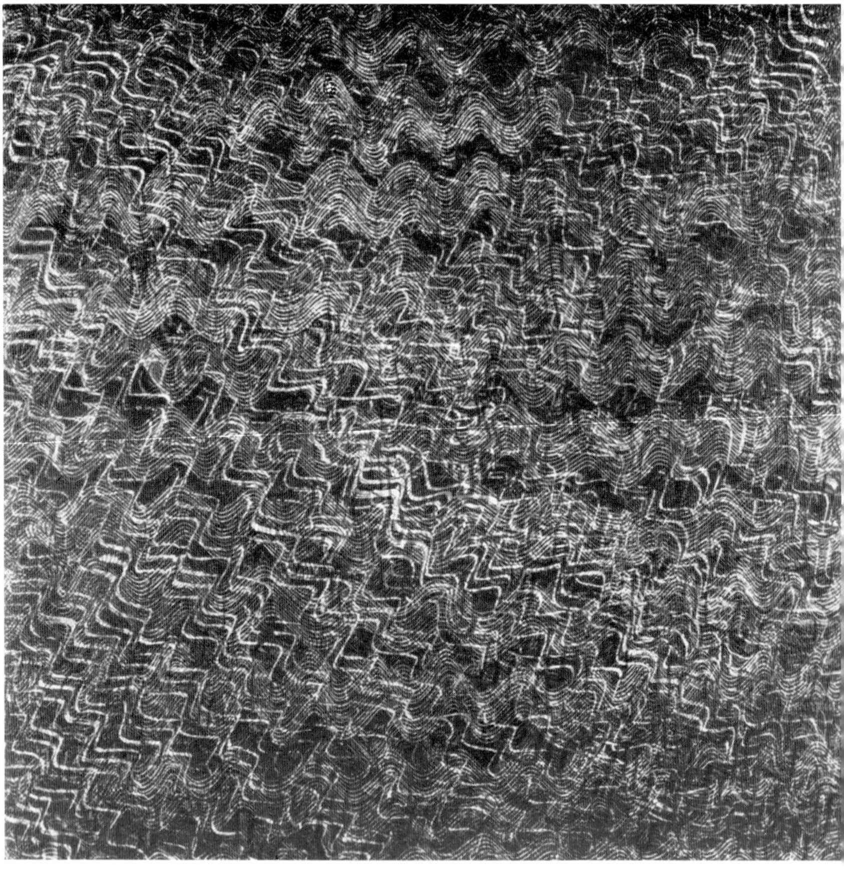

Weber is one of the most successful experimenters in mixed media printmaking. In fact, experiment is not the right word, so capably does she mold images and techniques into a unified statement. For *Opening Thoughts IV,* the artist rolled up and printed a rag board collagraph plate in red. She cut color Xerox and put it in place, and after it was run through the press with the etched Plexiglas plate, a second etched Plexiglas plate was added and run through the press. The artist printed on hand-made paper.

139
Stephanie Weber
(b. Lubbock, Texas, 1943)
Opening Thoughts IV
1978, collagraph, collaged Xerox, and etching, edition: 8
Image: 46.6 x 37.6 (18¼ x 14½)
Sheet: 60.7 x 48.6 (24 x 19⅛)
The Artist

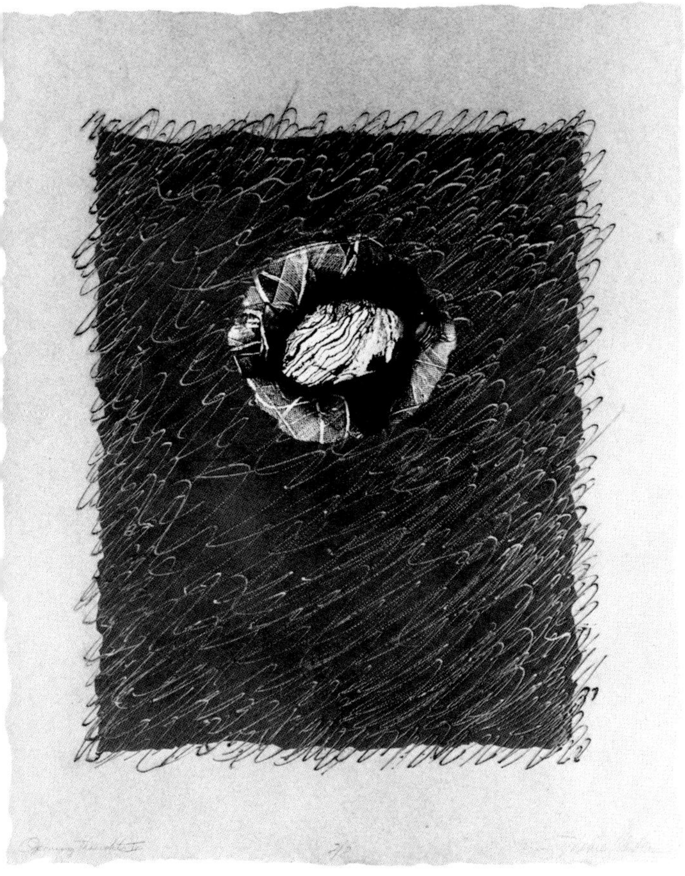

140
Stephanie Weber
(b. Lubbock, Texas, 1943)
Reliquary IX
1978, etching and embossing with collaged Xerox and hand-coloring, edition: 3
Image: 15.9 x 19.1 (6¼ x 7½)
Sheet: 36.5 x 50.5 (14⅜ x 19⅞)
Reproduced in color on page 10
The Artist

Weber makes consistent and expert use of collage in the production of her images. *Reliquary IX* was printed by her from two etched plates and one blind plate. When they were run through the press creating the block form, she cut Xeroxed images to size and ran them through the press with the blind plate. Later she added hand-coloring with watercolor. Paper is Arches Cover white.

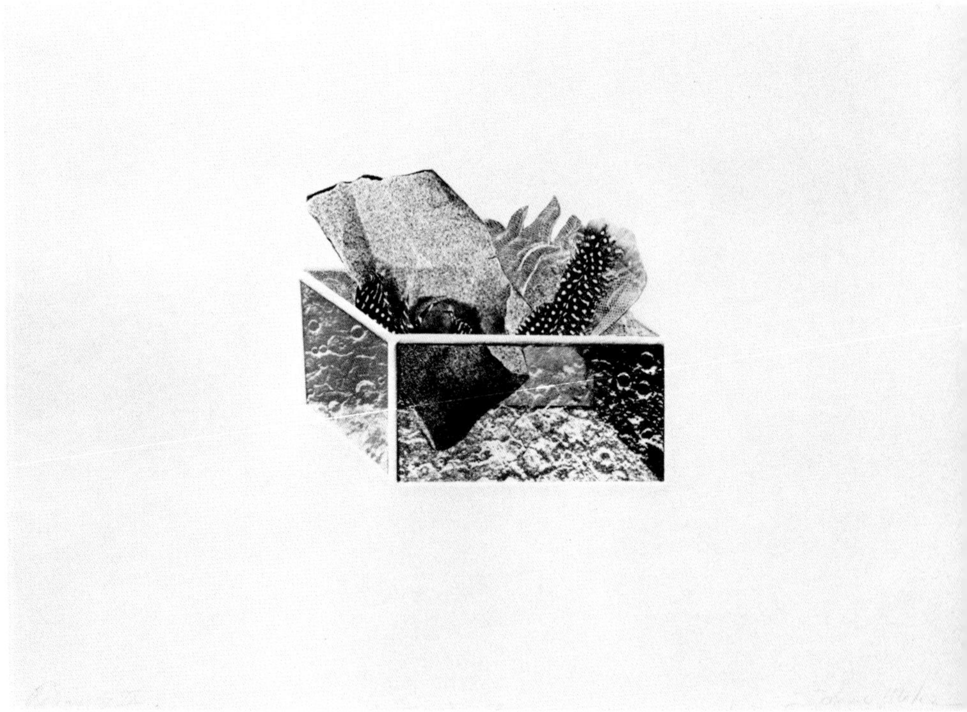

Wolff works expertly in a small format. In this fanciful etching on zinc, her image is indeterminate in scale (we may be experiencing a mountain), while the delicacy of the surface suggests intimacy. This trial proof was printed in Graphic Chemical Ink on Arches Cover buff by Rick Leal at Little Egypt Enterprises, Houston, Texas. The edition is printed on Twinrocker paper with the artist's watermark.

141
Dee I. Wolff
(b. Springfield, Minnesota, 1948)
Untitled
1978, etching, edition: 15
Image: 14.6 x 14.8 (5¾ x 5⅞)
Sheet: 30.2 x 30.5 (11⅞ x 12)
Little Egypt Enterprises

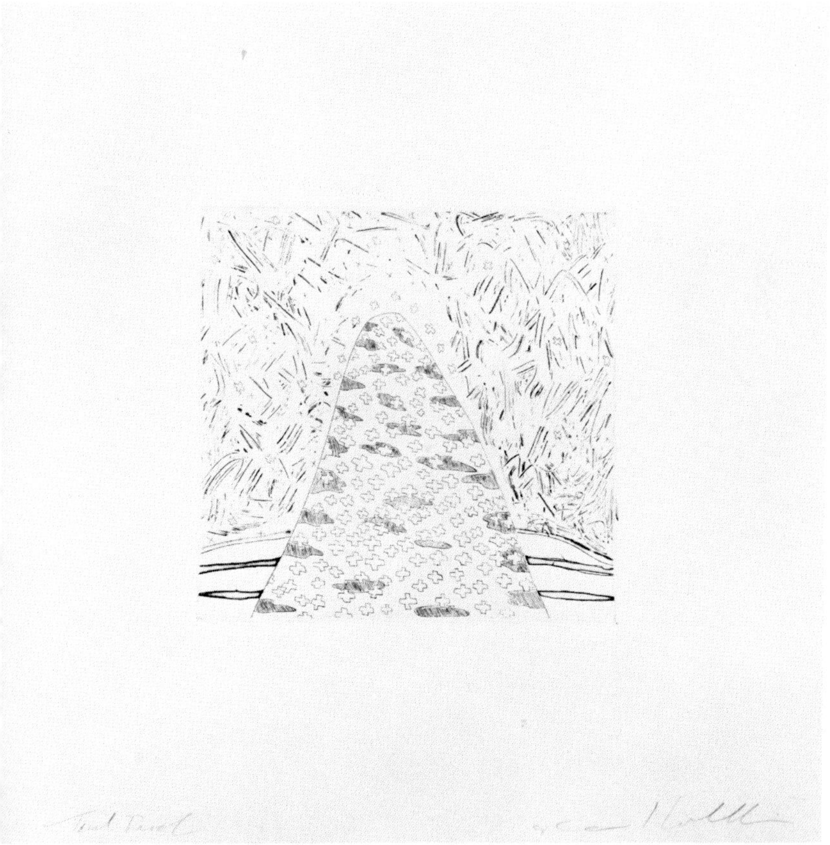

142
Dee I. Wolff
(b. Springfield, Minnesota, 1948)
Crossroads One
1978, lithograph and etching, edition: 21
Each:
Image: 14.7 x 14.7 (5¾ x 5¾)
Sheet: 21.0 x 21.0 (8¼ x 8¼)
Little Egypt Enterprises

Wolff's intriguing triptych *Crossroads I* was printed in four press runs. First, litho washes on an aluminum plate were printed in Vanson Transparent Green. Second, an aluminum plate was printed with Vanson Transparent Blue. The third aluminum plate was printed with lithographic crayon in Vanson Bright Gold. The final printing was a zinc etching plate in Graphic Chemical Brown. Printer for the edition was Katy Farr at Little Egypt Enterprises, Houston, Texas. Printing was on Twinrocker hand-made paper with the artist's watermark at the top of the sheets.

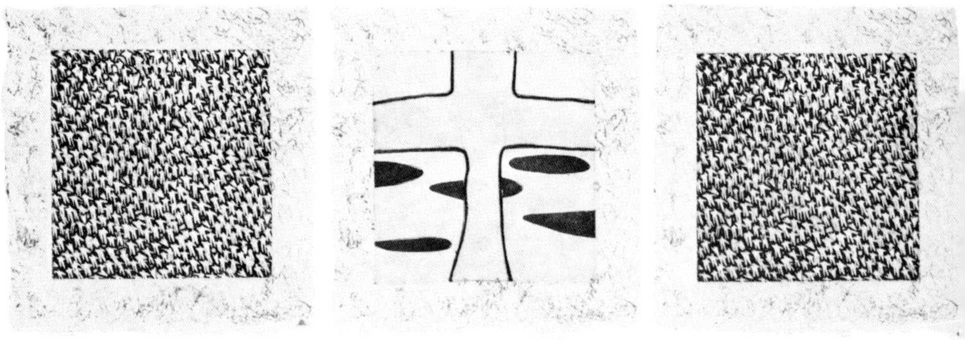

Wong's prints play upon paradoxes, upon the nature of identity and correspondence, upon the fact of flatness and the allusion to space, upon the image that is an amalgam of images found and arbitrarily disposed of. The prints are alive with incidents and with relationships that can be seen in several ways. In *Winds and Moods,* photographic materials are seen literally and illusionistically. The created structure involving these images, as well as notes and markings provided by the artist, raises questions of scale and pictoral energy. The artist printed in five runs from four stones and one photographic plate on Arches Cover white.

143
Paul K. Wong
(b. Fargo, North Dakota, 1951)
Winds and Moods
1977, lithograph, edition: 6
Image: 60.2 x 87.8 (23¾ x 34⅝)
Sheet: 60.2 x 87.8 (23¾ x 34⅝)
The Artist

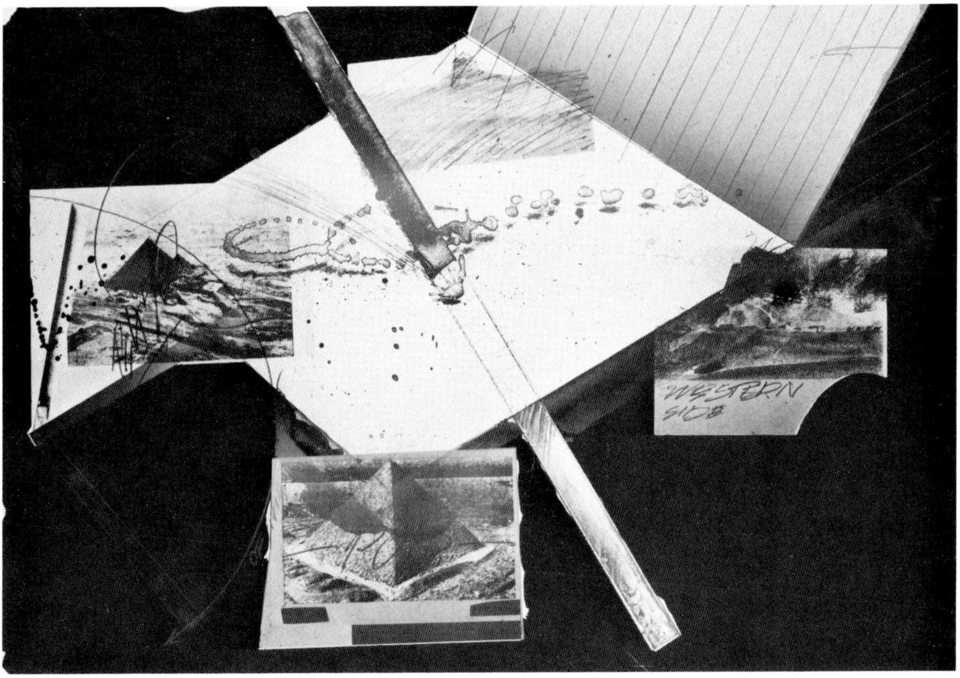

144
Paul K. Wong
(b. Fargo, North Dakota, 1951)
Sites for Three Sunken Trapezoids
1978, lithograph, edition: 12
Image: 59.7 x 92.7 (23½ x 36½)
Sheet: 63.8 x 98.2 (25⅛ x 38⅝)
The Artist

Wong's *Sites for Three Sunken Trapezoids* involved the selection and manipulation of photographic images, which, in a sense, exist apart from the artist's control. The process is essentially one of elaborating and restructuring, adding what is made to what is found—a process of discovery and rediscovery. The artist printed this lithograph in five runs from four stones and one photographic plate on Senishu Japanese white paper.

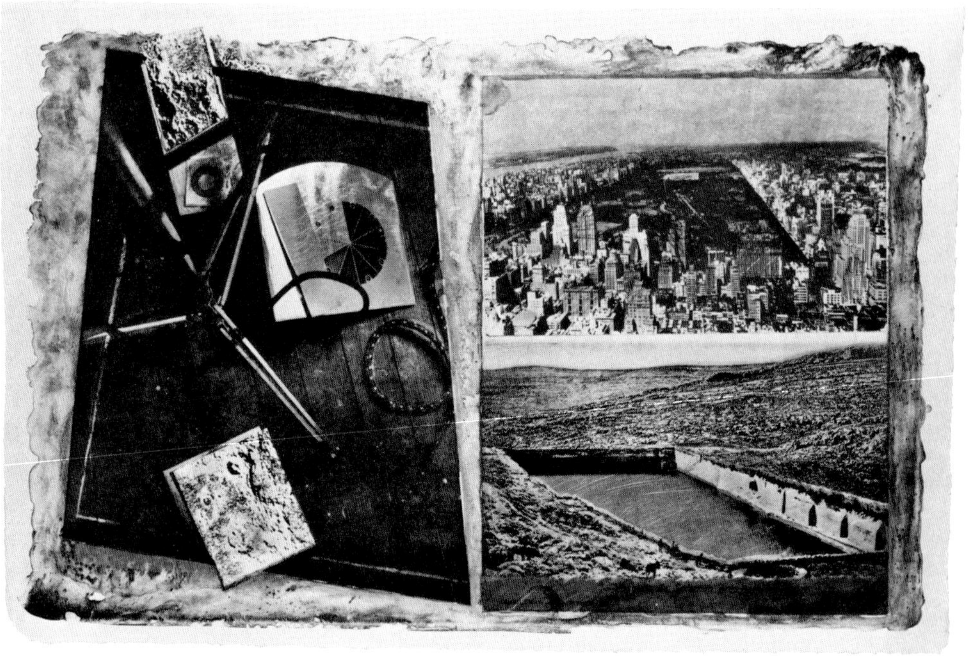

Worley's prints announce themselves as handsome images. But they have another sort of life when examined up close. They have surface interest that can also be absorbing. For *Interweave*, the artist made two six-inch-square papers from old prints that were torn up and blended and recast. This accounts, technically, for the coloring in the paper. The image was printed on both pieces of paper from a single copper plate line etched only. Then the two pieces of paper were fixed to a larger piece of Arches Cover white on which the artist had silkscreened a rectangle.

145
Taj Worley
(b. Monmouth, Illinois, 1947)
Interweave
1976, etching and serigraph, edition: 10
Image: 20.3 x 36.7 (8 x 14½)
Sheet: 60.8 x 45.8 (24 x 18)
Reproduced in color as the frontispiece
Davidson Galleries

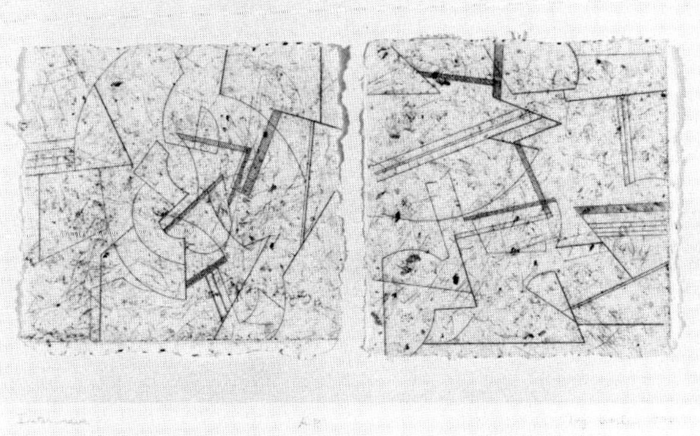

146
Taj Worley
(b. Monmouth, Illinois, 1947)
Pathways
1977, etching, soft-ground,
and some open-bite, edition: 9
Image: 30.2 x 30.2 (11⅞ x 11⅞)
Sheet: 41.0 x 37.8 (16⅛ x 14⅞)
Davidson Galleries

Worley's *Pathways* was printed by her from two plates on Twinrocker gray paper. First she printed a line-etched zinc plate in Hanco inks mixed to produce a blue-green color. Then she overprinted a copper plate using a gray-black ink. (The black ink was specially made for the Indiana Printshop by Handschy Chemical-Hanco.) The image on the copper plate combines straight line etching and soft-ground with some open-biting around the line in the form of small circles.

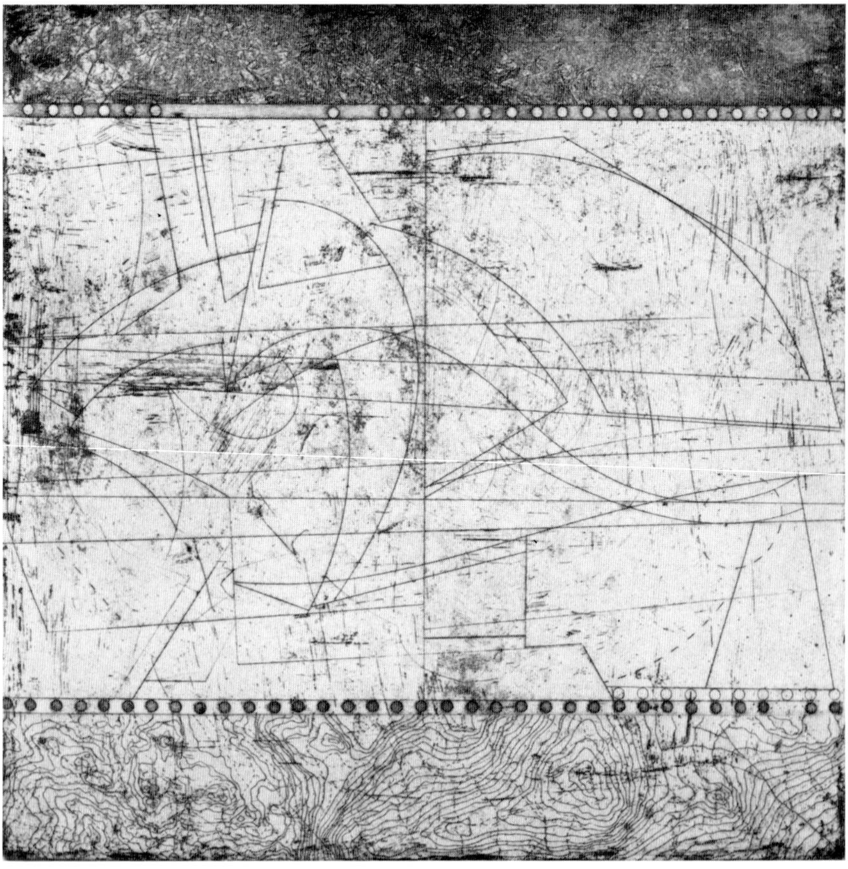

’ang’s prints are wonderfully simple and direct; they en-
apsulate in image and sensation the thing depicted. Their
ıncomplicatedness is part of their elegance. For *Cloud Bank*
he artist photo-etched a copper plate and cut chine collé
heets. She brushed the sheet with Japanese rice paste in
ppropriate areas instead of applying paste to her silk tissue
hine collé shapes. The chine collé shapes were positioned
y eye and printed in one press pass. Paper was Copperplate
)eluxe and inks Keach’s Prime Concern produced by
tephen Hazel.

147
Janet F. Yang
(b. Honolulu, Hawaii, 1955)
Cloud Bank
1976, photo-etching and
chine collé, edition: 10
Image: 42.2 x 30.2 (16⅝ x 11⅞)
Sheet: 68.5 x 48.3 (27 x 19)
The Artist

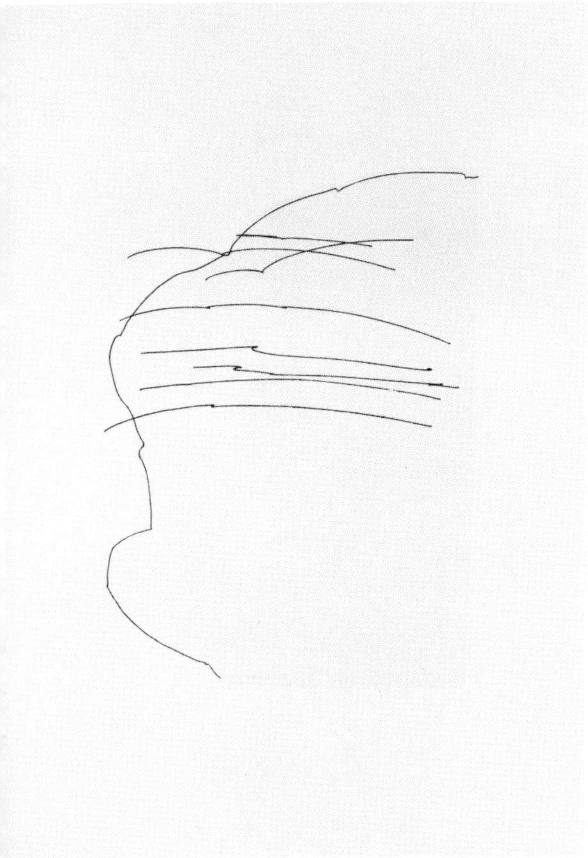

148
Janet F. Yang
(b. Honolulu, Hawaii, 1955)
Sunset: Hanalei
1977, photo-etching with aquatint, edition: 10
Image: 61.2 x 45.7 (24 ⅛ x 18)
Sheet: 61.2 x 45.7 (24 ⅛ x 18)
The Artist

Yang's *Sunset: Hanalei* was printed by her from a photo-etched copper plate that had been steel-faced. Papers (Japanese Kizuki Hosho) were hand-colored while dry then soaked in hot water to rid them of some sizing. The plate was printed intaglio in one run with Sinclair and Valentine inks. Hand-coloring with watercolor and gouache was with Windsor and Newton paints.

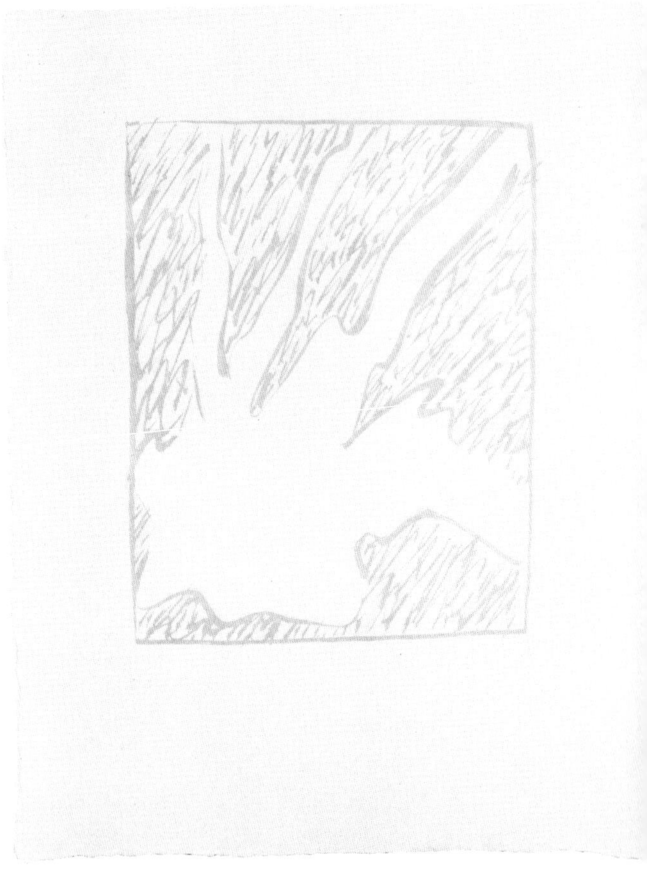

Zebrun's prints suggest an equivalence to natural spaces and processes. We look at things happening across distances through the tension set up by geometric shapes and more personal markings. *Ocean Song* was printed by the artist from a single stone in 50% copper and 50% black ink on Rives BFK buff paper. The artist later added hand-coloring with Prismacolor pencils.

149
Cameron Zebrun
(b. Clearfield, Pennsylvania, 1955)
Ocean Song
1977, lithograph, edition: 9
Image: 55.3 x 41.2 (21¾ x 16¼)
Sheet: 65.4 x 49.5 (25¾ x 19½)
The Artist

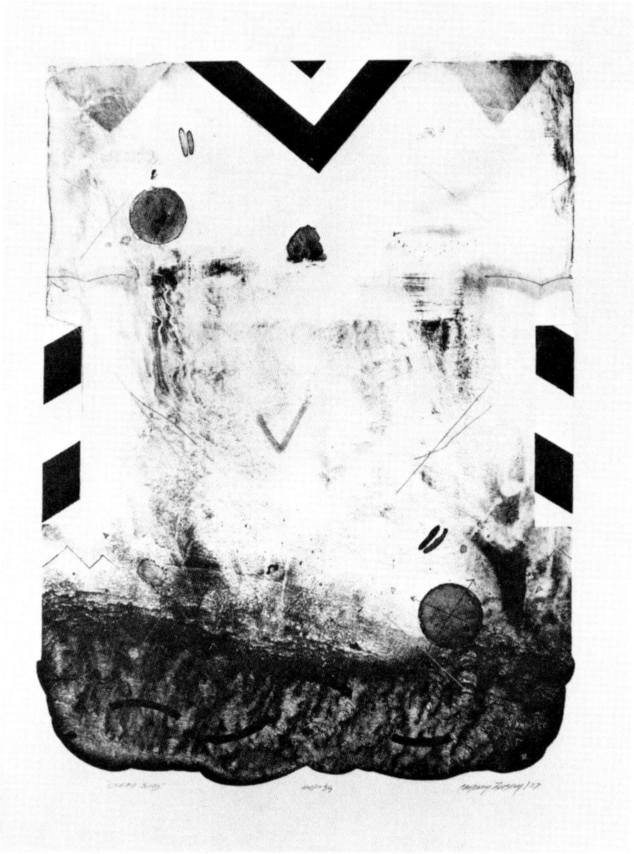

150
Cameron Zebrun
(b. Clearfield, Pennsylvania, 1955)
Triangle Landscape
1977, lithograph, edition: 9
Image: 59.7 x 39.3 (23½ x 15½)
Sheet: 65.7 x 48.0 (25⅞ x 18⅞)
The Artist

Zebrun's *Triangle Landscape* holds a variety of elements in tension across the picture plane. Deep space is suggested mainly by the unprinted paper. Again, the balance between formal and informal elements is maintained. The artist printed this lithograph from a single stone with 70% copper and 30% black ink on Rives BFK buff paper.

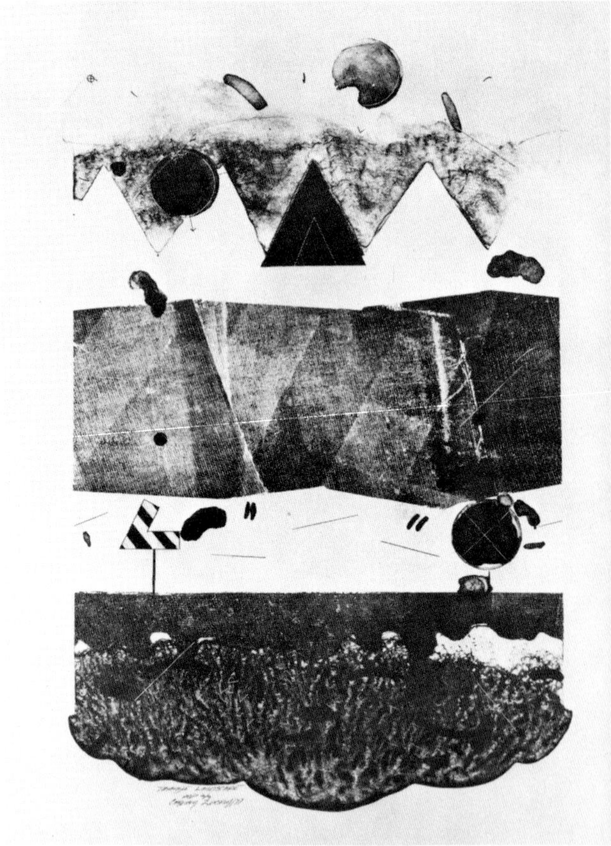

ARTISTS' STATEMENTS

Each artist selected for the Twenty-first National Print Exhibition was asked for a statement on his work and, more specifically, his concerns with the printmaking medium.

Nancy Andell

I am addicted to making prints. After being away from a print shop for any length of time, the smell of etching ink and toxic fumes has confirmed this repeatedly. And then some images simply demand to be etchings or monotypes, for which I find unique qualities in each printmaking process which are unavailable in other mediums.

However, I see my work in printmaking as very much connected to drawings and painting, towards which I feel an equal commitment. Each feeds the other, and all seem to benefit when being carried out simultaneously.

Peter Baczek

Depicting imagery in my immediate environment in a realistic manner but with a suggestion of a more personal attraction to subject matter is one of my concerns. There is another level in my art that may not be readily apparent to the viewer. These buildings are only a facade to an inner world suggested by the artifacts, textures, and movements surrounding them. In representing detail as faithfully as possible I maintain a strength of imagery necessary to the completion of my work.

The relationship between artist and viewer can be strengthened, in many cases, by recognizable imagery. There is a point, though, where the viewer may lose touch with the artist's intent. My scenes in prints have the immediate acceptance of reality and something more. There is a hidden world behind those doors and windows that attracts me—a feeling of something beyond the mere depiction of detail and texture that is the backbone of my work. There is not just an obvious reality, but a suggested fantasy world. It is a hope that this world does not elude the viewer.

Andrew G. Balkin

My art is the product of an intellectual and physical relationship with the world. It evolves through dynamic interactions and reflects organic unity which harmonizes form as a nonstatic and nonabsolute quality. I rely on the active response of the observer, as functioning poet performing a process which gives the art content form unlike those kinetic artists who rely on optical illusions. The drawings, prints, and paintings I create are the bridge, the mediation between the intellectual and the physical, between the organic and the inorganic.

Susan Hamilton Bolt

My prints turned in their present direction with an initial concern for the space of the paper as a physical element and a compositional concern. My affinity for the silkscreen process was in conflict with a disdain for the poster appearance of most silkscreen color. The use of very transparent color then allowed the paper to be more than a surface which accepted ink. In earlier work, the paper represented and was included in a cross section of a more atmospheric space. The space of my imagery is now in transition. I've grown more interested in the utilitarian use of paper and an interpretation of this function.

Martin Boyle

The inherent qualities of printmaking have been of prime importance to the thematic and technical developments of my work. Mirror image reversals and repetition of an image with variation are two central concerns within the medium. The repetition of an image for public distribution has been of less importance. Intuition and free association are used to find images which may have multiple meanings. Viewer involvement is invited through the use of ambiguity and words. I aim to present an ecological world view in which all things and events are interrelated.

Glenn F. Brill

These prints [Cats. 11 and 12] are an exploration into two seemingly opposing attitudes: surface activation of a two-dimensional plane and form manipulation on a three-dimensional surface. They are an attempt to combine these two attitudes, together with an alternative concept of how one can use the idea of "multiple images."

Influence upon my imagery has come from observing the never-ending palette and surface of nature and from living in 20th-century America where all products are decorated. However, the main influence upon my textures and form comes from being the mannequin for my mother when I was young and wearing garment after garment while she hemmed and sewed.

David Bumbeck

My decision to work in the intaglio process exclusively over the past fifteen years was due to its inherent richness in providing the unification of a draughtsman's concerns with painterly sensibilities. In developing an image, many layers (or states) include combinations of aquatint, line etching, open bite, and extensive scraping and burnishing. Passages of photographic process provide an informational point of departure in my recent work; its specificity coincides well with the overall development of these depictions. The relative softness of zinc allows for adjustment in building an image, but has necessitated careful printing procedures, a task I enjoy because it lends a unique, personal completeness to the final print object.

Romola Chrzanowski

In my work I see a complementarity between printing and painting. In both mediums color is most important to me, and the development of color and image is coordinated through several states. In etching, intensity and variation of color is controlled by type of aquatint, degree of transparency of ink, and color of overprinting. I have been working with two to four plates etched and aquatinted in related patterns, which are alternately etched and proofed in many combinations of colors and plates to evolve an image through manipulation of color.

Paul A. Clinton

Because of materials and process, I've found printmaking to be a sensitive, versatile, and complete medium for aesthetic expression. Therefore, I've spent the past several years collaborating with and printing for major American artists. As a result I found that the most successful prints were being made by painters and sculptors rather than the printmaker artist. This was because painters and sculptors brought to the medium idea alone without the concern for technical prowess unrelated to image that is typical of a lot of prints.

It was at this point, as an artist, that I began to eliminate all traditional kinds of imagery and began to deal with process and technique of printmaking without any other association. This was reminiscent of what had taken place in painting. The litho stone became the image to use and the point of departure. From there I began rendering the temporal visual aesthetic which takes place throughout process. Process and technique became image.

James Crabb

Technical concerns involved in intaglio printmaking are too many to talk about and are universal. My only real interest is to produce an image. It can be pretty, or "sweet," ugly, moody, eerie, mundane, but it must be honest. That's all I want from my work, my life, my world. As usual, I want what isn't.

Jack Damer

My motivation came from common source material. My intention was to authentically reveal that experience through the magic of lithography.

Robert W. Danner

In both pieces [in this exhibition] there is an attempt to balance random forms in controlled compositions. Trusting my instincts opens me to chaos. Energy enters from chaos and is structured in material form. Thus the process is one which moves from abandon to structure, spirit to material.

The printmaking process has conditioned me to see composition in terms of layers. I layer, free form, environments, textures, patterns, figures, photographic as well as hand-worked. The images vary from randomly selected to rigidly structured, as in the hair portraits.

Paul S. Davidson

I love lithography. It offers flat, matte, and mysteriously rich surfaces that cannot be had elsewhere. Fine papers are also a fetish. There is a unique marriage of ink and paper in the lithographic process. I find the process itself very romantic, and the end result is sometimes jewel-like. Enough.

Richard Davis

In art to be a realist is not just to convey what is seen, like a camera, but also to convey what is known and what is felt. More than just our eyes are at work when we take in our surroundings.

In my newest print, *Outcrop* [Cat. 28], for example, one of my desires was to express some of the faces of nature at work, the pushing up and wearing down of the landscape. Diagonal lines crisscrossing the picture are one of the results of this effort. The upward thrust of the dark foreground rock against the gray distant mountain is another. The looming clouds with their inevitable rain is another. Also in this print the overall dark tone becomes symbolic of the somewhat forbidden aspect of this landscape, while the warm tones of the sunlit central outcrop are a counterbalance and an invitation.

I use the conventions of realism because to me they remain the clearest language of visual art. My desire though, is to go beyond the purely visual reality to convey the other, more hidden, somewhat mysterious reality.

Craig Dennis

Art is medicine. I want to produce work that is administered through the senses, activates the mind, and infects the spirit. Because I know of no ultimate panacea, I make and do many different things. Each has its own effect on the body. When I make a print, i is because of the rich density of printed ink, the transparency of a flat color, the cumulative effects of two thousand years of history, or some other equally inherent print quality which will produce the most powerful potion. On any given occasion, my objectives might be more directly met through paint, metal, or a vidicon tube. I like to think that anything can become a vital ingredient and that all elements are important in psychosomatics. Regardless of the particular form of a given piece, it should become some type of plasma with potentials which can be catalyzed by the senses into new directions. I want to see a map of my hand because it knows things that I don't.

Michael Di Cerbo

My work is about the mountains, valleys, chasms, and precipices of the urban environment. It reflects the beauty and eloquence of the monumental geometry of the city.

Martha Erlebacher

I make lithographs of representational imagery with symbolic content, and with the help of my printer attempt to demonstrate the traditional beauty and richness of the medium.

Yasuhiro Esaki

I am trying to create images that convey the boundaries of realism and abstraction, which focuses on sections of natural objects, their textures, shadows, and highlights drawn with line-etching. I would like to transform an object with an intensity and tension that goes beyond the transcription of literal visual information.

Maurine Farmer

My primary concern is image: its color, legibility, and movement across the page.

Freddie Fong

The physical presence of materials (paper, pigment, canvas) and illusory space are the main concerns of my lithographs as well as my paintings. The wrinkled paper image of my print is first airbrushed on paper and then transferred onto an aluminum plate by a non–photo-transfer method. The technical process of printing records the natural qualities and processes of paper itself. Printed wrinkles and tears are juxtaposed with the actual characteristic of conventional printing paper: color, deckle, watermark, etc. Its expression confronts the viewer with the situation of reality and illusion.

Sondra Freckelton

I like to approach printmaking as an extension of my paintings rather than as a separate medium. This means using many plates and working on each one as though it were an individual watercolor, painting very light to dense touche washes. In standard lithography it is difficult to hold the delicate washes or to get more than three colors over one another without losing translucency. The offset press can maintain very thin, consistent inking and I can get the results I am after.

Deborah Grobman Furnback

In my stroke lithographs I am interested in the transition from two-dimensional surface to three-dimensional form. Some of the stroke prints in my Edition Variée have areas that are cut and removed, some have areas cut to be dimensional, and some are concerned with the illusion of dimensionality. My interest is to present brushstrokes as gestures isolated and eventually removed from the background while still maintaining a painterly relationship among them. Conceptually, these prints are concerned with the idea of image-making. My art is about making art.

Anita Gelman

Through the medium of intaglio, I have discovered the most satisfying method for personal expression. Its particular qualities—depth of line, subtlety of tone, the process itself—provide a lasting attraction. This medium continues to be a challenge, a mystery, and an intrigue—all essential for my creative environment.

Jane E. Goldman

I am an image-maker, concerned with finding the extraordinary through the ordinary. I make woodcuts, etchings, and lithographs. I love printmaking, first of all for its linear, textural, and color possibilities, secondly for the roundabout route, i.e. the process, through which you arrive at the "magic" of the printed image.

My images are autobiographical in that they reflect my past or present environment. I choose "scenes" that I see daily, so familiar to me that, having permeated my consciousness, they take on some aspect of my slant of perception: my plants, the row of apartment buildings across the street, the Texas neighborhood in which I grew up. Through this ordinary subject matter I try to define the particular, to create a comprehensive environment in a single image.

Robert Gordy

I find the surface look of screenprinting and the unneurotic nature of the medium extremely satisfying. Printmaking allows me to give an extended life to images I've developed and find especially successful—and to reach a larger and to some extent different audience. As I live completely off the sale of my work, the prints take off some of the pressure to produce and exhibit drawings and paintings regularly. I guess they help to see me through the "dry spells." About my work in general—it is primarily concerned with polishing the apple of illusion while keeping the surface inviolate—not very original concerns, I admit, but still quite viable. I really do find the work in the studio a joyous experience.

John Greene

My recent work is primarily concerned with natural qualities in the abstract. I wish to visually investigate the associations between nature's tactile realities and systems of linear or markmaking juxtapositions (artistic realities). The systems that were used for the two works in the exhibition were based on details of drawings by Tiepolo and Dürer. Nature's systems become analogous or visually identified with a series of marks in the works insofar as they relate a similar spatial essence.

Kathy Gura

My prints are about isolating, containing, condensing a particular set of colored, torn-out paper shapes in an image that is both literal and suggestive of the materials. I first print flat colors on rice paper, tear the rice paper (according to its natural qualities and suggestive color) and collage it onto the printing paper. In *Square Site I* [Cat. 54], the square format contains a deep space created through color and shape; in *Box Series II* [Cat. 53], the image is contained within itself, the box itself being the image occupying the shallow space of the paper from which it is fashioned.

Gary Hansmann

I feel that each medium I work in—painting, drawing, printmaking, etc.—has its own essential quality. I strive to find it, understand it, and transmit this essence into each of the pieces done in that medium. Within each piece are the formal elements that the artist deals with—line, form, space, color, composition, design, texture. Each of these has its essential quality and is in a state of constant change with each mark that I make.

In my work, I deal with the mystery of man, his fantasies, psychology, myths, and superstitions. I try to put together these mysteries by using the essences of the different mediums and pulling them together into a unity. I am currently exploring the possibilities and capabilities of the monotype. This medium combines painting, drawing, and printmaking. It is a full and abundant language for the artist to use. I will probably continue to explore this technique indefinitely, as well as apply what I am discovering to the other mediums I work with.

Clint Harelson

My recent prints are clearly autobiographical. Some are simply illustrations of events in my life. More often they evolve as I fantasize about particular experiences and/or daily concerns. Thus, in addition to the strictly visual considerations, each print recalls a memory or daydream.

William Heydt

From figurative painting in the sixties my work developed into pure abstraction in the early seventies with my concentration on color theory. Since then I have traveled throughout Europe and Asia, and my observations of people and their cultures influenced me a great deal. That visual experience is still my strongest influence. As a result, my imagery deals with figures, but in a personal, sometimes abstract manner. I work in Printmaking now because the processes give me a certain diversity and flexibility which did not exist for me in painting. By the use of line quality, shape relationships, and tonal intensity the subject matter and the created environment work together to describe a moralistic tale, a personal situation, or a particular personality.

Denzil Hurley

I consider my work to be about individualized metaphor through the use of a narrative relationship of time, form, and color. The intaglio process enhances my intentions toward my work because of its varied characteristics concerning line, texture, and tactility.

My prints evolve through several sessions of drawing and proofing that enable me to live within the process of an individual print and find connecting elements in the process that are relevant to my overall intentions about the particular print.

Anita Janoff-Katjanelson

The prints in the series [in this exhibition] were initially motivated by an impulse to record sound patterns. The treatment for this almost suggested itself by the use of *a priori* grid systems with inevitable solutions for each sound, human or otherwise. The image thus developed was, however, sustained over a period of several years, first by a continuing involvement with a system of signs, namely the indexical configuration and, on a metaphysical level, with the idea of entropy. For instance, the image at first used to record the recurrent beat of some barely audible wasp wing was replaced by complete disinterest in content the thrust becoming totally visual. For a brief period the work exhibited Op effects, with color playing the most important part. Vibrating dots pressing against the retina hopefully caused the viewer some mild to extreme discomfort. When my concern with entropy grew more important, it became apparent that I had to find an image which would allow my eyes to come to rest, to settle upon and to be transfixed by it. The image "in equilibrium" was found in Plates I, II, III and IV as seen individually. The tension set up between each dot in these symmetrical arrangements was magnetic, compelling my eyes to fix upon one cluster of dots or another. It was difficult to pull my gaze away after being rooted in an area for an hour or so. As each image became more densely populated by the addition of opposing grid systems, disintegration set in. The equilibrium was upset and chaos was the ultimate end. In recent work, the image is being further destroyed by the use of chine collé. Some prints are partially covered; others are totally covered with blank rice paper. The under-image is still visible, but less so. The raised dot is still seen, but the color on the structure beneath is veiled. The new direction I have been led to is still taking shape and is undetermined.

Lucas Johnson

The versatility of the graphic mediums (lithography and etching-drypoint) allows a richness of textures and effects simultaneously demanding total control of drawing.

Robin Kaneshiro

Essentially, I work within my own personal reality juxtaposed in a nonreal situation. However, in working with the process and its indirectness, I often find that the real becomes less real and the nonreal more real.

Anne Marie Karlsen

I am juxtaposing various images to create a visual experience reflecting my own emotional energy. That energy begins inside and is amplified by one's life experiences and perceptions. I am intrigued by its paradoxes, and its extremes, and try to utilize these to create an energized visual surface. In this sense my work is a constant and necessary cleansing process for me—a means of analyzing that emotion, that energy, and giving it concrete form.

David Kessler

I view my color lithographs and my paintings as having certain shared concerns. Keeping the quality of the realism intact is one of them. Dealing with the jump from using hundreds of colors in painting to only a handful of sequential, transparent colors in printmaking is what I find so challenging.

My current solution to this problem is to draw a very detailed key on stone. To achieve the spectrum of color I desire, I use aluminum plates and render each of these with an airbrush, giving the colors in the print a soft quality. Of course, the sequence in which the key and the color plates should be dropped is the trick; arriving at this singular formula in collaboration with the printer, without sacrificing, is to me the uniquely rewarding experience of printmaking.

Wayne Kimball

My work of recent years has gradually become less directly answerable to modern and contemporary developments in art and more dependent upon idiosyncratic tendencies and upon my perception of some movements of the past. There has been no attempt to break from or to ignore our time. I belong to this era and would not prefer to live in another. However, there has been a sense of kinship growing in me with Northern Gothic and Renaissance painters, viz. Robert Campin and Jan van Eyck, and with the Islamic and Indian miniaturists. Some values which, in my view, characterize those artists and which attract me are: 1) The evolution of entire worlds within seemingly very restrictive sets of conditions; 2) The invention of highly peculiar, unexpected forms which are immediately identifiable in objective terms, yet which reflect subjective—or even irrational—vision; 3) Exuberant response to tactility of both subject matter and picture-as-art-object; 4) Intimacy of scale which invites close examination, requires impeccable execution, and allows form to be read *before* process.

Pat Angle Kirk

I am obsessed with the medium of lithography. I think in terms of it and the majority of my drawings and paintings take on a quality of the lithographic medium. It is a challenging and exciting vehicle of expression. The execution from thought to the signing of the edition is an intimate and fulfilling pleasure.

I love my life and love to work—my work is a reflection of what I see and feel. I cherish every moment I am able to do "my stuff." It's a real joy to print.

Alison Kmetko

I have chosen to work in the print medium, not for its more obvious possibilities as a multiple, but for its value as a transfer technique. The demands of working from one surface to another are unique to printmaking.

Mark Kuchar

I'm concerned with structures and their relationship to the space within and around them. These structures usually have architectural references, as in aerial views. I imply relationships of figure-ground, form-void, openness-enclosure.

My approach towards making prints is an experimental one. The final image is vague in my mind when I begin, and I allow the creative decision-making process to take place while my work is in progress.

Leonardo Lasansky

Much of what you do should be thrown out. The less said about the rest, the better.

Michael Lasuchin

A puzzlement at the magic of life and at the infinite manifestations in the mysterious ways of art and intuition ceaselessly calls for tireless search and outreach. Both prints [Cats. 83 and 84], in different ways are embodying a dignified order of essentials; promising a gift of joy, a discovery of that happy equilibrium of life which is synonymous with the endless and the immortal; reflecting a symbiotic view of the universe in a form of a visual metaphor of the unity and integrity of life, a mysterious equanimity of forces inspiring awe, wonderment, and meditation.

Allan J. Lerner

Laughing Gas [Cat. 86] and *Laughing Cow* [Cat. 85] are a humorous personal world view seen through the windows of altered consciousness when sense of self is dislocated in time and space, and where shapes, colors, textures, and objects convey meanings apart from one's everyday, ordinary perceptions.

Ann McCoy

The Night Sea Journey, the journey of Hercules in the vessel of the sun, is for me a journey into the darkest regions of the psyche, previously unexplored lands of the soul. The watery abyss is a metaphor for the lapis angularis. The stories of Jonah, Beya, Aristaeus, universal myths. The prints depicting the Night Sea Journey are a personal exploration of this myth.

Michael McGowan

These etchings reflect my concern with arranging bundles of marks to create a visual tension between order and confusion. The marks are trapped within distinct stable areas or are allowed to float freely over the surface. They are nervous, blind, wanting to rest.

Stephan McMillan

A large part of my search for an image happens when I am looking through the viewfinder of my camera. At times I will see something that demands that I photograph it. My choice to take a photograph comes out of an intuitive sense rather than any formal rules I happen to know about photography. I have a love and fascination for the rhythm and profound beauty of the visual poetry around me. Aquatint etching is well suited to my love of detail and texture. I work freehand directly from the photograph, which I have cropped to the desired composition. Either a small watercolor brush or a burnisher is used to meticulously draw the image onto the plate. The photo graph is used as an image source, and often etching is far removed from it in mood and, at times, in content.

Deng Ming-Dao

My art is deeply involved with nature. I feel my relationship with nature to be spiritual, constant, and passionate. Since I believe art must also have these qualities, I therefore apply these standards to my printmaking. At sudden moments in nature, the human heart feels a particular emotion. It is a moment when there is an abrupt shock of recognition, full of poignancy and feeling. It is this feeling that I wish to express.

Philip Mullen

My current work may be called visual meditation. In meditation one repeats a mantra, which is a mystical formula of invocation or incantation. While I do not think of them as especially mystical, I invent visual mantras, then repeat them, allowing variations and developing their richness. Sometimes I juxtapose different visual mantras. When this is done the art works result.

Mark A. Nelson

Primarily I've been concerned with the idea of fossilization—layers of objects, images, forms, or colors caught in full motion or in complete stasis—frozen and dying within the picture plane.

Art in this sense becomes a very introspective statement, a personal reaction to the stimuli offered by my environment. Printmaking becomes the tool of selection and preservation, placing natural forms in new settings and structural environments. The image, as recognizable image, is not as important as its essence or its force.

Thomas Wilson Northington

I care more than I hope to say. I have more to say than I care to write. Thus I hope my art will say more. If one reflects on the artist as a musician, then a printmaker is an artist that practises more than he plays. I no longer prefer to edition my prints, for creativity is the essence and only variety can quench curiosity.

Michael Nushawg

My primary concern with my prints is the color relationships that are achieved; the spatial relationships that evolve are desired and needed but not what is sought after when a print is begun. The prints are created by intuition; there is not a set image. I initially began working on large prints hoping to attain a research grant for large prints. I soon discovered that the presence of large prints gave me what I was seeking all the time.

Eva Pokorny

The concept of the single impression in printmaking interested me since my first acquaintance with the classical methods of printing. The technique of monotype and its versatility liberated me to work in the spontaneous, direct way that no other printing method permitted me. Characteristically for monotype, the process extends its visual possibilities from the field of printing into the area of drawing and/or painting or the combination of named mediums.

My aesthetic development can be traced to two dominant influences in my life. The first is my early exposure to traditional artistic training in Czechoslovakia. The second abiding influence on my aesthetic development was determined and clarified by my exposure to philosophical models and current artistic concepts in the United States. My interest in Slavic literature conducted me to the creation of the miniature monotypes—the visual commentaries on Dostoevski's, Gogol's, Pushkin's,and Chekhov's philosophical themes. However, my monotypes *My Life* [Cat. 103] and *In the Ravine* [Cat. 104], included in this exhibition, are not traditional illustrations with the principal concern of "illustrating" the stories. The majority of illustrations executed in the last few centuries either supported the most important event in an episode or mainly described what the writer already stated in it. I see only limited possibilities in this approach, which gives such an inferior role to the illustration. My aim was to reach back to the Gothic to renew the traditional relationship between the visual and literary statement, with the basic orientation on equal importance of those two mediums. Although Medieval illustrations appear to be formulated within the range of ornamentation and decoration of the books, their perfect joint visual function with the text should remain the valid property of today's illustrations. My preoccupation with the symbolic forms and the psychological properties of the colors of the ornamental motifs from early illuminated manuscripts enriched fundamentally my present artistic vocabulary.

Madeline Poster

Printmaking offers a variety of techniques that are compatible with my approach to making art. I find the problem of using similar repeating shapes to form a composition intriguing. Using textures and values to enrich the composition complicates the problem further. The addition of color in silkscreen adds another element.

My choice of subject matter is predicated partly on the image's potential for treatment through repetition, varying textures and values, and color. My work grows from a belief that survival in urban situations is based on one's humor.

Scott Reeds

I would like to see a situation where there was little if any distinction between work and play in an everyday sense not just in the imaginary "artistic" way.

The strongest intent in my work is that it reflect my total spectrum of living and that the object of art evolve from that living rather than technical methodology or academic discourse.

Minna Resnick

My concern has been to create an isolated space in which a figure or figures exist. This space sometimes takes the form of a stage where an unidentified drama is in progress.

Ronald L. Ruble

In my work the initial image is first mentally visualized and is conceived of imagined rather than real experience. It is a very private world relating to a fascination for dreamlike arrangements either associated with past or would-be situations.

Once this image is mentally conceived, I work, rework, and refine it in my mind until I feel it is ready to be tried on paper.

On rare occasions, once on paper, the image works immediately. In most cases, however, I continue the process to further define my original thought. I change, rearrange and in general force the image to struggle for its survival.

Following this procedure and momentarily satisfied that the drawing is completed, the plate is etched and the edition is run.

I then begin a third and, personally, a very important evaluation process. I question: Is the image complete? Could it be slightly changed in structure? Would a different environment serve it better?

It is because of this third process that certain images in my work repeat themselves, slightly changed or with different props, time and time again. This repetition serves my purpose. As in life, images exist in many environments; time does pass, locales are altered; and movement occurs ever so slight.

In brief, these are some of my feelings and beliefs that I feel are expressed in my poetic images.

Shunji Sakuyama

I am trying to describe the recognition of the artist's side which means where is the artist in the printing subject.

Douglas K. Semivan

The Print Artist works with an intuitive sense toward an image that can appear as a multiple. The Work of Art, then, can be seen as an image-set, or edition, where one impression serves as a part of a larger and more profound whole. A print's effectiveness in communicating its own metaphysic is determined by the artist's choice of content—content and technique are less separable in prints than in most other mediums. Concrete Poetry could not have come about without the invention of the typewriter. Likewise, with prints the interest is in delivering an image that has an inherent ability to appear as more than one, a multiple; not so each impression exists as merely a by-product of the artist's created matrix. The choice of content is influenced (metaphorically) by the multidimensional, multidynamic environment.

Carl F. Smith

Printmaking affords me the luxury of a more complete image, whether it be in etching or relief, or a combination of the two. The imagery I deal with could only be realized in a print, because of the properties of the medium and the nature of that imagery.

D. G. Smith

I am interested in adapting methods and materials from all two-dimensional image-making systems, including hand and commercial printing systems, painting, and photography. Through doing this, I get insights into the powers and weaknesses inherent in the medium. Also, it is a marvelous way to educate oneself about the effects these systems have had on social change.

Scott Smith

I am at a transitional period as far as my skills are concerned. My images are constant though—the bird, the hat, and the mask. The bird allows me to dream, the hat covers my faults, and the mask allows me to talk in the dark.

William Kane Smith

My use of the print medium as a means of expression evolved from a fascination with the transformations which occur between the stencil and image. It is at this point in the printing process that I gain the most enjoyment from the print itself. Many times the next image idea procedure begins here in my print work, as my search for imagery most always comes from a revelation through the process of printing.

John Sommers

Basically, my main intent is unity. Secondly, I want stirring beauty. A major concern is color realization and not unimportant are subtlety and vigor. Concurrent with these there must be content; it is a very personal reading of nature and my relationships in it.

Currently, the lithographs are concerned with the simultaneous creation and destruction of two images, their interaction, tension, and retention. I am concerned with the expressiveness of the edge and of the inner frames and their ability to contain and yet allow the space that the images must have to exist. While the frames create limits, the imagery must expand and spill out of their containing influence. Another concern is the creation of depth and relief and of floating and anchored forms coexisting in shifting space.

Since my medium is lithography, I take into account the aesthetic aspects of ink; paper, and lithographic materials as well as the technical considerations involved in printing from limestone and metal plates. I want my prints to have the fullest realization of the lithographic potential that I can envision. In the struggle to fully realize the art in that potential a new potential is revealed. This becomes the impetus for each new work and the means of a fuller expression.

Steven Sorman

Baldasare Forestiere said: "Any fool can make something straight but if you make it crooked and it looks nice, that is good." William Morris said: "Have nothing in your houses that you do not know to be useful or believe to be beautiful."

Norman Stewart

My concern in *Bias* [Cat. 130] was the integration of a weave of regular diagonal (bias) lineal elements against a field of autographic, garishly pigmented forms in an arbitrary fiber-like configuration.

In *Cranbrook Suite: Gossamer* [Cat. 129] I am dealing with the interaction between 1) a layering or veiling of translucent white ink, 2) a field of predominantly horizontal streamer-like lineal forms of a wide chromatic difference, and 3) the gray of the paper.

David Sullivan

A screen's complete lack of sympathy makes it an ideal companion on the search for visual truth.

Evan Summer

In my work, the elements of time, change, and deterioration play important roles. The architectural and geometric imagery provide the formats by which time may be defined in terms of change. These structures and objects are at once both timeless and decaying. They were created by man but abandoned to the eternal forces of nature.

Robert Thorn

My approach to screenprinting is from the printer's point of view. As a printer I must be able to transform my mental image from an idea into a print, using the print process to its fullest extent rather than being limited by it.

My prints are made up of lines which, from a distance, show up only as masses of color. On closer inspection they can be seen as a matrix of lines ⅛ of an inch apart over the entire field of the print. Layer upon layer of transparent and opaque ink are used to create the textured fields. Areas are blocked out with various materials which are brushed, thrown, and splattered onto the screen and allowed to dry before being printed. The lines are done by the photo process to create precise lines across the entire print, causing value changes in the color of the background. For the viewer to appreciate the print fully he must look at it from a distance and also close to. On close inspection he will see subtle changes in color and tactile qualities not evident at a distance. The design, the interaction of color, and the actual printing process fascinate me and lead me to new ideas.

Marilyn Torre-Whitesell

Interest in combining the illusion of texture with geometric patterning.

Applying color to paper the way a painter would to canvas, avoiding the key plate tradition of color intaglio printing.

Keeping techniques at a minimum to avoid making plates rather than images on paper.

Stephanie Weber

I am concerned with the blending of different mediums. I want to move from crisp illusionism to human gesture, from photocopy images to abstraction and back again. I find that a very eclectic and experimental approach—working into metal plates, plastic plates, adding rapid copy images, etching on top of that, layering Xeroxed acetates over etched areas—is freeing. It allows the immediacy catch mood of the piece and flexibility.

Dee I. Wolff

A note to myself: Remember those things which are important to you. Select your own universe from the field of perception. Concentrate on it. Enlarge it. Destroy it.

Paul Wong

A perspective of space-time environment which contains my currect reaction; one changeable, the other struggling for permanency, magnetizes by tension. A coherent motion catching chaos and order carries the substance of what appears. My impulse best arrests this distinction between readability and confusion. In my terms, I can draw the expanse of any distance and location, through measured miles as well as millennia. I discover these stimuli through found and captured photographs outside of my control. The puzzle falls in place. By stifling intuition, parts and pieces become cognizant wholes. I am reinvestigating the flexibility of given knowns about a universal comprehension concerning various photographic documentation; closer to flash cuts of layered action happening simultaneously. The print further confuses the flatness of an irregular sheet of paper with the falsities of a deep space.

Taj Diffenbaugh Worley

What excites my drawing is the ability of rhythm, movement, and directionality of line to convey an idea or feeling. At the same time I value the mark-making for itself. Often there is a coexistence of rather austere geometric and loose random elements in my work. My images have revolved around such themes as "journeys," aspects of "male and female," "camouflages," "emergings" (birth), "embellishments"; I see the images as metaphors for these themes.

Janet Yang

Making pictures as cricketsong
A biological noise of the species
Little model voices to sing the human song.

Cameron Zebrun

That printmaking permits the artist a distance between himself and his subject is central to my work. The studio requires the artist to clarify and specify, in an economical sense, his idea and intent.

I have found that through this process I have had to develop a personal language, through invention and discovery which the studio provides ample supply of, to interpret my ideas intellectually and technically.

INDEX BY MEDIUM

Each work is preceded by its catalogue number. When more than one printmaking technique has been used, the work is indexed under all mediums involved. For example, a work made with etching and relief is indexed under both etching and relief.

Aquatint

Balkin, A. G. 6: *Future Memories I*
Bumbeck, D. 13: *An Actress*
Bumbeck, D. 14: *Moods of Miss J*
Crabb, J. 19: *No Deposit, No Return*
Crabb, J. 20: *Departure #8*
Heydt, W. 60: *The Proposal*
Hurley, D. H. 61: *Other Places #I*
Hurley, D. H. 62: *Other Places #VIII*
Kaneshiro, R. 68: *Untitled*
Kmetko, A. 78: *La Bajada*
Kuchar, M. 79: *Line #2*
Kuchar, M. 80: *Perimeter Series #1*
Lasansky, L. 81: *Orientalia*
Lasansky, L. 82: *Tomás*

Engraving on Plexiglas

Smith, S. 121: *Friday Night*
Smith, S. 122: *House on the Hill*

Etching

Andell, N. 1: *Picnic at Crane's Beach*
Boyle, M. 9: *Wan Was Wax*
Boyle, M. 10: *Triptych: Conundrum I, Omnidirectional Translator, Conundrum II*
Bumbeck, D. 13: *An Actress*
Bumbeck, D. 14: *Moods of Miss J*
Chrzanowski, R. 15: *Untitled*
Chrzanowski, R. 16: *Untitled*
Crabb, J. 19: *No Deposit, No Return*
Crabb, J. 20: *Departure #8*
Di Cerbo, M. 31: *Untitled (77A)*
Di Cerbo, M. 32: *Untitled (78C)*
Esaki, Y. 35: *Fourth Iris*
Esaki, Y. 36: *Jacket*
Gelman, A. 45: *The Serpents*
Goldman, J. E. 48: *Castle Place Reflections #1*
Greene, J. 51: *Untitled*
Heydt, W. 59: *Femme de la Nuit*
Hurley, D. H. 61: *Other Places #I*
Hurley, D. H. 62: *Other Places #VIII*
Janoff-Katjanelson, A. 63: *Yellow Afterimage*
Janoff-Katjanelson, A. 64: *Plates X, II, and I*
Johnson, L. 66: *Homage to Tamayo*
Kaneshiro, R. 67: *Standing Alligator II*
Kaneshiro, R. 68: *Untitled*
Kuchar, M. 79: *Line #2*
Kuchar, M. 80: *Perimeter Series #1*
Lasansky, L. 81: *Orientalia*
Lasansky, L. 82: *Tomás*
McGowan, M. 89: *Untitled*
McGowan, M. 90: *Untitled*
Nushawg, M. 101: *RE-4*
Nushawg, M. 102: *(Dové Te) Destiny Kinnel*
Poster, M. 106: *Festival of San Gennaro—Mulberry St.*
Ruble, R. L. 111: *Dying Rhino*
Semivan, D. K. 116: *Black Maru (liner maru)*
Summer, E. 134: *Untitled*

Hand-coloring

Lithograph

Roulette

Goldman, J. E. 48: *Castle Place Reflections #1*
Lasansky, L. 81: *Orientalia*
Semivan, D. K. 116: *Black Maru (liner maru)*

Rubber stamp

Furnback, D. G. 44: *Strokes Given Linear Momentum by Hand*

Scraping

Bumbeck, D. 13: *An Actress*
Bumbeck, D. 14: *Moods of Miss J*
Kmetko, A. 77: *Collage Series*
Kmetko, A. 78: *La Bajada*

Screenprint

Gordy, R. 49: *Dog*
Gordy, R. 50: *Sister Act*
Ruble, R. L. 112: *She Who Controls Dreams (Violet Haze)*

Serigraph

Bolt, S. H. 7: *Declination Reparation*
Bolt, S. H. 8: *Box Making*
Danner, R. W. 23: *I Bombed the Taj Mahal with Art (What's Steven Got in His Hand)*
Danner, R. W. 24: *1973 Birdnest, Rose, and Capital*
Davis, R. 27: *Bottles*
Davis, R. 28: *Outcrop*
Farmer, M. 37: *Summer Salads*
Farmer, M. 38: *Little Floaters*
Harelson, C. 57: *Locking Horns*
Harelson, C. 58: *Strongman*
Lasuchin, M. 83: *Trans*
Lasuchin, M. 84: *Triad*
Lerner, A. J. 85: *Laughing Cow*
Lerner, A. J. 86: *Laughing Gas*
Mullen, P. E. 95: *Kathmandu Eccentric*
Mullen, P. E. 96: *ADI Blue*
Nushawg, M. 102: *(Dové Te) Destiny Kinnel*
Poster, M. 105: *Rockefeller Center*
Stewart, N. 129: *Cranbrook Suite: Gossamer*
Stewart, N. 130: *Bias*
Sullivan, D. 131: *Facade*
Sullivan, D. 132: *Asymmetry*
Thorn, R. 135: *160 Lines*
Thorn, R. 136: *It's All the Same*
Worley, T. 145: *Interweave*

Soft-ground

Balkin, A. G. 5: *Life's Flight into Water: Harmony*
Balkin, A. G. 6: *Future Memories I*
Chrzanowski, R. 15: *Untitled*
Chrzanowski, R. 16: *Untitled*
Gelman, A. 46: *Self Portrait II*
Heydt, W. 60: *The Proposal*
Kuchar, M. 80: *Perimeter Series #1*
Lasansky, L. 81: *Orientalia*
Lasansky, L. 82: *Tomás*
Smith, W. K. 123: *Houses in the Rain*
Torre-Whitesell, M. 137: *Mosaic Vision*
Worley, T. 146: *Pathways*

Spit-bite	Andell, N. 1: *Picnic at Crane's Beach* Kaneshiro, R. 67: *Standing Alligator II*
Sugar-lift	Hurley, D. H. 61: *Other Places #I* Hurley, D. H. 62: *Other Places #VIII* Lasansky, L. 82: *Tomás*
Transfer	Lerner, A. J. 85: *Laughing Cow* Lerner, A. J. 86: *Laughing Gas*
Woodcut	Greene, J. 52: *Untitled* Ming-Dao, D. 93: *Rain Basin* Ming-Dao, D. 94: *Cloud Shadows* Semivan, D. K. 115: *Receiver II*
Xerox	Lerner, A. J. 85: *Laughing Cow* Lerner, A. J. 86: *Laughing Gas* Weber, S. 139: *Opening Thoughts, IV* Weber, S. 140: *Reliquary IX*

INDEX TO LENDERS

ADI Gallery: 3, 4, 28, 39, 40, 53, 54, 73, 74, 91, 92, 93, 94, 101, 102
Associated American Artists, New York: 33, 34, 111, 112, 131, 132
Associated American Artists, Philadelphia: 7, 8, 83, 84
Brooke Alexander, Inc.: 41, 42, 87, 88
The Brooklyn Museum: 27, 35, 44, 57, 63, 71, 72, 75, 81, 82, 95, 105, 106, 109, 113, 114
Davidson Galleries: 19, 20, 99, 100, 145, 146
Impressions Workshop, Inc.: 1, 2, 135, 136
Little Egypt Enterprises: 141, 142
Moody Gallery: 65, 66
Van Straaten Gallery: 37, 38, 76
Vermillion Editions, Ltd.: 127, 128

All works not listed here were lent by the artists